WASHINGTON'S GOLDEN AGE

WASHINGTON'S GOLDEN AGE

Hope Ridings Miller, the Society Beat, and the Rise of Women Journalists

JOSEPH DALTON

ROWMAN & LITTLEFIELD
Lanham • Boulder • New York • London

Published by Rowman & Littlefield
An imprint of The Rowman & Littlefield Publishing Group, Inc.
4501 Forbes Boulevard, Suite 200, Lanham, Maryland 20706
www.rowman.com

Unit A, Whitacre Mews, 26–34 Stannary Street, London SE11 4AB

Distributed by NATIONAL BOOK NETWORK

British Library Cataloguing in Publication Information Available

Library of Congress Cataloging-in-Publication Data

Names: Dalton, Joseph, author.
Title: Washington's golden age : Hope Ridings Miller, the society beat, and the rise of women journalists / Joseph Dalton.
Description: Lanham : Rowman & Littlefield, 2018. | Includes bibliographical references and index.
Identifiers: LCCN 2018012464 (print) | LCCN 2018019263 (ebook) | ISBN 9781538116159 (Electronic) | ISBN 9781538116142 (cloth : alk. paper)
Subjects: LCSH: Miller, Hope Ridings. | Women journalists—United States—Biography. | Women periodical editors—United States—Biography.
Classification: LCC PN4874.M4915 (ebook) | LCC PN4874.M4915 D35 2018 (print) | DDC 070/.92 [B]—dc23
LC record available at https://lccn.loc.gov/2018012464

Printed in the United States of America

CONTENTS

INTRODUCTION

Growing up in Texas, I always heard the name of my elder cousin—Hope Ridings Miller—spoken with a certain reverence. She was an East Coast institution, a point of pride, a star of accomplishment and success. I come from the Ridings side of her family tree. Hope and my maternal grandfather, Olan Ridings, were first cousins. My full name rings with the same cadence: Joseph Ridings Dalton.

I remember Hope's three books proudly displayed on the coffee table in my grandparents' living room. Issues of her magazine, *Diplomat*, must have been on hand, as well. Once I was well into researching this biography, certain covers of the magazine resonated for me, evoking a little boy's curiosity and wonder at faraway glamour and elegance.

Missing the chance to call on Hope during a visit to Washington would have been like skipping the Smithsonian. When I was a sophomore in high school, I attended a weeklong model Congress on Capitol Hill. My mother made sure that along with my suits, sport coats, and ties, also safely packed away was cousin Hope's phone number. Once in town I called her from a pay phone and introduced myself. Without hesitation, she invited me to lunch the next day at the National Press Club.

I must have been pretty nervous during that phone call because I wrote down the wrong address. I would have been terribly late if I'd kept going on foot from wherever I was in downtown to wherever I thought I should be. So I hailed a taxi. That was a new experience. We didn't have cabs in Fort Worth, not much of a downtown either, and D.C. sure did feel like a big city. Luckily, the driver knew the Press Club, which turned out to be practically around the corner.

I wondered how Hope and I would recognize each other, not realizing that I'd be the only 15-year-old showing up alone for a midweek luncheon. As I stepped out of the elevator, she was sitting contentedly on a bench right in front of me and offering a sincere little smile. Maybe she could tell I was flustered. After she rose and we clasped hands, she leaned forward to give the tiniest embrace. That kind of cheek hug became our customary greeting during the ensuing years of friendship.

Our meal was interrupted several times by Hope's friends and colleagues who came by to pay respects. Looking back, I fear that my manners weren't up to snuff. I didn't stand when I was introduced, and I could have ordered something less sloppy to eat than a roast beef sandwich au jus.

For all the learning and growing that was still ahead of me, Washington seemed like a great place to start. I returned two years later to serve as a Congressional Page in the House of Representatives. It was early 1981, the beginning of the Reagan years and a thrilling time to observe politics and government at work. Pages had unique access to the House floor and virtually every corridor of the entire Capitol Hill complex. Thanks to my well-connected cousin, I also made it to other places of power.

Just a week or so after I'd arrived, Hope took me along to a reception at an impressive colonial-style home in Georgetown. The small gathering featured a screening of a short documentary about Jim Wright, the House Majority Leader who was also my Congressman. During his twenty-five years in Congress, Wright had appointed countless pages. I think it's safe to say that I was the only one of them who appeared out of nowhere at a private Georgetown party. The impression I made just by being there that one night illustrated the point that Hope had spent her career articulating in one article after another—that the social scene was a valid and effective way to get ahead in town.

Twenty years later, when my career turned from arts administration toward journalism, I recalled that there was another writer in the family. Delving into Hope's books, I flashed on the idea of writing her biography. It's been a labor of love for the better part of a decade. The research has encompassed reading more than 1,200 columns that she produced for the *Washington Post*, and perusing twelve years of *Diplomat* magazine, along with the correspondence and photos that she left behind. Sometimes I'd feel a flash of inspiration and sense Hope nearby, saying, "It's all there, dear."

I hope that this book paints a picture of a gentler side of politics and diplomacy. Things like dignity, courtesy, and respect once mattered in our

nation's Capital and they were Hope's stock-in-trade. Politics was still contentious, that's its nature. But rumors and potential scandals made their way
around the city mostly by whispers, not by promulgation on 24-hour cable
news shows. Most importantly, things got done. Maybe the legislators in Washington found it harder to attack each other by day when they'd broken bread
together by night. It feels like another world.

PRELUDE:
DINNER AT THE WHITE HOUSE

Tonight would be intimate and off the record, but dinner with the Roosevelts in the White House family quarters was still an occasion and Hope Ridings Miller took nothing casually.

Before leaving her desk at the the *Washington Post*, she phoned her husband Lee to make sure he'd finished his rounds with patients and was also on his way back to their 16th Street apartment. Returning home to change from office clothes into evening attire was part of Hope's regular work routine. Collecting Lee wasn't. But whether she went solo or coupled, her evenings were usually spent "going about," as she often put it. A cocktail party or two, an embassy reception, or a formal dinner at a private residence, she was invited to everything. And the next morning she'd be alone with the typewriter, recounting the names and titles of whom she saw and what they were talking about. This evening at the White House would be unique though, and spouses were essential.

The dance for the Fourth Estate was one of the White House's lighter affairs. In past seasons the Millers had been part of the throng of 1,500 reporters and editors who enjoyed an evening of beer and dancing at the executive mansion. But now they were invited to come early for dinner, a tradition reserved for the top officers of the various press organizations. The Millers were still in their early thirties and had only been in Washington for six years. Prominence had come quickly. As president of the Women's National Press Club, Hope would sit alongside leaders—all men—of the White House Correspondent's Association, National Press Club, and the Gridiron.[1]

They arrived at the White House gate at the same time as Raymond Clapper, president of the Gridiron, and his wife Olive. Though Clapper and Hope were colleagues at the *Post*, that was more a coincidence than any particular evidence of status for the paper, which was still running in fifth place among the city's five major dailies. But publisher Eugene Meyer recognized talent. He promoted Hope to Society Editor after three years as a staff writer, while Clapper, an aggressive political reporter and commentator, had been recruited away from his position as bureau chief for United Press.

When the two couples arrived on the second floor of the White House, they were greeted by the First Lady. Though not big on small talk, Mrs. Roosevelt was on familiar terms with the young Mrs. Miller, who attended her weekly press conferences. Mrs. Roosevelt passed along regards to Hope's parents back in Texas.

Soon the President arrived in his wheelchair and the evening was fully underway. Also on hand were the Secretaries of the Treasury and of Agriculture, plus their wives, and the White House press secretary. When Roosevelt invited everyone to have a drink before dinner, Hope observed Mrs. Roosevelt abstaining from alcohol. Only some of the gentlemen joined the President when he insisted on a second round.[2]

Conversational topic number one was the same as at every other Washington gathering in the early summer of 1939: the upcoming arrival of the King and Queen of England. The first visit to U.S. soil by a British monarch would be of huge geopolitical consequence, given that the Brits were desperate for American aid in their resistance to German aggression. But the events were prime territory for society reporters, who were already filing daily stories about the imminent goings on. Guest lists, wardrobe choices, and all matters of etiquette were never more important than when royalty was at hand.

President Roosevelt asked Hope if she found the British embassy to be cooperative. Or at least more cooperative. Just weeks prior, the British Ambassador and his American-born wife, Lady Lindsay, had each taken to calling press conferences. This was to make up for the lack of information coming from Lady Lindsay's curt assistant, who had been so obstinate on the phone as to bring one of Hope's own underlings to the point of tears. But direct contact with reporters had only made matters worse, as the Lindsays' verbal gaffes kept hitting the headlines. Perhaps there really was no other way to describe a formal garden party than as elite and exclusive. But Americans weren't having it, and, even worse, too many Washington women weren't getting invited.

Everyone at the dinner was already aware of the predicament. In responding to the President's inquiry, Hope's natural inclination was to be both positive and discreet. She gave a confident little smile and a knowing nod.

"Oh yes, Mr. President," she said, "Lady Lindsay seems to be doing the best she can with something she doesn't quite understand."[3]

At that, the President tossed back his head and gave out a hearty laugh. "Well, I'm sure everything will work out alright," he said, as the First Lady echoed her husband's sentiments, and the party took their seats for dinner.

1

COFFEE MILL CREEK

Hope Deupree Ridings came into the world on Christmas Eve 1905 in Bonham, Texas, population circa 5,000. It was a home birth that took place practically in the shadow of government. The little frame house on West 5th Street was only a short walk to the town square and the Fannin County Courthouse, an imposing three-story structure made of Texas limestone and capped with an ornate clock tower.

A budding political connection played into how the young family obtained the dwelling where their first and only child would be born. Alfred and Grace, the proud new parents, were renting from John F. Rayburn. The following year, John's younger brother Sam would win his first election to the state legislature. Six years after that, he headed to Washington where he began his ascent toward becoming history's most powerful and longest serving Speaker of the House.

Samuel Taliaferro Rayburn and Alfred Lafayette Ridings had been friends since boyhood, when they attended a one-room country schoolhouse in the area known as the Blacklands. The policy in those days mandated a school within walking distance of every child's home. Those walks were a tough slog when the dirt roads became deep and thick with mud that weighed down the children's shoes. A typical school term ran for just four months since all available hands, no matter their age, were needed on the family farms. Even the littlest ones could be taught to clear rocks.

Agriculture had been the primary business of Fannin County since its establishment in 1837. Cotton, corn, and wheat were the crops grown year after year. Sometimes the small tracts of land became worn out by repeated

1

plantings. How much income the soil produced also depended on the unpredictable rainfall, the intense summer heat, and the occasional sudden arrival of tornados that blew through the flat and open expanses.

At its northern border, about thirteen miles from Bonham, Fannin County abutted Oklahoma, which was Indian Territory until it achieved statehood in 1907 (Texas joined the Union and became a state in 1845). The circuitous state border was the Red River, so named for the burnt orange sand that covered the banks and could tint the water a soft pink. Midway between Bonham and the Red River was Coffee Mill Creek where the soil was as dark and heavy as used coffee grounds. Yet the name itself comes from the fact that in pioneer days some unknown traveler nailed his coffee mill to a tree and then left it behind. The device came in handy for future campers and became a kind of landmark.

The county and its seat of government were both named after fallen heroes of the Texas Revolution. James Fannin died at the Goliad massacre, James Bonham at the Alamo. So the region was every bit Texas, though it was never about cowboys or cattle. Besides farming, the other economic engines were cotton mills and the railroads, which arrived in the 1870s. The nearby town of Sherman, some thirty miles due west in Grayson County, became known as the Athens of Texas because of its many teachers' colleges and church-run academies. Also, about thirty miles away, but back to the east, was another town with cultural aspirations. It was named Paris.

If a settler was looking to find ranching and roundups, he'd have to head on past Paris, Bonham, and Sherman and on toward Tarrant County and its center of commerce, Fort Worth, proudly branded "where the West begins." The major city closest to Bonham was Dallas, located about seventy miles to the south. Men in big boots liked to say, "That's where the East peters out."

The Ridings family lineage usually starts with Charles Calvin Ridings, a 49 year-old blacksmith, who with his 40 year-old wife Jane Kennedy Ridings, set off for Texas from Cherokee County, Alabama, in 1855. They traveled in two covered wagons with their nine children, ranging in age from toddlers to teens. The family stayed for a spell with an uncle in Mississippi so that Charles could work his trade, mostly shoeing horses or fixing tools and other equipment, and thus he could afford more food and supplies for what lay ahead in the 800-mile journey.

At some point after crossing from Arkansas into the Lone Star State, they learned that no corn was grown in Tarrant County, their ultimate destination.

That didn't suit Charles's intentions, and so they came to a halt in Bonham. The family Bible cites December 8 as their date of arrival. At the beginning of January 1856, Charles purchased a house adjacent to the main square (the courthouse had not yet been built). Nearby, he also opened the Buckhorn Blacksmith Shop.

After their arrival in Texas, Jane delivered another child. A trait of all the Ridings was their modest height. But Jane and Charles's brood was also hearty. All of their children lived to adulthood, an unusual distinction for the era.

Perhaps life in the center of town just got too confining for the large family or maybe the new railroad was just too noisy. In the early 1870s, Charles purchased a tract of land eight miles to the north, right near Coffee Mill Creek. Many generations of his descendants would make their lives there, expanding the property holdings and working as farmers, teachers, and merchants. The settlement became known as the Ridings Community.

Perry Pinkney Ridings, Charles and Jane's second child, was fifteen when the family came to Bonham. Like many of his brothers, he apprenticed with his father at blacksmithing. After he and Mildred Davis married in the late 1860s, the couple left Bonham to join the family's settlement. Later, they donated a portion of their land holdings to the Corinth Baptist Church, which still holds services and is the only surviving remnant of the Ridings Community. Perry had a noted flair for craftwork with a variety of materials. He made shoes for his children, drop earrings for his wife, and a pulpit for the church. Maintaining ties to Bonham, he was a member of the Fannin County Board of Commissioners when the courthouse was erected in 1888 and he contributed to the design of its clock tower. Perry and Millie had five children: Texanna Belle, Ewell Wright, Charles Calvin, Alfred Lafayette, and Lilly.

Alfred, known as "Lafe," was born in 1879. After completing primary and secondary schooling in Fannin County, he retraced his grandfather's path back east to study medicine at the University of Louisville. He practiced in Fannin and Grayson counties his entire career and delivered the children of many longtime residents, as well as some passing strangers. Among the latter was Virginia Adele Gash of Arkansas, whose son Henry Leon Blythe was born in Sherman on January 17, 1938. The father of the boy was Virginia's ex-husband, William Jefferson Blythe. Eight years later and with another wife, Blythe would have a second son born in Hope, Arkansas. That child (the half-brother of the boy that Dr. Ridings delivered) became the 42nd President of the United States, William Jefferson Clinton.

Grace Deupree Ridings's roots go back to the town of Ivanhoe, which was also on Coffee Mill Creek and hardly a stone's throw from the Ridings Community. The settlement was founded in 1845 and originally named Hawkins Prairie. It was renamed a full forty years later when the U.S. Postal Service demanded a new name. Joseph Emory Deupree, one of its more literary residents, borrowed the new moniker from the novel by Sir Walter Scott.

Deupree was born in 1840 in Pickens County, Alabama, and orphaned at a young age. He was brought to Texas by his maternal grandfather Nathan Smith and other relatives, who established a plantation on the banks of the Red River. After schooling in Bonham, Deupree attended Baylor University and was salutatorian of the Class of 1859. Sam Houston was at the commencement ceremony. After hearing Deupree's oration, he proclaimed, "Young man, you'll go far in this life ahead of you."

He soon did. Deupree was studying law in Tennessee when the Civil War broke out two years later. "I found the whole country aflame with excitement over the great impending war," he wrote in a memoir. "The boys were forming companies, and the pretty girls were giving picnics, and threatening to send hoop skirts to all who failed to join the Southern army. So I soon caught the war fever."

He joined the Noxubee Cavalry and fought in their ranks for some twenty months. He then reconnected with Baylor classmates as part of another cavalry unit, Waul's Texas Legion. In Mississippi during June 1863, he was captured by Union forces and taken to the prison at Fort Delaware. After four attempts to escape with a three-mile swim, Deupree was finally released under the name of a dead man as part of a prisoner exchange on April 10, 1865. Long after the war ended, he was still known by his rank and was referred to as Captain Deupree.

News had traveled back to Deupree's people in Texas that he had died. Though he was welcomed back and glad to be home, he was disheartened by how the Smith plantation had fallen into utter disrepair. It would not return to any lost glory.

"If I were asked at what time in life I had rendered the most efficient service to my country, I could readily answer that it was during the dark days of reconstruction," wrote Deupree.

Drawing on his antebellum studies at the Cumberland University, Deupree was able to pass the first bar exam offered after the Civil War. With those credentials, he became counsel for the Red River District, settling all manner of disputes in the territories on both sides of the river. It was a contentious, sometimes life-threatening job that he held for ten years.

In 1869, Deupree married Amelia Wofford, whose cousins back in South Carolina founded and endowed Wofford University. Joseph and Amelia had one son and three daughters. The third born, Grace, was just five years old when Amelia died in 1883. Two years later, Deupree remarried Annie Erwin. Within months after exchanging vows, the couple left Bonham and settled into a farming life in the community eventually known as Ivanhoe, where four more sons were born.

On top of managing his properties and raising his large family, Captain Deupree returned to an early passion—writing—that he'd been forced to put aside, first for the war and then for aiding the local redevelopment in its aftermath. True to his worldly nature, he didn't keep his writings private. He published essays in the *Bonham News* using the byline J. E. Deupree, and also under the penname "Ajax," drawn from Greek mythology. Today's associations with Ajax as an abrasive cleansing agent make it an apt moniker, for Deupree wrote sharp opinion pieces, "his pen dipped in caustic alkali," as one observer put it. But that some reader also said, "He frequently wrote from smiles to tears, from love to hatred."[1]

The ability to communicate through writing, an appreciation of great literature and a devotion to the Texas countryside were all things passed along to Captain Deupree's only daughter, Grace. She became one of the state's finest poets. Her most widely remembered work is probably the three-stanza "Calling Texas Razor-Backs." It begins:

> Where Coffee Mill Creek rolls along
> And zig-zag rails are high,
> When hickory nuts begin to fall
> And wild geese dot the sky,
> Along the path by the old creek line,
> As far and straight I go,
> I hear again the familiar strains
> A voice of the long ago.[2]

Some of her other titles—"Peach Tree in Bloom," "The Eagle of Ivanhoe," and "San Jacinto Battle Cry"—convey her range and focus.

Young Grace, though, was no idle belle lounging on the veranda with pen in hand and waiting for the muse to speak. Most of her poetry came later in life, as memories of girlhood days. Instead, Grace received a formal education and graduated from Ravenna College in her early twenties. She went straight into teaching school. But in a one-room schoolhouse full of children of all ages, strict discipline was the first order of business. Grace had that in her constitution as well.

Grace continued to teach after she married Alfred Ridings and also, in time, after giving birth to Hope. During the period when Alfred was studying medicine in Kentucky, Grace and Hope moved in with other Deupree family members in Bonham. When Alfred returned in 1910, it took most of his attention to establish a practice and see patients. House calls were not uncommon and sometimes involved trips well outside of town. So Grace was in charge of the home and also of keeping Hope in line.

"Daddy showered me with attention, complimented me often and made me feel very special," recalled Hope. "Mother as a rule didn't mind. When she thought he went overboard and warned that he was spoiling me, he replied that there's no way on earth anybody can spoil a nice girl."

Grace probably didn't linger long in feeding baby talk to Hope. She made reading time an opportunity to draw her daughter into stories such as *Alice in Wonderland*, *Peter Pan*, and *The Wind in the Willows*. Not surprisingly, literacy came fast and easy to Hope. By age twelve, she was reading on her own such classics as *Vanity Fair*, *David Copperfield*, and *Pride and Prejudice*. Many of these titles were readily available in a handsome set of leather-bound volumes on the shelf in the family home.

Along with the distant journeys and exotic adventures that reading itself provided, Hope was given further incentive. Her mother, inspired by a well-publicized catalogue of "The 100 Best Books in the English Language," drew up her own list of eighty great books and promised to pay her daughter a dime for every title she finished "within a reasonable length of time." Hope kept up a steady pace of reading and earning.

Starting at age seven, she was also enrolled in weekly elocution lessons, which covered the finer points of public speaking and also encompassed diction and grammar, proper manners, and how to present oneself. If up to this point shyness was anywhere in her makeup it got thoroughly wiped away. Before long, the little girl was on a local circuit giving recitations to women's clubs and fraternal orders and at various other civic functions. Frequent roles in school pageants and plays also encouraged Hope to shine.

In 1917 the family moved from Bonham to Sherman where Hope entered high school. The relocation served Dr. Ridings's business, as he joined a colleague in forming a clinic located in the Commercial Bank Building. Within just a few years he also became the city physician and saw patients at

City Hall. Both locations were within walking distance from their home on South Travis Street.

The new house provided easy access to places of worship. The Baptist Church was right next door, the Christian Church just across the street. Since Alfred was Baptist and Grace was Christian, the Ridings family visited both churches regularly, usually on alternating Sundays. Though Grace was the more religious of the two, it was the Baptists that ultimately claimed Hope.

One or two Baptist revivals may have tipped the holy scales. Hope attended them with her dad a few times in the evenings when he served as resident physician. The annual North Texas Baptist Encampment ran for a full week and drew thousands of participants from counties near and far. Making camp together or lodging in nearby homes, they quickly formed close community. Evening services carried on long into the warm nights, as the preachers exhorted the crowds into a fevered worship, imploring the Holy Spirit to come down and cleanse their souls from wrong. Hymns of consolation, conversion, and triumph rang out across the countryside.

> Why should I feel discouraged
> And why should the shadows come?
> Why should my heart feel lonely
> And long for my Heavenly home?
>
> Jesus is my comfort, a constant friend is he.
> His eye is on the sparrow and I know he watches me.
> I sing because I'm happy,
> I sing because I'm free.
> His eye is on the sparrow and I know he watches me.

Back home at First Baptist Church, the prayers on a normal Sunday morning didn't often reach frenzied peaks. But the rounded and tiered sanctuary, erected in 1914, could easily hold a congregation of a couple hundred souls. With the pipe organ playing and all voices raised in song, the music could be heard by neighbors and probably the Almighty as well. So if it was a Sunday that the Ridings family crossed over to the Christian Church, Hope could still turn an ear to at least some of what was happening at First Baptist. Returning into the fold of Baptists on Sundays would remain a constant throughout the rest of her life.

In the Ridings household, it wasn't just religion where Alfred and Grace had disagreement. They could diverge on politics, as well. Sam Rayburn, of course, had the support of the whole family, as well as the devoted allegiance of most every registered voter in the region. There were years when a strong opponent ran against him, but generally speaking, "He was just next to the President and the Lord," as one local put it.[3] But when "Mr. Sam" wasn't on the ballot, Alfred and Grace sometimes parted ways. One time, a county judge who was also a friend of Alfred's, was running for reelection. Grace decided to vote for the challenger, who won by a single vote. No hard feelings arose afterward. To Hope it provided a clear lesson, that a woman, married or otherwise, was empowered to make her own decisions.

But a child making declarations about her future was another matter entirely. On Hope's thirteenth birthday, December 24, 1918, she informed her parents that she was destined for a life in the theater and that it should start as soon as possible. In her mind, that meant immediately after high school. Scratch the plans for college. Thanks to a regular slate of summer courses, Hope was already on track for an early graduation. That was just eighteen months away. Stardom was nearly at hand!

Her parents were firm that the educational path laid out for their only daughter would continue unabated and that it included college. The confrontation made for a dark holiday. But by this point, Grandfather Deupree had taken an avid interest in Hope's prodigious reading program and also served, at times, as her confidant. Offering both consolation and reason, he explained that no matter how much talent or determination one had, the chances for success in acting were slim. Amid the tears and rants, he gently turned the conversation toward writing and suggested she might keep that in mind for the future.

Meanwhile, Grace was making efforts to submit her poems in some journals and she faced an issue—the ungainly spelling of Deupree. She asked for her father's blessing in dropping the first of the many e's in the family name. Hope was in the room at the time and heard her grandfather recount the French Huguenot origins of the name. He then acknowledged that not only was it difficult to spell and also pronounce (dew-PRAY was the preference), but it had already appeared in many permutations over the centuries. So go ahead with the change, he told his daughter, who thereafter wrote under the name Grace Dupree Ridings. Hope was still imagining how her name would look on a lighted marquee rather than the printed page. But not too many years later when she began her own career as a writer, she did her mother one better, dropping another "e" and became known as Hope Dupre Ridings.

Keeping up with her accelerated academic load while also taking dancing classes, and some private lessons in piano and violin, Hope completed high school at age fifteen. The school administration allowed her to participate in the graduation with her class the following year. Given her age, though, going away to college wasn't in the cards and she remained at home while she took classes at Austin College in Sherman for the next two years. Her junior year she finally departed home for the city of Austin, where she enrolled in the University of Texas. A year in the women's dorm was followed by a move into the Phi Mu sorority house. At both residences she reveled in having a house full of sisters.

Along the way at both Austin College and at U.T., she participated in theater, either with elective courses or on an extracurricular basis. After receiving her Bachelor of Arts in 1925, Hope was still bursting with curiosity and ambition. A penpal from Chicago who'd just completed undergrad work at Northwestern University wrote to say that she was applying to Columbia University and suggested that Hope might join her there. Thinking that a capital idea, Hope got on the train to New York where she was enrolled in a one-year course of graduate-level study.

She lived on campus in Whittier Hall but didn't limit herself to staying on the Upper West Side. Once a week, she went downtown for classes at the Lucy Faegan School of Dramatic Arts. It was the go-to place for aspiring actors. One of its later and more famous alums was future Broadway star Angela Lansbury.

After enough study and practice to gain some confidence in the city's theater scene, Hope auditioned for the Washington Square Players. She was a noticeable young thing—standing hardly more than five feet tall, with wavy blond hair, a prominent nose when seen in profile and hazel eyes that conveyed a combination of wisdom and mischief.

Though she wasn't cast, that tryout led to an offer to join the Provincetown Players for a season of summer stock on Cape Cod. Also in Manhattan at this point was Hope's mother Grace. She'd come to New York for an extended visit, a stay long enough that she even enrolled in some writing classes at Columbia. Alfred appeared too, just in time to witness Hope receiving her diploma, an M.A. in English. Together, the folks prevailed on their girl to return home.

Now twenty-one years old and with two degrees in hand, Hope was back under her parents' roof just in time for a blazing summer in East Texas. She struck out where she could. Just making its way to Sherman was the Little Theater Movement, a nationwide effort at staging intimate live plays. The scale was appropriate to the struggling economy and also served as an affordable alternative to cinema. With her one year of experience in Manhattan, Hope had theater chops like nobody else in town and she became director of several productions. Typical of the theater, each experience was exhilarating and also completely exhausting. Yet she kept signing up for new productions every few months, once or twice even directing and starring in the same show.

Her voracious appetite for books, still in place long after completing her mom's ambitious reading program, sparked an idea. It involved writing. She strode over to the *Sherman Daily Democrat* and proposed to editor Newell Jenkins a weekly book page. He expressed interest but wondered about her ability to deliver good copy. She returned two days later and presented typed reviews of some popular recent titles, including Sinclair Lewis's *Elmer Gantry*. Jenkins set the pages down on his desk and sent her away. Within a couple hours he telephoned to inform her that she was now the editor of the *Daily Democrat's* new Saturday book page.

The pay was modest, the experience great. Hope soon got a good taste of newspaper journalism and all that it entailed: Editors who were always busy and distracted but also with a constant need to fill pages; the requirement to write fast, concise, and simple, and to deliver on deadline; the gratification of seeing your work quickly appear in print. And starting the process all over again for the next edition.

Hope worked from home and returned to the newsroom each Wednesday morning with a fresh story. Jenkins gave her some quick lessons in style.

"He took time with me to explain any changes he made in my copy to bring it up to easy-to-read newspaper style, achieved by using short sentences, familiar words and conversational contractions, such as isn't, doesn't and the like," Hope recalled. "He said to just write as though you're talking to and not writing to your readers. That turned out to be one of the best bits of advice I've ever had from an editor."[4]

With a network of family and friends spread across the region, other opportunities were bound to arise. Near the end of summer 1928, Hope heard from a high school classmate who was teaching at the recently formed Paris Junior College. She'd suggested Hope as a candidate for a position that opened up only weeks before the start of the fall term. After one interview, Hope became head of the English department.

P.J.C. had been established just four years prior for boys and girls of Lamar County who could not afford the travel, room, and board required for study at a four-year college. Yet many still struggled to make the tuition, often paying with money earned picking cotton or scrimped from meager family food budgets. They arrived with widely divergent knowledge and skills because country schools had no standardized curricula or commonly available texts. Many of these new college students aspired to return to the school system as teachers themselves in just one or two years' time.

After holding classes in the high school for its first year of operation, the junior college opened in a renovated former post office. The building occupied a full city block just two streets over from the vibrant town square. A rare dash of urbanism, it became known as the "concrete campus." For students from the farm country, or a rookie teacher who was missing Manhattan, it was more stately than the nickname implied. Recessed Roman columns framed the entrance, which led into an arched central atrium with pendant lights. A latticed metal grillwork adorned the high front windows. Classrooms had hardwood floors, large sashed windows and tin ceilings, and long, wall-mounted chalkboards. Everything felt new and full of potential.

In her English literature classes, Hope lectured about authors as if they were real people and assigned memorization of selected passages so that the lines from plays or novels could take deep hold in the students' minds. She was also the adviser for the yearbook, named the *Galleon*. And as faculty sponsor for the Collegiate Players, she directed and sometimes also performed in productions of one-act plays.

With kindness and good order, charm and patience, she usually won over each new class of students and made them want to please her. Especially the boys. At least two of them wrote poems about their fair teacher. What's more, they even had the courage to present to her their rhyming efforts.

"THE SECRET"

> I wonder if you know
>   Of whom I speak.
> She is little, and she's neat
>   And she's very petite.
> To me she always speaks
>   When we meet upon the street.
> For the warmth of her smile
>   I would walk a mile;
> There is no beguile
>   In the twinkle of her Irish eyes
> When she laughs or is surprised.
>
> She has freckles on her face,
>   Even they accentuate her grace
>   As she leads us a lively chase.

After notebooks I heard her say,
  "They must be in at roll-call
  Or I'll not accept them at all."

Would it be any harm
  If she should lean up on my arm
  And give me Hope
  While we were Riding?
That I might be the lucky fellow
  Wouldn't all the boys turn yellow?
                    —J. P. N.

"AND HER NAME WAS HOPE"

In a junior college classroom
Sat a very pensive youth
Who kept tapping with a pencil
The enamel on his tooth.

His eyes were glued upon her,
Nor shifted he his stare,
But continued to survey
Every feature, and her hair.

She had taught him bits of grammar
Attempted argumentation,
But the most that he absorbed
Was the poets and narration.

There was some power about her
That fascinated the boy
As you've seen some gay apparel
Lead a child away from its toy.

Silent he admired her,
And he said, "I guess it's love,"
For her very presence soothed him—
A benediction from above.

Gradually he realized
Such a romance could not be
So in order to forget her
He made plans to go to sea.

Time came when this feeling
Was revealed in its true light,
As expanded admiration
Soaring to a greater height.

Each day from her classroom he went
Feeling wiser than before
Thinking she must have eaten the apple
Of life clear down to the core.

And now he could write prose to her
Or just a friendly letter,
And from a literary point of view
The merits might be better.

But only poetry can express
The things he wants to say,
And the whole is that he'd like to be
Back in her class today.
                    —Patrick Tobin

Hope preserved these poems in her scrapbook. The other pages show girlish fantasies (cute bunny rabbits, lots of plump cupids, photos of Hollywood starlets); admiration for the greats of arts and letters (magazine profiles of Edna St. Vincent Millay, Oscar Wilde, and Sinclair Lewis, among others); and an inquisitive spiritual life (countless poems and sayings drawn from across the ages).

After a semester of commuting from Sherman, Hope rented a room in Paris. She was proud to be paying her own way and began to think of the town as home. She ended up spending five years on the faculty of Paris Junior College, though she would later claim that her tenure lasted only a couple of years. It was the first occurrence of a few deleted or overlooked years that contributed to the long and great mystery of her age.

At the end of each spring term, Hope would return for frequent and extended summer visits back with her parents. But in May 1930, Sherman entered the most violent and convulsive period in its history.

On Saturday, May 3, George Hughes, a 41-year-old black farm worker, allegedly assaulted his white employer's wife at their home five miles south of town. When tracked down by a deputy sheriff, Hughes fired twice before surrendering. While in custody, he confessed to rape. On the Monday following, he was indicted, and the trial was set for that Friday. Early in the week, sheriffs took Hughes out of the county jail to an undisclosed location in order to prevent violence. But every night, mobs of increasing size gathered, demanding the prisoner.

On the morning of the trial, a crowd surrounded the courthouse. An American flag was paraded around the grounds to incite action and rocks were thrown at the windows. Though the noise interfered with courtroom procedure, a jury was empaneled by noon. After a reading of the charges, Hughes pleaded guilty. As the first testimony from witnesses began, the mobs began storming the front doors of the building. Tear gas did not deter them. Women and children escaped the courthouse by ladders. The judge halted the trial, considering a change of venue. By 2:30 p.m., the building was set afire with gasoline.

Hughes had been secured in a vault, which by 4:00 p.m. was practically all that remained of the 1876 courthouse. In late evening, the crowd had swelled to 5,000 in number. Around midnight, dynamite was used to finally blast open the vault. It killed Hughes, yet his body was chained to a car, dragged to the black part of town and strung up on a tree in front of a pharmacy. The entire block of businesses was then set ablaze.

Law enforcement came from across the state, with a force of 225 members of the Texas National Guard in place by morning. At the request of some fifty community leaders, the governor imposed martial law in Sherman. The order was made on Saturday evening, May 10, and remained in effect for two weeks. Throughout the period, machine guns were mounted in the town square and also at the jailhouse.[5]

"My father was the physician who treated the wounded Negro before he was lynched," Hope recalled decades later.[6] Dr. Ridings was also likely one of the town elders who, as a last resort, petitioned the governor to impose martial law. As soon as safe transit was viable, Grace fled to be with family in Ivanhoe. Hope remained in Paris.

The trauma affected the entire region. Another lynching occurred on May 16 in the community of Honey Grove, near Bonham. Fourteen leaders of the Sherman riot were indicted but the first trial wouldn't take place for more than a year. The courthouse wasn't rebuilt until 1936. Within a year or so after the melee, Grace and Alfred left their house on South Travis Street and moved about a mile from the center of town.

Hardly more than a month after the turmoil, Hope and Grace were even farther away, finding welcome distraction on an extended tour of Europe. The last section of Hope's scrapbook opens with a map on which she traced their elaborate route. Their crossing on the *Ile de France* ended at a British port near Plymouth. From there, they saw London, rural England, Dublin, and Belfast, then on to Amsterdam, Rotterdam, Brussels, Berlin, Prague, Lucerne, Vienna, all the major cities of Italy, the French Riviera, and finally up to Paris before departing home from the northern coast of France. Though Grace had been to Europe before, the trip proved to be more than an escape from Texas. It was an extended period of bonding between mother and daughter, and of cultural immersion and discovery for them both. The return train ride from New York included a stop in Washington, D.C.

Typed-up portions of Hope's European diary remain, her first experience as a travel writer:

> The train to London is one of the best in England. The cars of the train are small and high in comparison with our American ones, and I wondered, at first, if they could possibly be comfortable. Once inside, however, this fear was dispelled; they are small but roomy enough. But they are so different from American train cars for the aisles are on the side, and each car seats six or eight people, depending on the class of the car. Oh, yes, I soon became accustomed to classes in England. Each train has a first and third. The latter is for those who do not know better.

At home once again in Texas, Hope became far more lyric and succinct about travel. The following poem by her ran in the *Chicago Tribune* in late 1930 and has been widely quoted ever since (often without attribution):

LINES TO A TRAVELER

Oh you have seen the pirate moons
    that shine in old Bombay,
And you have glimpsed gay waterfalls
    In a land once called Cathay;

> You love to tell how in Japan
> Pale cherry blossoms blow.
> But here, I've seen a cardinal
> Against a bank of snow!

Back in Paris (Texas), ardor awaited, and not just from lovesick schoolboys. At a country club dance in spring 1932, Hope met Clarence Lee Miller. He was handsome and debonair, had a head of rich, dark hair, and was a good bit taller than Hope. Lee was born in Monmouth, Illinois, as one of six children. His medical studies had taken him to St. Louis and Chicago and, since 1928, he'd been in Paris working as an osteopath in a practice with his brother, Lamoine.

Hope and Lee formed a quick and close connection. They remarked at the similarities of their birthdays—Lee's was on New Year's Eve the same year as Hope's—and they found a natural poise and rhythm together on the dance floor. Lee's ready sense of humor reminded Hope of her father's wit.

Hope still had an eagerness to try life in a larger city and Lee joined in the sentiment. He'd considered returning to Chicago for more studies, but yes, he told her, he'd consider Manhattan. In fact, he knew a faculty member at N.Y.U.

The couple married on September 26, 1932, four months after they first met. Rather than have a lavish event, Hope wanted to save the funds for their time in New York. So, their small ceremony took place in the living room of Hope's parents' home. Four hours later, they were on the train for New York. "Hardly anybody knew, and we were gone," recalled Hope.

An autumn in Manhattan would serve as an extended honeymoon. Hope prevailed on Lee that they should head straight to Greenwich Village where they found an apartment on the northern end of Bedford Street, an intimate and historic stretch running only nine blocks between Christopher and West Houston streets.

Around the corner from their place was the experimental Cherry Lane Theater and practically across the street was Chumley's, a former speakeasy that had also served as a hangout for legions of early twentieth-century writers including some of those Hope most admired, among them Millet, O'Neil, Cather, and Steinbeck.

While Lee was immersed in a postgrad program, the great city lay before Hope, her budding skills of observation and reporting at the ready. She wrote some pieces on spec about the history of various Manhattan neighborhoods, and on quirky institutions like the Salmagundi Club, an artist collective founded in the 1870s and situated on lower 5th Avenue.

The young couple also did plenty of exploring together, with Hope leading the way. "Lee said if he ever lost me in a strange city, he knew he'd eventually find me—in a library or an art gallery or the antique shop closest to the place he last saw me." Just such a locale was the mammoth Old Curiosity Shop, a combination antique store and junkshop located in desolate Hell's Kitchen west of Times Square. Legend had it that a Rembrandt had once been found amid its deep and dusty inventory. After a weekend visit together, Hope returned to interview the owner and then turned it all into a feature story.[7]

As winter set in, Hope nestled in their little apartment and took new stabs at creative writing, attempting a stage play and completing a few short stories. No sooner did she discard them and conclude that fiction wasn't her thing than she received word from a Texas publisher. Her submission of a short story titled, "A Study in Psychology," had won third place in a competition and would be published in the collection *Love Stories of the Southwest*. It would be her last piece published under the name Hope Dupre Ridings. The story opens at a party.

2

CITY DESK

Making their way back to Texas, the Millers stopped in Washington on the day of Roosevelt's first inauguration, March 4, 1933. As they exited Union Station into the winter chill, the Capital was alive in a rare spirit of celebration and they joined the throng of half a million Americans that had come together to cheer the new president. But the patriotic banners, marching bands, and repeated choruses of "Happy Days Are Here Again" only went so far in masking the poverty and neglect that held a tight grip on the southern city. As throughout the rest of the country, the effects of the Great Depression were everywhere. At the White House, exterior paint was yellowed and peeling. Coffee shops operated with a system of I.O.U.s for regular customers.[1]

Planning to stay only a few days, their Washington itinerary included some of the typical attractions but top of the list was calling on Sam Rayburn. The old family friend, now with twenty years of seniority in Congress, took the young couple to lunch. They told him of the exciting months spent in New York, and the thrill of the recent inauguration. Rayburn inquired as to their plans for the future. The latest thinking was that Lee would move his practice to Sherman and share offices with his father-in-law. For Hope, there was setting up a household, trying to find some new and worthwhile writing opportunities, maybe directing more community theater.

As the meal progressed, they saw in Rayburn a Texan prospering in a dynamic East Coast environment. Eventually, Hope shared how Washington was stirring up feelings of intrigue and possibility. She floated the idea that maybe they could stay. Rayburn was encouraging, but Lee had misgivings, primarily about money. Hope countered that Lee might continue his education toward an M.D. and she would get work.[2]

19

And that was pretty much that. The couple took an apartment on H Street NW in the area known as Foggy Bottom. Lee enrolled in a cardiology program at the University of Maryland in Baltimore. Hope plunged into the life of a freelancer.

With a population of just over half a million, Washington was still a long way from being a cosmopolitan center and in many ways Hope was still a country girl. But the Capital offered a potent mix of people and cultures. Plus, the New Deal was quickly getting under way. Coming up with ideas for stories in such an environment would never be a problem for Hope, though selling her initial pieces was going to require some hustling. The burgeoning world of Washington newspapers presented opportunities.

On the newsstands were five dailies. Leader of the pack was the *Evening Star*. Privately owned and full of advertising, it also boasted of having the influential political cartoonist Clifford K. Berryman whose depiction of Teddy Roosevelt led to the Teddy Bear. Also hitting stands in the afternoon was *The Daily News*, a tabloid owned by the Scripps Howard syndicate.

Then there was the morning *Herald* and the evening *Times*, which from the days of World War I were owned by William Randolph Hearst. Editor of them both since 1930 was the determined and competitive Eleanor Josephine Medill Patterson. "Cissy," as she was known, had close family connections in the business. She was a cousin of *Chicago Tribune* publisher, Robert McCormick, and her brother was *New York Daily News* publisher Joseph Medill Patterson.

Bringing up the rear was the *Washington Post*. Derisively referred to as the "daily miracle," it was on a slimming diet, eventually shrinking to just eighteen pages, with less than nineteen columns of display ads and fewer than two full pages of classifieds.[3] By virtue of inheritance, Edward Beale McLean had been its owner and publisher since 1916. A serious playboy but a negligible businessman, McLean lived a profligate life with his glamorous spouse Evalyn Walsh McLean, who was also a moneyed heiress. When at the *Post* headquarters, McLean rendezvoused with his mistresses and assigned more reporters to covering baseball than presidential elections.

McLean refused an offer of $5 million for the *Post* back in 1929. The prospective buyer was Eugene Meyer, a successful investor who had served in the administrations of Wilson and Coolidge as a "dollar-a-year man" (basically a volunteer with a government position) and was appointed by Hoover as chairman of the Federal Reserve. Meyer's ambitions to purchase and run a newspaper had also been rebuffed by Hearst, who said, "I buy papers. I don't sell them." But Meyer kept an eye on the *Post*. When McLean had all but bled the operation dry, it went into receivership and was put on the block in 1933.

The auction occurred on the steps of the paper's headquarters and was such a scene that the crowd rivaled the opening day of Congress. Bidding by proxy, Meyer won rights to the failing operation for the sum of $825,000. Cissy Patterson was furious. She could have beaten that price with her own funds but was an employee of Hearst whose representatives withdrew from bidding at $800,000. After she found out the identity of the successful buyer, Patterson and her papers entered into a battle royal with the *Post* and Meyer, its novice but well-heeled publisher.

Meanwhile, Hope had set out to conquer the city, one story at a time. What she lacked in experience, she made up for with industry. As with her recent months in Manhattan, each self-guided walking tour also functioned as an independent reporting expedition. Back at their little apartment, she wrote stories on spec and shopped them to editors. She visited the newsroom of every paper and made initial sales to the *Star* and the *Herald*. When she returned to deliver her finished copy, she made pitches for new assignments.

Hope found consistent success at the *Post*, where new talent was sorely needed. As with her hometown paper, book reviews were her breakthrough. Her first byline in the *Post* appeared on October 11, 1933. The article was a review of *A Nice Long Evening*, the latest book in Elizabeth Corbett's home-spun "Our Mrs. Meigs" series. Quickly added to a steady stream of short reviews was the occasional responsibility for an on-going column on the publishing trade, "No End of Books." Her first interview for the paper was with a young woman author who declared, "I would advise anybody not to write if she can do anything else in the world."[4]

Hope didn't listen. A growing infatuation with all things Washington spawned a stream of story ideas. Her first visit to Embassy Row was for research leading to "Christmas Around the World in Washington," a kind of holiday sampler that outlined the yuletide traditions of different countries as described and practiced by foreign nationals.[5] It ran in the *Post* on Christmas Eve and spilled out across a lavish, illustrated two-page spread, or "double truck" in newsroom lingo. Alas, her byline was missing, an unfortunate mistake, according to her assigning editors. But that same day, "Christmas Legends and Stories of Many Lands," a piece of similar international flavor, ran in the *Evening Star* and with due credit given her.[6] By this point, some months into her freelance hustling, the competing papers had to have known of her ambitions and professional promiscuity. Whatever the reasons for the withheld byline at the *Post*, major stories appearing simultaneously in two different papers still made an auspicious occasion out of Hope's first birthday celebrated in Washington.

Relations with the *Post* were only strengthened as she continued to pitch and they continued to publish. "Real Martha Washington Now Revealed" was given generous space and large graphics, even if it mostly drew on previously published sources and its revelations were as modest as Mrs. Washington herself.[7] A six-part series looked at the evolution of literary heroines from the 1860s to the 1920s in the popular genre of dime novels. The second day's entry began: "Fainting and flirting—two feminine arts that have never been improved upon—reached their zenith in the '70s. Weeping was an almost equally popular device. In no other era did women capitalize so much upon their foibles and frailties. . . . No woman dared to begin reading a popular romance without a stack of handkerchiefs at her elbow."[8] The tone of mild amusement was not contrived. After stumbling on a trove of Victorian-era romances at the Library of Congress, Hope considered the subject rich enough for a book and found time to expand her research into a monograph a few years later.

Whether she was casting about for ideas or just enjoying the sights, a visit to the National Museum (later named the Museum of Natural History) inspired some quick research and resulted in a timely story. Before her in a display case was a life-size bust of an Indian chief with braided hair, a feathered headdress, and stern visage. "Who is this old friend?" Hope wondered. The identifying placard said that he was Two Guns Half Calf of the Blackfoot tribe, whose profile is seen on the Buffalo Nickel. After reaching into her purse, she compared the likenesses and began wondering how this particular Indian had come to receive such an honor.

Her next stop was back at the Library of Congress where an hour or so of investigation revealed that Two Guns was one of five prominent Indian chiefs who modeled for designer James Earl Fraser. The image on the nickel was actually a composite of all their likenesses. "Old Two Guns did me a special favor," Hope later wrote. "The day after I picked up his trail, he died. Afternoon newspapers carried a brief report that the Indian on the Buffalo Nickel, at the age of 78, had departed from his Dakota home for his happy hunting ground. I wrote a correction and took it to the city editor of the *Washington Post*."[9]

The story ran on March 25 and the following day, Hope went from being a stringer to an employee of the *Post*. Besides being the linchpin in landing her a job, the nickel story also solidified what she described as "an ungovernable desire to be a reporter."[10]

Already she'd shown her prolific inclinations were no flash in the pan, so the *Post* editors probably figured it cheaper to make her an employee than to keep paying her piecemeal. Though her income declined from her best periods at freelancing, it was a relief to no longer be pitching stories all over town and to have a desk outside the home. With the Great Depression still going and Lee in school for the foreseeable future, she understood the value of a steady paycheck.

Hope's work for the *Post* so far had mostly appeared in the general news or Sunday sections. But publisher Meyer was launching a new women's department. Leading the effort was editor Malvina Lindsay, who came to the *Post* after pursuing general news and women's features at two Kansas City papers.

Lindsay reminisced about those early days of working together upon the publication of Hope's first book thirty-five years later:

> I feel vindication in a premonition I had when Mr. Meyer called me into his office and told me he had hired you. "Now Mrs. Miller has great potential" he said, "in time she might become a society editor." I felt outraged and I almost exclaimed, "Oh, surely she can become much more!" I was already familiar with your work and in those days I was determined to drive everyone with talent into becoming a *writer*. All I ever did for you was to show you some technique for getting the attention of the common reader, whoever that may be. You already had the basic knowledge of how to write and what a comfort that was.[11]

The women's pages and the personnel behind it quickly became a point of pride for the *Post*. "Written by Women for Women" was the title of a substantial overview of the new direction. It explained that in contrast to a typical paper where the women's section would be full of syndicated material, the *Post* was emphasizing a strong local focus.

"The publisher has accorded women a free hand in managing this department," the article declared. It proceeded to introduce the contributors and editors starting with Lindsay, who began a daily column, "The Gentler Sex," full of light satire and sometimes composed in verse. Next in order was Elizabeth Young, Lindsay's assistant, with her own column of armchair psychology. Penned under the byline Mary Haworth, it became hugely popular and nationally syndicated.[12]

Next came a dozen reporters, with where they had come from and what they would be covering. Hope appeared first. Though her weekday beat was general assignments of interest to women, her refined manner was recognized because she was assigned a Sunday etiquette column. "Be gracious and friendly;

the rules of etiquette count—but not so much as charm, natural or acquired. This is the essence of Hope Ridings Miller's social philosophy, stated in her weekly column and exemplified in her personality."

Each of Hope's etiquette columns carried a tone of complete confidence, as readers' queries and quandaries were dispensed with in a succinct and definitive manner. Some examples:

> A personal letter or thank-you note must always be written by hand.[13]
>
> Eight o'clock is the proper hour for a formal dinner. The hostess is never served first at either a formal or an informal dinner.[14]
>
> Sizes of visiting cards very according to lengths of names, but a woman's card is usually $2^{3}/4$ inches high. Very young girls usually selected a card about $^{1}/4$-inch smaller. A man's card is narrower and from $2^{1}/2$ to $3^{1}/2$ inches long depending on the length of the name. Cards may be made of white or ivory kid-finish cardboard.[15]

The etiquette column only lasted until early 1935, at which point Hope took responsibility for an even more sophisticated domain—poetry. Each week, she curated selections by contemporary writers, often drawn from current literary periodicals. Now and then she also read verse on radio station WJSV, a CBS affiliate broadcasting out of a building next door to the *Post*.

Not mentioned in the article introducing the staff of the women's page was a temporary member of the new department. She was 17-year-old Kay Meyer, daughter of the publisher, who served as copy girl and all-around gofer during her summer between high school and college. The low-level job was an early step in her long but steady march to eventually becoming the legendary publisher Katherine Graham.[16]

In these years, Eugene Meyer was investing heavily in staffing rather than upgrading facilities. The paper's headquarters on E Street, adjacent to the National Theater, was "perilous and problematic," as Graham later recalled. The whole place shook when the presses were rolling. The gloomy front lobby had a counter where the public could purchase recent issues, pay for classifieds, and the like. A porter operated a rickety and undependable cage elevator. On the second level was the city room, busy, smoky, and manly. The third floor housed the editorial and women's departments, offices of the managing editor and the publisher.[17] The condition of the building may not have aided in recruiting new staffers, but perhaps it served as an incentive for reporters to spend time away from their desks and out in the city chasing down news.

Hope's output only increased once she went on staff. She averaged ten bylines a month in 1933 and 1934, not counting her etiquette and poetry columns. During this era in journalism, bylines were not guaranteed and many of Hope's stories on artists and entertainers—among them, actresses Ginger Rogers and Marlene Dietrich, violinist Fritz Kreisler, and writer Gertrude Stein—ran without attribution.

Of her pre-society days, Hope would recall:

> I interviewed and wrote about women of every shade and description. Writers, actresses, government works and distinguished visitors from foreign lands, intellectual Amazons and mental pygmies, diplomatic hostesses, dowagers and debutantes, immutable Cassandras and peripatetic philosophers. Some were inspiring, a great many entertaining. A few, caught in the inevitable struggle between ego and the opportunity to be quoted in print, talked as though they'd been vaccinated with a phonographic needle. Others were so reticent they allowed me to answer my questions for them, and then were delighted to find themselves superbly articulate in print. Still others responded so smoothly and gracefully that the interviews seemed to write themselves.

Whether talkative or reticent, they could be volatile. Hope, a calm and polite Texan, was warned as much. "One of my favorite Capital wags, probably quoting someone else, once quipped, 'The world is full of women who seem to have sampled gunpowder along with their mother's milk.' "

A case in point was Margherita Sarfatti, an Italian arts patron and journalist who was also Mussolini's official biographer and sometime lover.

> A statuesque blonde, she greeted me with a dramatic flourish and an apology because her hair was disheveled and her Mayflower suite littered with magazines, books and newspapers. She dislodged a stack of manuscripts to vacate a chair for me. I asked her about her journalistic work with Mussolini. "I do not discuss Il Duce!" she replied firmly. Then would she tell me something about the women of Italy? Were they becoming more interested in public affairs? "I know nothing about the interests of women!" she shouted.[18]

Back in the newsroom, her hands shaking at the typewriter, Hope managed to crank out a tepid version of the conversation with Sarfatti. She was "reputed to be the most influential woman in Italy," and was "lavish in her praise" for American women, and "enthusiastic about the President and First Lady," who had received her at the White House a few days prior.[19]

Encountering such an array of personalities and agendas at breakneck speed proved wearing to Hope, a cub reporter in a new a city, a woman in a man's profession, and a newlywed whose husband was a full-time student. But once in a while, an interview became a genuine two-way dialogue. Stage and screen actress Jane Cowl fostered a sympathetic and encouraging exchange. Hope called on her in a dressing room at the National Theater.

> She must have sensed that I was inexperienced and perturbed. She put me at ease by describing her qualms when she landed her first big role in the theater. Then she began asking me questions. She inspired confidence. I told all. "Working women all have similar struggles," she said finally. "Success in any field depends more on energy and management than on talent, and a sincere desire to contribute, rather than receive. If you remember that, you'll go far."

In the subsequent story, Hope kept the bonding moments to herself and instead shared Cowl's musings on how the mix of beauty and ambition can aid or hinder an aspiring actress.[20]

On top of the constant flow of personality stories, Hope also wrote a number of series that delved into contemporary issues. Bringing historical background into the Capital's current discourse would become a specialty of her journalism practice in the coming years. An early example was a three-part series on the issue of school teachers being married or spinster. It was prompted by the D.C. education system's repeal of a "marriage clause," something that had gone into effect some twenty years prior and became reinforced by the "back-to-the-home" movement. Hope's lead acknowledged the reality: "Spinsterhood and pedagogy became one. The title 'school teacher' came to be inevitably preceded by 'old maid.'" Her survey of successful women teachers stretched from the Greek philosopher and instructor Hypatia (single) to the American education pioneer Emma Hart Willard (married).[21]

Another weeklong series looked at the growing phenomenon of married women who work outside the home. Presented in the context of the Great Depression and the general paucity of jobs (for men), the matter was viewed by some with alarming importance. Hope ran with that angle, opening one of the stories with: "Do working wives imperil the welfare of the race?" At the ready with an affirmative answer was a male anthropologist. "It is woman's business to be a good home-marker. If she sidetracks that duty . . . she is working against the laws of Nature." Hope's own views, as well her still nascent experience as both wife and professional, did not enter the discussion. But she closed that same day's story with remarks from a confident missus: "The woman who has unusual talent, such that the world would lose if she directed most of her interest to her home, should be allowed to continue her career, whether she happens to marry or not."[22]

No counterbalancing opinion came in a rather brief personality profile, whose subject declared, "The modern woman's Victorian manner is completely spoiled by the cigarette which hangs from her lips." The home, she continued, "offers an outlet for her intellect, her energy. It is a self-sufficient career." And so on. The speaker was Annie Nathan Meyer, founder of the all-female Barnard College.[23]

Rare was the profile of a progressive woman of a more recognizable and demonstrative type. In town on a lobbying effort in February 1935 was Margaret Sanger, who coined the term *birth control* and made it her cause. "Perhaps no woman, in the last 21 years vitally concerned with any cause, has battled against greater odds. . . . Yet there is nothing of the fighter in Mrs. Sanger's appearance. Mild in manner and calm even while discussing the most turbulent of her experiences, she is the antithesis of the proverbial feminine champion of Amazon proportions, booming voice and mannish attire." After further description of Sanger's clothing, hairstyle, and complexion, all part of Hope's normal introductory method, the story goes on: "One senses beneath that composed exterior, however, a steel that has sustained this courageous woman in the face of ridicule—a steel that has strengthened her through arraignments and even a prison sentence and prompted her to continue her fight for a cause that seemed hopeless two decades ago."

The story explains how the Comstock Law, dating from the post-Civil War era, prohibited the distribution of obscenities and thereby constrained the practice of medicine for women. Hope makes an effort to address what birth control is—mostly information and education, in those days—and what it is not, "the taking of life." Never mentioned was the term *abortion*, nor for that matter was the word *pregnancy*. The last word is given to Sanger: "Ultimate victory will come only after every intelligent voter has been awakened to the importance of proper birth control legislation."[24]

More typical stories were light and appreciative in tone, domestic or artistic in focus, with a constant emphasis on the women's angle. Headlines from three consecutive articles by Hope in just the week after the Sanger profile give the gist: "Dorothy Stone 'Adores' Gardening, Shuns Kitchen;" "Miss Styron Interested in Keyboard Music of 17th, 18th Centuries;" and "Father's Political Methods Are Good Enough for Her, Reba Doughton Says."

Amid the tonnage of newsprint that made up the women's section at the *Post* is a decades-long chronicle of political and economic progress. When "For and About Women," as it was eventually titled, got replaced in 1969 by "Style," the executive editor, Ben Bradlee said, "Traditional women's news bored the ass off all of us."[25] Yet in the midst of that climactic period, a dedicated forum for the systematic coverage of the women's movement had been yanked away. It would take time and a new generation of unflinching women reporters to move issues like day care, abortion, and pay equality out of the realm of "soft news."[26]

After eighteen months with the women's department, Hope transferred to the city room where she was the only woman reporter alongside some fifty men. She'd tired of having to stick with the woman's angle and her editors thought a change would broaden her outlook and benefit her writing. At the start, she was well deployed, doing deep research on D.C.'s adoption laws and practices. The first story in that series earned placement front page and above the fold. It began: "What price babies? Anyone asking this question can easily find the answer here in Washington, where at least three 'baby marts,' dealing in illegitimate children, function openly and entirely within the law. In one, the price of a baby 4 months old or under is $250."[27]

"This was the only time I did a stunt thing," she recalled. "I went to a woman who had an adoption agency, and I asked her about adopting a child. She took it that I wanted to adopt and I never corrected her on that. They tightened the law in the District after that. But see, the men didn't mind that. That was a woman's story."[28]

The placement of Hope's desk may have changed, but the shift in assignments was slight: feature-length stories loosely tied to local and federal issues, predominately in the feminine or familial realms. Child welfare and other youth matters were follow-ups to the adoption series, and there were daily reports on the national conventions of the Daughters of the American Revolution and the Parent-Teachers Association.

An exception to the confines of stories related to women came when Hope was sent to the Washington convention of the National Association for the Advancement of Colored People. She couldn't help but wonder about her assigning editor's motivations, "Here I was just a little southern girl and the only woman." She filed two news stories on the conference, during which delegates urged Congress to pass an anti-lynching law. Presiding over the gathering was Walter White, who, as the organization's executive secretary from 1931 to 1955, succeeded in persuading President Roosevelt to issue an executive order prohibiting discrimination by defense contractors and also advised President Truman on the desegregation of the military. Toward the end of the convention, White introduced himself to Hope and complimented her writing. He also asked where she grew up. Given the circumstances of their meeting and the infamous lynching in Sherman less than a decade prior, this may have been the only time in her life when Hope had anything less than all-out pride in her Texas roots.[29]

Hope also made a number of visits to Capitol Hill and not just to interview the wives. On the opening day of the 75th Congress, she cornered each of its six women members and filed a composite story about their respective agendas. "Every one of them knows exactly what type of legislative housekeeping she wants done this session."[30]

A couple of months into the term, she wrote short profiles of eleven new members, the most famous among them Senator Henry Cabot Lodge, Jr., of Massachusetts, the political scion and future diplomat. Each story was accompanied by a caricature of the subject and most contained repetitive tropes about the gentlemen's outside interests including baseball, football, scholastics, and cow punching. The history of Charles Arthur Anderson, a 37-year-old former prosecutor from Missouri, provided some welcome drama. He walked with a cane, his limp the result of a serious car accident that occurred the night after a conviction in a mafia-related kidnapping trial. "A close call, yet Anderson has been in law long enough to know that around an attorney's head the bullets of hatred fly just as freely as bouquets of admiration."[31]

When Hope found herself in the vicinity of the Capitol, she'd frequently stop by Sam Rayburn's office. If it wasn't a busy day for the House, they'd sit down for a private conversation.

"He liked to chat with me about things because he knew I wasn't going to run out and tell anybody. If I did that one time, then he'd never tell me anything else. I think I was one of the few people that he really talked to, aside from Lyndon and his pals," she said, referring, of course, to Lyndon Johnson who was first elected to the House in 1937, the same year Rayburn became Majority Leader.

Hope didn't probe for news items, though political jockeying in the city was a natural part of her conversations with Rayburn.

"I never used him as a source for stories. If I wanted background and he could give me any, yes, but I never regarded him that way. I was just always proud to see him. He knew a lot of stories."[32]

During one of Hope's visits to the Hill, she dropped by the Senate Office Building to call on Democratic Senator Henry F. Ashurst, whom she had recently met socially. Ashurst took his seat in 1912 as one of Arizona's original legislators. The kindly Senator greeted Hope as he was escorting out another visitor, Mrs. George Mesta, who was lobbying on behalf of the National Women's Party. As they all stood in the reception area, Ashurst introduced the two ladies and suggested that as a reporter Hope might be able to help out Mesta's cause.

"Oh, Mrs. Mesta, what is your cause?" Hope inquiredy politely.

"I'm working for equal rights for women and the National Women's Party," she replied. "And I do need your help."

"Well, Mrs. Mesta, I can't help you," Hope demurred.

"Why not?"

"Because I don't believe in equal rights for women, only special privileges."

Mesta let out a laugh and pressed on, "Oh, I'll change your mind. Come have dinner with me tonight."[33]

Hope's policy never waivered—equal rights for men, special privileges for women. But she soon built a close friendship with Perle Mesta, who was on her way to becoming one of Washington's great hostesses. Adding to the bond that they strengthened over many years of parties was the fact that they were raised in the same part of the country. Though born in Michigan, Mesta spent her early childhood in Galveston and her family moved to Oklahoma City just after the turn of the century. The family's fortune came from oil, her father being an investor in the famous Spindletop field near Beaumount. That, plus the wealth of her husband, a Pittsburgh steel manufacturer, made possible Mesta's political activisim and lavish party giving during the 1940s and 1950s.[34]

Looking back on her eight months as the only woman in the city room of the *Post*, Hope repeatedly stressed that she never experienced any discrimination because of her gender. But some extra chores in her daily work routine undermine that argument. One of her duties was to open her editor's desk and see if he had enough liquor to last the night. Otherwise, she had to run across the street and buy a bottle.[35] As for her fellow reporters, "They bothered me a lot, asking how to spell things, because none of them would go to the dictionary. 'Miller! How do you spell. . . .' Just time after time after time. I could hardly get my work done."[36]

3

SOCIETY EDITOR

"Why, why, there goes Mrs. Roosevelt!"

"This muffled cry of surprise rippled through the rain-soaked crowd of men and women assembled in the open-air press section of the Inaugural platform yesterday as the First Lady made an unexpected and fleeting appearance there approximately five minutes before the President took his oath of office."

"With her son, John, a grim-faced Secret Service man and a couple of drenched newspaper women at her heels, Mrs. Roosevelt minus umbrella and galoshes threaded through the crowd and ran up one aisle and down the other, scanning faces eagerly—looking for somebody, and incidentally, establishing a precedent for wives of Presidents."

"Unmindful of the rain that splashed down unmercifully on her blue flower-covered turban, slanted across her three-year-old black broadtail coat, and showered the bouquet of violets she carried in her white-gloved hand, Mrs. Roosevelt hurried on. . . ."[1]

When Publisher Eugene Meyer and Managing Editor Casey Jones sat down with Hope to discuss the position of society editor, they envisioned more than just the whirl of parties. They offered her the First Lady. That came as a relief, since Hope's initial instinct was to decline the new job, saying, "I don't want to be a Society Editor and write about what people eat."[2] The possibility of covering Eleanor Roosevelt was another thing entirely.

Hope assumed the position of Society Editor in May 1937. But components of the beat were foretold in that front-page report on the January 20 Inauguration. To start, there was simply following Mrs. Roosevelt's busy schedule and then reporting the who, when, where, and always what she was wearing or planning to wear. There would also be the benefit of proximity and the constant underlying awareness that this was a First Lady of a new order. (As to that "somebody" Mrs. Roosevelt was frantically searching for on the inauguration stand, if only to share a moment of greeting, it was Marion Dickerman. One of the First Lady's most intimate friends, Dickerman was also head of the Todhunter School in Manhattan and had been a principal in Val-Kil industries, a furnishing and housewares operation based on the Roosevelt property at Hyde Park. The balance of Hope's article detailed the First Lady's many activities through the course of Inauguration Day.)

Though the Roosevelts had already occupied the White House for four years, the city establishment was still getting accustomed to their ways, especially how they entertained. During the time of the Coolidge and Harding administrations, which was also the era of prohibition, "the general air of official parties was one of frustration bordering on plain crossness. Almost everyone seemed over-trained and worn out," as Hope later wrote.

With the arrival of the Roosevelts, White House parties became not just a place of distinction but also a time of enjoyment. A widely remembered symbol of the change was the moment when Mrs. Roosevelt appeared at her first formal White House reception without gloves. According to Hope, "she revolutionized the social picture from the top down, introduced an air of informality at White House parties, and while maintaining the basic decorum, augmented the official calendar with innovations that forever horrified conservative Washington society."

FDR did his part as well, also with the simplest of gestures—greeting guests by their first names. "In official reception lines formerly noted for stuffiness, his wisecracks began crackling up and down like snappers popping at a children's birthday party. Now and then a particularly good retort rated a reception guest an invitation to one of the celebrated Sunday night suppers at which Eleanor Roosevelt presided over a chafing dish and served scrambled eggs."

Society was no longer its own game but was once again an extension of government business.

> Society that mattered became recognized for what it had actually been since the beginning of the Federal City—company town society, in which everybody of national importance was either an employee of U.S.A. Inc., or had some significant connection with it. And under the energetic aegis of Eleanor Roosevelt, everybody sooner or later had the chance to meet The Management.[3]

Coverage of Mrs. Roosevelt would no longer be a literal chase, as it had been on that inaugural platform, nor was it limited to nighttime duty at formal affairs. Hope also became the *Post*'s eyes and ears at the First Lady's weekly press conferences, which were the exclusive domain of women reporters.

For a good spot at the Tuesday gatherings, a competitive race took place among the scribes as they dashed up the White House stairs to the Monroe Room on the second floor.[4] After the press corps was assembled, Mrs. Roosevelt would read her schedule of appearances and speeches for the coming week. That would lead to questions as to why she was going there and what she hoped to accomplish.

Groundbreaking as those gatherings were, and as legendary as they have become, headline news did not exactly spill out of them in profusion. One of Hope's earliest stories as society editor recounted the transitory substance of a typical conference in May 1937: Mrs. Roosevelt intended to slow down her pace during the coming summer months although how to accomplish that she "hadn't the faintest idea." She also found it difficult to christen airplanes, since smashing champagne bottles can lead to splashes on one's dress. Upcoming appointments included: an afternoon meeting with Belgian author Mme. Claire de Hedevary; a visit to the Red Cross headquarters to receive a book translated into Braille; a gathering at the State Department to participate in opening the phone line to China; and taking along some students to settlement houses established under the Works Progress Administration. Hope included a paragraph laying to rest the question of the First Lady's interest in astrology and palmistry, which was apparently prompted by a recent visit to the White House of a woman who claimed to be a psychic and took an impression of Mrs. Roosevelt's hand. "I certainly don't take it seriously," said the First Lady. Then came some family matters. There was the big upcoming wedding of Miss Ethel du Pont to Franklin D. Roosevelt, Jr.; also in July a crossing to the continent by John Roosevelt and Sara Roosevelt, the President's mother.[5]

Hardly a glamorous or important hour spent at the White House, but it was enough to fill some columns. The conferences served as a convenient means for reporters to collectively keep abreast of the First Lady's agenda. And week after week, month after month, Mrs. Roosevelt was giving a level of job security to women of the press and at the same time building rapport with them.

The press conferences weren't the only time when the First Lady welcomed the newspaper women to the White House. Each year, on the same night that men of the press and leading political figures gathered for the Gridiron roast, Mrs. Roosevelt hosted the "Gridiron Widows," for women of the press and the administration, plus wives of diplomats and of legislators. Satirical skits and lighthearted songs were performed and it became a high point of the year.

Still other ways that the First Lady and her staff were attentive to the journalists included hosting their children for play dates with the Roosevelts' grandchildren and inviting their parents to social functions at the White House, even when the parents lived in another part of the country. As one participant recalled, a reporter could expect to receive "flowers from the White House greenhouse if she stayed home even a day with the sniffles."[6]

Once in a while during her conferences, Mrs. Roosevelt might address emerging policies or forthcoming actions of the administration. "She didn't get really into the hard news herself, but she did skirt it," said Hope. Should the First Lady tread too far, her secretary, Malvina Thompson, was at the ready to walk it back. Also on hand at every session was the social secretary, Edith B. Helm. But even some members of the press were known to chime in and not with questions but interjections to protect the First Lady.

"You could depend on Martha Strayer or Ruby Black, one or the other, to speak up and say, 'Mrs. Roosevelt, are you sure you want that on the record?' And then she might say, 'I do want that off the record,'" recalled Hope, referring to her colleagues working for the *Washington Daily News* and United Press, respectively. "But you see," continued Hope, "we felt if she did that, we still were on the inside and she was giving us background. So we didn't resent that at all."

Hope regularly left the sessions with leads for other stories as well, often on matters not even directly related to the administration. What's more, upon her return to the *Post* headquarters in the late morning, male reporters sought her out to inquire if anything good had come up.

"You could ask her anything and she would answer. I never knew her to avoid a single question while I was there or to sidestep anybody," continued Hope. "It must have been a source of some embarrassment for her that they were always quizzing her about divorce in the family. You see, her children were always divorcing, it seemed, always getting married and divorcing. But she would say, 'It's their lives, and I can't interfere with that.'" The five Roosevelt children would ultimately have a total of nineteen marriages.

"I thought she was the most remarkable person I almost ever knew in my life, in the way she handled all of us," said Hope. A general admiration for Mrs. Roosevelt was common among the women reporters, but some were more obviously protective. Besides Strayer and Black, others in this group were Bess Furman and Beth Campbell, both of Associated Press, and Gene- vieve Forbes Herrick of the *Chicago Tribune*. "We all knew (Mrs. Roosevelt) had certain favorites," said Hope. "I was not one of them, which was all right, because that made me more popular with the rest of them."[7]

Admission was limited to one representative of each local paper and each wire service, plus some magazine correspondents and visiting reporters from out of town. It was quite literally a select group and Hope now belonged.

Almost simultaneous with her promotion at the *Post*, Hope became a member of the Women's National Press Club, a body formed in 1919 as an alternative to the National Press Club, which only admitted men. The WNPC brought together reporters from the political and city beats, often referred to as "front- page girls," with the society editors and features writers, sometimes called the "Green Room Group," a curious reference to the theater world.

The camaraderie was a welcome reminder to Hope of her two years at the University of Texas when she lived with "sisters." But the club was foremost a professional organization, intensely active in providing educational support and networking opportunities to its members. This occurred primarily through a weekly speaker series that took place over lunch in the Cabinet Room of the Willard Hotel, a practice modeled on that of the National Press Club. Guests were notables from the fields of politics and diplomacy, entertainment, and culture. Their presentations often resulted in members leaving with fresh mate- rial for news stories.[8]

A highlight of every year was the club's "stunt party," during which elab- orate skits spoofed the goings on of the day, in much the same manner as occurred at the Gridiron. The event was produced in the early spring as the centerpiece of a busy weekend of related events that brought together women from all avenues of Washington life and also female journalists from around the county. The party itself began with dinner followed by an entertainment that was far more than a short satirical skit. While still in the spirit of a spoof, it was a lengthy theatrical undertaking, with singing, dancing and costumes, all written and performed by the club members.

The shows gave Hope a regular opportunity over the ensuing decades to reconnect with her performing ambitions. She made an auspicious debut by starring in the 1938 revue as Miss Lotta Business, opposite Franklin DeLayno, portrayed by Esther Van Wagoner Tufty, an independent reporter with her own news agency. The scenario was a film shoot. The primary target of the humor was the president's difficulties with industry and labor.

The parting curtain revealed Lotta, gowned in white satin and laden with orchids, looking anything but pleased with her leading man. Franklin looked like Franklin, eyeglasses, cigarette holder and all. The hero and heroine scowled at each other, while the directors scowled at them both and the cameraman looked bored, in a strictly professional fashion. The director pleaded with the stars to remember this was the Supreme Courtship—"The public's demanding a love scene between you two, and it's gonna get it. See?" Meanwhile, Franklin had declared that all Lotta wanted to do was to "sit around and play Monopoly!"

"Oh, I do, do I?" Lotta snapped back. "You haven't left me anything to sit around on! Everywhere I look there's nothing but tax, tax, tax!"

In desperation, the director threatened to fire Franklin at the expiration of his 1940 contract.

In the six scenes that follow, there's an appearance by the child star "CIO-ley Temple" (referencing the labor federation) who gleefully calls the President "Daddy"; also a Boycott Ballet; and a send-up of Clare Boothe Luce's hit play "The Women." The latter scene takes place in a beauty parlor where a call goes out to the First Lady informing her that the false eyelashes she ordered had come in.[9] That tied back to a month prior when big fashion news was made by Mrs. Roosevelt appearing at a press conference wearing, for the first time, some lipstick and "a hint of rouge."[10]

An audience of 500, including Eleanor Roosevelt, witnessed the fun and the entire guest list was printed in the *Post*. Another crowd of 300, this time including some husbands and sundry newspaper men, gathered at a post-party event the next day where dinner was again served. Lotta and Franklin reprised their scene and Hope again got to deliver the line: "He pinched me on my undistributed profits!"[11]

Another new club member accepted during the 1937–1938 term was the First Lady herself. After considerable debate within the club, which had a policy of admission only to women of the working press, she was accepted by virtue of her credentials as writer of the column, "My Day," which was syndicated to hundreds of papers by United Features. While never a regular attendee at the club's functions, Mrs. Roosevelt was often the honor guest at the Stunt Party and an end-of-season banquet.

Among Hope's many new colleagues, she found a mentor and ally in Ruth Jones, the society editor at the *Washington Herald* who wrote under the name Jean Eliot. A native of Washington, Jones was born with deep ties to the city's power structure. Her father was an influential lawyer, her great uncle had been in the Senate and her great grandfather was the city's second mayor. Jones began her career in 1914 covering the social scene at the *Washington Times*, which named her society editor the following year. She held the same spot at the *Post* from 1928 to 1930 and by that time she'd become established as the premiere society editor in the city. That made her prime pickings for Cissy Patterson, who upon taking over the *Herald* persuaded Jones to come aboard.[12] Jones is remembered as the first to write society reports in a narrative fashion . . . rather than as a series of brief notes and facts . . . set apart by three dots. She was twice elected president of the WNPC and was the only society writer on the original committee of women that came together to advise Mrs. Roosevelt on her plan to conduct regular press conferences.[13]

Despite the gap of almost a decade between their tenures at the *Post*, Jones was essentially Hope's immediate predecessor. A few different women did hold the job for brief periods after Jones. But in the years immediately prior to Hope, most society items in the *Post* ran without any indication of authorship, a likely indication that the position was vacant.

"She was so sweet to me when I didn't know anybody. I'd go to parties and she'd help me with names and everything," recalled Hope. "If she hadn't helped me out a few times, I don't know what I would have done. I didn't know anything about society in Washington. I didn't know who was who or anything, except that if you stayed with it, you could sort it from the top—the President and the Vice President, the Cabinet, and so on."

The welcoming spirit that Jones showed Hope indicates the sense of fellowship that existed among women of the profession, even when they were competing with each other for stories and stature.

"Oh, there was competition," said Hope. "Ruth Jones and I were awfully good friends but we were competitive. We were covering the same parties and you weren't going to scoop on the party. The only thing you could do was to out write each other."[14]

Hope had little time to get acclimated after her start as society editor in May 1937 before plunging into coverage of a late June wedding that would bring together two great families of American aristocracy, the Roosevelts and the du Ponts. In ten separate articles, large and small, that ran during the month prior to the wedding of Ethel du Pont and Franklin D. Roosevelt, Jr., she conveyed every available detail: names of the attendants, of the presiding Episcopal reverends and of the celebrity dress designer; invitations going out, gifts coming in, thank-you notes written by hand; and cherished hymns for the wedding, favorite popular songs—with orchestra—for the reception.

Hope's tenure in the City Room had given her a heightened skill and determination for reporting that she put to good use, since information was not being doled out in the normal Roosevelt fashion. Too many calls from reporters were being fielded by the butler at Owls Nest, the du Pont home in Wilmington. That led to the family of the bride hiring a publicity agent who stanched the flow of information. Hope let her readers know:

> Each day brings a flood of reports as to plans for the wedding, but they don't come from Fred H. Uthoff, the high-powered publicity man hired to take care of the press. From his office has been sent some material—three long, single-spaced pages, to be exact—filled with facts, but few sidelights, and prefaced with the suggestion that "this information is sufficient for several stories in advance of the wedding." So it is. Stories that could just as easily be combed from Who's Who, the encyclopedia and the social register. In reading through the whole discourse, I found nothing new except that Owls Nest is spelled without the apostrophe. But from another source in Wilmington comes some livelier news. . . .[15]

A voluminous story for the Sunday magazine section played up the Montague-Capulet comparison that had become the talk about town. "New Dealers and Old Dealers, staunch Democrats and loyal Liberty Leaguers will sit shoulder to shoulder to witness a wedding that will unite two of America's oldest and proudest families. Differences in political leanings apparently will be laid aside by elders in both families as a Roosevelt and a du Pont exchange their vows." Next, Hope jumps back a century or so to when ancestors of the families arrived on these shores, and then she marches the chronology forward.[16]

For another item in the wall-to-wall coverage, she considered the wedding in the context of the season and recent history.

> Wednesday remains the most popular day for weddings, probably because so many persons remember the ancient rhyme: *Monday for health, Tuesday for wealth, Wednesday's the best day of all. Thursday for losses, Friday for crosses, and Saturday's no luck at all.* I wonder if Ethel du Pont and Franklin D. Roosevelt, Jr., chose their nuptial day, Wednesday June 30, because they knew that rhyme. And that reminds me—the Duke of Windsor married on Thursday. For losses? Well, merely a throne.[17]

The day of the ceremony brought news that the du Pont home would be guarded by 300 federal soldiers, a force equal in size to the number of invited guests.[18] Hope filed a lengthy report that was carried on the front page. It was so full of detail that every blossom got a mention. The maid and matron of honor "carried oblong bouquets of single blossoms arranged of hortensia maculata, nizza levkoja, stephanotis and primulus with a soft tinge of wisteria blue and hydrangea purple. These botanical names completely stumped a Wilmington florist yesterday morning, who wondered why the blossoms 'weren't called by more familiar names, since the wedding is supposed to be such an unpretentious affair.' "[19]

Reporting and writing were only a portion of Hope's new responsibilities, since the "Editor" part of her title was no mere honor. She assembled and supervised a staff charged with filling two pages in each daily edition of the *Post*. Besides coverage of Mrs. Roosevelt's every movement and all White House receptions, society also encompassed the constant surge of embassy events; the regular flow of weddings, engagements, and debuts; plus club meetings and functions, and countless comings and goings. As examples of the latter, "Notes of Society: Official and Residential" from one Thursday in early September 1937 contained thirteen short items. Among them: a British attaché and his wife entertained at the Shoreham; an American consul sailed for France; a couple closed their Newport cottage and motored to Canada before returning to New York; and a woman is entertaining at her home in Bethesda.

It was the Facebook of its day, at least for people of a certain class. More than once during her tenure at the *Post*, Hope was told by appreciative readers, including men of high position, that after reading the front page they turned directly to society, "to see what's really going on." The depth of coverage fit within the larger news effort at the *Post*, where a Sunday paper in 1937 typically contained 100 pages but sometimes as many as 180 pages. A parallel but distinct entity from society pages was the women's section, which included fashion, gardening, and cooking. Performing and fine arts were also handled separately.

Hope's own stories took top position on the society pages, often accompanied by a "headshot" of her with a wavy bob and a knowing, sideways glance. A smattering of shorter stories as well as the regular "Society Notes" column usually carried no byline, which suggests that Hope herself may have sometimes written the various items. Yet she was building a staff that would soon establish their own voices in the *Post* and over time their own distinguished careers.

Dudley Harmon, a Smith College graduate, had joined the women's department in 1935, starting with stories on domestic appliances and tasks. She came over to assist Hope on advance research for larger events, making calls to embassies and residential hostesses about guest lists, menus, and the like. Harmon also had her own regular column, "About the Town." Later working for the United Press, she became one of the first female overseas correspondents during World War II and also covered the Nuremburg Trials and early sessions of the United Nations.[20]

Harmon's most harrowing adventure came immediately after leaving the *Post* in 1941, when she headed for Africa to work with the Free French effort. She and a missionary were returning to the States aboard a Norwegian freighter that was torpedoed. Her account of spending a night aboard a life raft conjures up the image of Tallulah Bankhead, the unflappable, bejeweled reporter in Hitchcock's *Life Boat*. Harmon paints the scene: "I gazed at the water and remembered tales of submarines which rose and machine-gunned survivors. I kept quiet though. I even recall grinning. But my stomach felt funny and my hand shook as I lit a cigarette."[21]

To strengthen the *Post*'s reporting on establishment Washington, "the cave dwellers" as they're still known, Hope recruited a native, Betty Beale, who was also a Smith girl.

> I was doing Junior League work, writing press releases and taking them to the society editors of Washington's newspapers. They must have been acceptable, because out of the blue, Hope Ridings Miller, society editor of the *Washington Post*, called to ask if I would do a weekly column for her section. I hesitated. How could she count on me to produce them on time? She wasn't worried. She asked me to write up the party I was going to that evening as a sample. I did and I was hired. . . . I thought I'd try it for a year. Just maybe it would lead to something better. I hadn't a clue that I was being propelled into a lifetime profession.[22]

As a freelancer, Beale was given charge of the modestly titled column, "Top Hats and Tiaras." She was with the *Post* from 1937 to 1940. After a five-year hiatus from the field, Beale became society editor for the *Star*, a position she held until that paper folded in 1981.

Many a time, Hope began a column remarking at the rapid pace of social events in Washington despite it being either in the heat of summer or the deep freeze of winter, the Christmas holidays or the period of Lent, with Congress in town or out of session. Her mailbox was constantly filled with invitations. But there was a single factor determining the schedule of Hope's stories and also when hostesses could schedule their soirees with some certainty of gathering a respectable assortment of notable guests. Everything revolved around the White House social calendar.

For the season running from autumn 1937 until just before Ash Wednesday 1938, the executive mansion would host separate state dinners honoring the Vice President, the Cabinet, the Supreme Court, the Speaker of the House, and the Diplomatic Corps. Receptions would be given to honor Congress; the Treasury, the Post Office, and other departments; and the Army and Navy.[23] Each gathering featured distinguished guests in formal attire, resplendent hospitality and enlightening entertainment. Yet for a mass of spectacle as well as formal protocol laced with political calculation, still another event—the Diplomatic Reception—outshined all others.

Hope's first outing at the annual affair was on December 16, 1937. The event honored fifty-four nations, had more than 1,000 guests, and resulted in another front-page story that continued with a two-page spread accompanied by photos on the inside jump. Hope's account balanced color and detail worthy of a screenplay with scrupulous attention to names of the most important guests and their proper titles.

At the opening hour, the scarlet-coated Marine Band struck up the tune of "Hail to the Chief," and the President, preceded by military and naval aids, led the way to the Blue Room. . . . Before a bank of smilax and fern, the Chief Executive and the First Lady, attired in a gown of plum and pink with orchids on her shoulder, received their guests. . . .

Envoys from countries which have instituted drastic changes in recent years for the most part wore formal dress, American fashion, with few, if any, decorations. Others—such as the British Ambassador, the Japanese Ambassador, the Chinese Ambassador, the Hungarian Minister and envoys from Norway and Sweden—were turned out in full diplomatic regalia with gold braid, medals, swords and plumed, cocked hats. Diplomatic hostesses, also appearing in their gayest and most elaborate plumage, set a new high in fashionable attire, which vied in beauty with that of Cabinet hostesses and others. The reception as a whole marked the one Washington event thus far this season at which the female of the species was less 'diked out' than the male. . . .[24]

Less than six months prior, the Marco Polo Bridge Incident had launched the Second Sino-Japanese War. Representatives of the two nations were in attendance that night and maintained a studied detachment.

One of the tensest moments of the evening was noted shortly after the staff of the Chinese Embassy, leaving the Blue Room and proceeding through the Red Room, arrived in the dining room. Not long before the Japanese staff had entered and had formed a little island to themselves near the center of the room.

But differences were masked in smiles, and Oriental envoys on both sides proved themselves masters of diplomacy. Each little group stayed clear of the other without being too obvious about it, and if any of the Japanese were isolated in any sense, it was of their own choice. At 9:35, after greeting a number of other guests quickly, somewhat nervously, the entire staff departed. They stayed at the reception exactly 30 minutes. Not long afterward, the entire Chinese staff left. The Dean of the Diplomatic Corps (Sir Ronald Lindsay) however remained until after the last guest had passed down the receiving line and the President had retired.[25]

Society editors, more often than not, get little more than a passing aside in the histories of the press. Even the studies of women in journalism move quickly to expound about the pioneering political reporters, those who had the "real jobs." Hand in hand with this comes the notion that covering society was as easy and relaxing as afternoon tea. It's a misconception akin to the view of performing arts critics as lucky folks sitting back and enjoying lots of shows, or even sports reporters who get to hang out with the guys and root for the home team. But excellent coverage of any of these fields—society, arts, sports— requires knowledge of history, keen and quick perception, a flair for analysis, and a way with words. Respected reporters in these arenas do get a special benefit though: ringside seats for the action.

"If you have a society column or you're society editor, you get invited to everything—everything!" recalled Hope. "The White House sent us engraved invitations to every reception they had and once a year to a state dinner. At that time there were about 50 embassies and legations in town and they were fascinating to me, this little Texas girl meeting all these 'ferners.'"

In contrast to how a newspaper person would review a performance or cover a game from a removed distance, society reporters took part in the show. Thus, another prerequisite was grace and refinement, plus a sizeable wardrobe.

"I never carried a pad and pencil to a party in Washington," said Hope. "I went as a guest and hoped that they'd forget I was a reporter, and mingled among them. I got a lot of good stories that way, stories that I never would have gotten if I'd been standing there with a pad and pencil."

First infiltrate the scene, then go beneath the surface.

"The usual reporting had been who was there, what they wore, and what they ate. I was trying to find out what they said and how they acted. Anything offbeat. I didn't go with the idea to catch them off guard or get anything scandalous, but I was trying to get as much interesting material as I could."

Even a young mind can't retain every conversational tidbit.

"Many times I would take myself off to the ladies room and whip out a pencil and put down something in a little notebook that I had in my bosom, and then rush back."[26]

Morning-after reports painted the general scene, but mostly stuck to the facts, including size of the crowd backed up by generous lists of dignitaries in attendance. Always a part of the accounts were descriptions of the ladies' outfits. Observations on fashion trends and details of specific ensembles worn by prominent women were a valued part of society coverage that dated back to its mid-nineteenth century origins. Before photography was pervasive, women relied on the written word to stay in touch with the latest styles. Over the decades, such reporting evolved into the popular television coverage of celebrities on the red carpets.[27]

Saved for Hope's columns, or "think pieces," were the broader contours of Washington social life plus choice disclosures from the discussions going on about town. "Teacup talk," as she called it, would take on a greater portion of her writing as she integrated further into the scene and as the social discourse turned increasingly to international and military affairs.

Hope was exacting in her writing and attentive to nuance. Not long after becoming Society Editor she took issue with certain changes made to her stories by the copy editors at the *Post*. "They got a few things tangled up, so I complained to Casey Jones and showed him the carbon copies of the original articles." Jones instructed her to send all her copy direct to the composing room, where type was placed on pages before printing. Skipping the copy desk meant from then on, Hope's duties included editing stories written by her staff and also composing the "heds," or headlines, for everything appearing on the society pages.

"In order to be sure that I could get my pages exactly as I wanted, Mr. Meyer suggested that I go down to the makeup room. Many times I'd be down there in an evening dress at 11:00 or 11:30, after having been somewhere to a party, seeing that they were putting the columns in where I liked them."[28] It probably didn't hurt Hope's standing that Meyer was also in the habit of dropping by late at night while wearing a tuxedo, just to check on things.[29]

Apart from the long hours, Hope's productivity was reflected in the count of her bylines. She was now clocking in an average of twenty stories per month. And not everything was a party report. The first Tuesday in October 1937, she went to the opening of the Supreme Court's new term where Justice Hugo L. Black took his seat for the first time. As to what cases were being argued, you'd have to turn back to the front page to find out. Still hewing closely to the women's angle, Hope painted the scene of what was happening in the rest of the courtroom. She described how, prior to the official business getting under way, Mrs. Louis D. Brandeis, wife of the eldest Justice, warmly greeted the young Mrs. Black. Also seen among the other spectators was the suffragist Elsie Hill.[30]

During the course of that month, Hope also covered the opening of the Theatre Guild's season with a production of *Madame Bovary*; noted the arrival to town of a British novelist and a Finnish minister, among many others; and repeatedly built anticipation for the December visit by the Duke and Duchess of Windsor. Doing her part for the Community Chest campaign, she expounded on the good deeds that come from society and said, "The list of women working on one of the most important annual campaigns in Washington reads like page after page from the Social Register or the Junior League membership book."[31]

One might even describe a typical column by Hope Ridings Miller the same way. Even when covering a modest "at home," during which a resident hostess welcomed all callers, Hope could easily mention fifteen or twenty names. Multiplying that by the number of stories she was producing shows how a sizable swath of Washington was garnering favorable notice in the *Post*.

While official protocol stipulated strict ranking for seating at a banquet, more flexibility was allowed for the placement of names in a society report. Mix liberally the attendees from the various branches of government, diplomacy, and residential society but do start with any heads of state. Lead with the celebrity hostess and gather commentary from the most sensational raconteur available.

By Hope's estimation, the best parties in Washington history were given by hostess Evalyn Walsh McLean. The daughter of an Irish immigrant turned Colorado gold prospector, McLean titled her life's story, *Father Struck It Rich*. She knew little of the ways of money, except how to spend it in profusion. On top of the world travels, grand estates, and lavish parties, there was the Hope Diamond, which she purchased in 1911. She would be its last private owner. Though cautioned, repeatedly, that the 45.52-carat stone came with a deadly curse, she wore the blue gem as a signature adornment. "I put the chain around my neck and thereby seemed to hook my life to its destiny of good or evil," she wrote.[32] And misfortune did follow. Her alcoholic husband Ned, former owner of the *Post*, died in a sanitarium. Their 10-year-old son was struck and killed by a slow-moving car. A 20-year-old daughter married a

Senator thirty-six years her senior, the same Senator whom Evalyn had been dating. Four years later, the daughter died of a drug overdose.

Despite all the troubles that life brought her, McLean gave parties of unceasing pace and unprecedented scale at her Washington home named Friendship. Sunday evenings meant dinner for 200 close friends. There were special occasions on top of that. William Borah, the Idaho Senator, once said to her, "This sort of thing is what brings on a revolution."[33]

Hope was at many of the affairs and also shared enough private moments with McLean, who was her senior by twenty years, that the two formed a bond. The following letter reveals McLean's admiration and fondness for the new society editor at the *Post*:

> September 20, 1938
>
> Dearest Hope:
>
> I just read your article last night about life in Washington and I think it is very very interesting. I am so glad you are getting started and I know you are going to make a great success of anything you undertake.
>
> In the first place, you are so fair and square about everything and you also have such an interesting way of expressing your thoughts.
>
> If there is ever anything I can do, dear child, to help you, don't hesitate to call. If I hear any news at all I will get in touch.
>
> with my love, affectionately,
>
> Evalyn McLean

The admiring sentiments went both ways. A decade after McLean's death, Hope wrote: "Beneath her glittering jewels beat a heart as big as the be-plumed Lillian Russell hats that she wore to her Thanksgiving luncheons and Easter breakfasts. She was generosity personified."[34]

Still later, Hope said in a television interview: "I thought she was a darling person. A kook, you know, but of course we love those in Washington."[35]

Hope's most thorough account of an evening at Friendship was filed on New Year's Day, 1938. The complete story included the names of ninety Washingtonians:

> Nearly 900 guests watched the old year out and the New Year in at Mrs. Edward Beale McLean's party at Friendship last night. A gay company, studded with social notables and headliners, blinked their eyes as lights were lowered at midnight and the streamer "Happy Near Year 1938" flashed on.
>
> A cry of "Happy New Year!" rippled through the crowd from room to room, and as the orchestra struck up, younger guests whirled into the dance

once more. In a few seconds Friendship again was ablaze with lights, and the ball moved merrily through the early hours of the New Year.

Before the dance, Mrs. McLean entertained 330 guests at dinner. Receiving them in the long drawing room, decorated with traditional Yuletide accents of green and red, the hostess wore a gown fashioned of paillettes, ranging in shades from sapphire to dark blue, blending with tones of her famous Hope Diamond but almost out-dazzling it.

Dinner was served at round tables in the long dining room and on the big, glassed-in porch. Rare plates and glassware, of which Friendship boasts one of the finest collection in the country, were set on gold satin clothes, each table being centered with a bowl of roses, red, yellow or white.

Featuring an elaborate menu, the dinner lived up to the McLean tradition of hospitality, with nothing left to be desired. After the dinner, while tables were being cleared, additional debutantes, dowagers and social notables invited for the dance were making their way—admission cards in hand—through the barricade of detectives stationed three-deep around each entrance.

In the interval between the dinner and the dance, guests gathered once more in the small room to the east. Others assembled in small groups on the front terrace and portico, which this year, as last, had been walled in, heated, draped with dark green sateen and decorated with fir boughs. This formed a long promenade between the drawing room and the ballroom, presenting a glamorous picture with its silver and poinsettia accents.

The dancing began about 10 o'clock, and from then until well into 1938 the music, furnished by Hal Kemp's and Meyer Davis' orchestras, was continued.

Champagne and other wines were served throughout the party. Late in the evening, a buffet supper was spread at a long table. The cocktail room, equipped with a new mirrored, maple-lined bar and small tables, was popular. For those who did not care to dance, there was a series of games in progress in one of the rooms.

Dancing, however, proved the most popular type of entertainment. And every step, from the stately and staid waltz to "the big apple," "the shag," and "the little peach," had an inning before the party was finished.

Glimpsed among the guests were a fair sprinkling of diplomats, many persons from official groups, scores of out-of-towners, and a number of debs, sub-debs and post-debs, accompanied by collegians enjoying the last of their holiday vacations.

Holding a little court of her own was Mrs. Nicholas Longworth. Justice and Mrs. Owen J. Roberts and their daughter, Miss Elizabeth Roberts, also were centers of attention. Senator and Mrs. Millard E. Tydings, the latter in a simply cut gown of black satin, arrived with Mr. and Mrs. Aldance Walker, of

New York. Mrs. Walker's gown was one of the prettiest there—grey crepe heavily embroidered with silver sequins.

Lucius Beebe, sartorial and journalist celebrity, was present; also Joseph Hergesheimer, the writer, and Mrs. Hergesheimer . . . Charles A. Davila, the Romanian Minister, was among the early arrivals, as were the Austrian Minister and Mrs. Prochinik, the latter in a handsome black velvet gown, set off with three big roses outlining the low neck. . . . The Secretary of War and Mrs. Harry H. Woodring were there . . . also Representative and Mrs. Sol Bloom, the latter in a dark green taffeta frock with a full skirt and short sleeves. . . . In fact, anywhere you looked, society with a capital "S" was in evidence.[36]

4

PRESIDING OFFICER

Joseph P. Kennedy had a full agenda in early 1938 after being appointed by President Roosevelt as ambassador to Great Britain. A priority was whether to side with Prime Minister Neville Chamberlain in broaching some form of appeasement with Germany's Adolf Hitler. Among Kennedy's lesser duties was something of crucial importance to elite families across the United States. It was his duty to decide which American debutantes would be presented at the Court of St. James's, as the royal sphere in London is officially known. Prior to heading overseas, Kennedy, accompanied by his wife, Rose, spoke at a January luncheon of the Women's National Press Club, which Hope noted drew a record turnout of members and their guests.[1] His remarks were off the record, but soon there was a buzz about town that change was afoot. Hope kept her readers apprised:

> It may seem nonsense to some, but it's still sacred tradition to some—this business of making a formal bow at a royal court. . . . Our new envoy, Joseph Kennedy, is toying with the idea of arranging no bows at all. He was at least, before he left Washington. As he sees it, or saw it, such a step would save a lot of heartbreak for those who can't make the grade, and a lot of trouble for an ambassador who will be busy enough negotiating weightier matters. In the past, the matter of examining thousands of applications accompanied by family histories, high-powered endorsements, and what-not has been a job within itself. Shortly before leaving Washington, Mr. Kennedy confided to a close friend that he had hopes of stopping the American bowing business altogether. He added, however, he would not force the issue if he discovered such a procedure would be distasteful to the British court.

Chances are the latter won't care one way or the other, and that Ambassador Kennedy can inaugurate something new under the diplomatic sun. If he does, he may disappoint the 20 or 30 American debs and dowagers in line for a curtsy and a look at a king, but on the other hand he probably would endear himself to millions of Americans bred in the tradition of Mark Twain, who consider formal presentation to a royal court the acme of snobbishness.[2]

In early April, the State Department announced a change in policy that was a diplomatic, middle course. Henceforth, the presentation of American debs at Buckingham Palace would be limited to daughters of officials stationed in England or of families who are domiciled there.

Minor news? the *Post* ran it top of the front page alongside Senate passage of a $5 billion tax bill and talk of riots in Paris. The story had no byline, but Hope's voice is obvious, especially in the playful, if lengthy, accounting of historical background:

> Kennedy's policy was made known last night in a letter to Senator Henry Cabot Lodge, Jr. (Republican), of Massachusetts, who had written the American Embassy regarding the presentation of a young Massachusetts woman. The 36-year-old Senator, of whose ancestors it was said that "Lowells speak only to Cabots, and Cabots speak only to God," wrote a reply to Kennedy in which he said: "I think this is a good decision and that you have adopted a truly democratic policy." Ambassador Kennedy's Irish ancestors were fighting the English when the Cabots and Lodges were entrenching themselves socially in Boston's elite Back Bay section. So, too, were the ancestors of Mrs. Kennedy. Her father, popularly known as 'Honey Fitz' Fitzgerald, was once Boston's mayor. . . .[3]

After that, the dowagers of Washington seemed to be on alert for challenges to their domain and prerogatives. They viewed an academic paper that analyzed and critiqued Washington society as a wounding affront. In one day, four different women complained to Hope on the phone, off the record mind you, of the writer's attempts to build up "class hatred." Hope reported the dustup with a tone of mild disbelief at the dudgeon on both sides.

"Among points emphasized in the study is that 'The society girl is a person who participates to the fullest extent in three institutions: the finishing school, the debut and the Junior League.' Pretty hard hitting, that. But the doughty Miss Mary Elaine Ogden had only begun when she wrote that in the introduction. Pitching in with verbal boxing gloves later in her thesis, Miss Ogden pounds away in harsher terms." More quotes follow about snobbery and how a society girl's debut year is one long romantic escape capped by a wedding.

Said dowagers also gave Hope another earful over lunch: "As one wise woman pointed out yesterday, 'Miss Ogden has confused real society with what sometimes passes for it. And she might do well to look a little further into the scope of the Junior League . . . and that it stresses its social connections far less than its ability to serve the needy.'"

All that made decent fodder for a week or so of chitchat about town and half a column in the *Post*. Hope's story carried a second item about a matter that had a bit longer shelf life. It flowed out of another June wedding by another son of the president, John Aspinwall Roosevelt, to Anne Lindsey Clark. The ceremony took place in Cape Cod with nearly as much fanfare, security, and press coverage as garnered for the Roosevelt–du Pont union almost exactly a year prior.

The maid of honor, 18-year-old Sally Clark, sought to extend her period in the spotlight by hurling "a verbal bombshell at society," according to Hope's description. The offending remark in full: "The people you meet in the theatrical world are so much more interesting than those you meet in society."

Hope replied, "Some of us who observed her cool, detached manner at the wedding of her sister last month can hardly imagine her being excited over anything. Poised as a princess at a court ball, she acted as if being a maid of honor was all in a day's work."

"Rumors were going around that if Miss Clark's upcoming singing engagement at The Ritz-Carlton goes over well, Hollywood will be angling for her services."[4]

There followed a few stories over a few months touching on what Hope variously called torch-singing, warbling, and trilling and with thoughtful consideration of its propriety for women of the married state and the social set. As for Miss Clark's destiny with fame, no recording contracts or film offers apparently arrived. Not that either kind of product would have found an audience in Hope, who damned up the young lady's publicity stream with an unusually opinionated wedding announcement.

"This business of society butterflies flitting about in the professional world just for the fun of it is getting to be a habit. Time was when the upper crust left such jobs as torch-singing, modeling and what-not to the girls who had to support themselves. But since money-making has become a high feminine fashion, every other debutante and socially registered matron you meet seems to be out to try her hand at something."[5]

While challenges to the dignity and prerogatives of those in society would ever continue, Hope was making new strides with her own professional stature. Gaining a following of devoted readers plus a bank of reliable sources, she was also building respect among her peers. After only a single year of membership in the Women's National Press Club, she was elected its president in May 1938. Nominating her for the top spot was outgoing president Doris Fleeson, political columnist for the *Daily News.*

Hope would recall that she ran unopposed, but the club's leadership positions were taken seriously and certainly not given away by acclamation. On election day, the 100 or so active members had a full day to visit the polls at the Willard Hotel. Ballots were counted in the evening and an inauguration ceremony followed a month later.

Hope's election marked the first time in a decade that a society editor had achieved the presidency. Sallie V. H. Pickett of the *Washington Star* and Ruth Jones of the *Washington Herald* each took the post for successive terms in the late 1920s. But since then and also in the years after Hope's tenure, the club leadership always went to the so-called hard-news reporters.[6]

As Hope and her fellow officers were putting together a schedule of events, top of their list was inviting the First Lady for a luncheon. They received a favorable reply and were pleased to accommodate the First Lady's request for a particular date, October 11. Turns out that would be Mrs. Roosevelt's 54th birthday and the club took the opportunity to have a celebration. Cake and candles were presented, there was probably singing, and a photograph went out over the A.P. wires. Before a lavishly decorated banquet table stands a grinning Mrs. Roosevelt, wearing a hat and gloves. She's about to cut the sizeable cake as the candles flicker. Standing beside her is the more petite and composed Hope, wearing a simple, dark, and belted dress with short sleeves and a matching dark hat.

Among the club's other noontime guests during Hope's year as president, there was a genuine star, actress Mary Pickford. One observer noted how Pickford and Hope, seated side by side, looked like sisters.[7] As for her remarks, Pickford eschewed Hollywood anecdotes and gave a high-minded talk on the dangers of fascism, titled "American Liberty Against Madness."[8] Still other celebrity speakers included the playwright, not yet a congresswoman, Clare Boothe Luce, and actor John Barrymore and his wife, actress Elaine Barrie, all of whom had come to town for work with the National Theater. There was also the racing pilot Jacqueline Cochran, several authors and a drama critic, a batch of foreign dignitaries, and the Texas Congressman Martin Dies, chairman of the Special Committee on Un-American Activities, which was ramping up its pursuit of communist infiltrators and sympathizers. The speaker series concluded with a tribute to two Texas writers, novelist Laura Krey and poet Grace Dupree Ridings, Hope's mother, fresh from attending the World's Fair in New York, where she was awarded a gold medal as the outstanding poet of her state.[9]

At the 1939 stunt party, Hope was even more at the center of the action. As president of the club, she presided as hostess and emcee rather than performing in a character role. The style of the show this time around borrowed liberally from Thornton Wilder's recent Pulitzer Prize-winning play *Our Town*, especially its minimal set. For this audience, "Our Town" meant Washington, D.C., and most of the good-humored story revolved around the upcoming visit of the King and Queen of England, and British-American relations all around.

As they appeared onstage, the royal couple were greeted by deep bows from everyone and everything, including the Washington Monument. "The Secret Service then searched the King, explaining, 'Just looking for matches, Your Majesty. There's something about the White House that makes a Britisher careless with matches.'"

"As Act II began, the Queen was taking a nap, reclining over the stepladder representing her suite on the second floor of the White House. She was awakened by a brash young woman fooling with the crown, and screamed in horror: 'A lady in His Majesty's bedchamber!' 'That ain't no lady, Queen. It's a newspaper reporter,' the impudent creature replied, hauling out her pencil and paper. . . .'"

After security removes the reporter, who'd started asking questions in rhyme, a couple of hard-boiled dowagers arrive.

> With exaggerated English accent, from which she occasionally lapsed, Mrs. Marchmont Whippoorwill announced, "Your Majesty, we represent the Amalgamated Mothahs of Washington Debutantes. . . . We want to know who this man Kennedy thinks he is that he can keep our daughters from being presented at court." They hand over a petition signed by 1,000 mothers of Washington debutantes past, present and future.

The bewildered Queen finally says she'll take the matter up with her mother-in-law.[10]

The program concluded, as it had in previous years, with Mrs. Roosevelt making a few off-the-record remarks. Earlier in the evening, she and her mother-in-law, Mrs. Sara Roosevelt, managed to put on a spontaneous private show that was intended just for Hope.

"I remember Mrs. Roosevelt was on my right and the President's mother was on my left and they commented about everything just right across me, as though I wasn't sitting there. They were very cute, saying amusing things. They knew that I was listening to everything, but it was as though they'd decided they were going to amuse me. It was wonderful."[11] And it's an extraordinary moment, since it was well known that the two Mrs. Roosevelts weren't keen on each other.

On the Monday after the stunt party weekend, Mrs. Roosevelt left Washington for a month-long trip across the United States that combined a variety of public appearances with extended visits to three of her adult children, Elliott in Fort Worth, James in Los Angeles, and Anne in Seattle. During a weeklong stay in Fort Worth, she made visits to the cities of Dallas, Waco, and Abilene. And on Sunday, March 19, 1939, she came to the small town of Sherman.

The evening of events took place during the worst dust storm that any of the locals could remember. "Suddenly, we began to smell and taste the earth," wrote Mrs. Roosevelt, describing in her column the ninety-mile drive.[12]

Nevertheless, things began on schedule with an intimate one-hour dinner in the home of Alfred and Grace Ridings at 318 West Belden Street, where the guests also included the mayor and his wife and Mrs. Roosevelt's private secretary Malvina Thompson. After the meal, the party adjourned to the city's municipal auditorium where the First Lady was scheduled to make an address.

There was a festive environment on the park-like grounds of the stately red brick building, later named the Kidd-Key Auditorium. Construction had begun on the facility in 1928 but it took support from FDR's Works Progress Administration to complete it. Assembled on the front steps was an honor guard made up of 100 Camp Fire Girls. A capacity crowd of 1,500 residents had come from across the region and they were eagerly awaiting the First Lady inside the theater, where the art deco fixtures were polished to a gleaming perfection and the high school orchestra furnished music. The official sponsor of the event was the Texas branch of the League of American Pen Women. In her capacity as its president, Mrs. Ridings was given the honor of introducing the First Lady from beneath the arched proscenium of the vast stage.[13]

During her hour-long address titled "The Problems of Youth," Roosevelt said that she heard regularly from young people who had completed their education but could not find work. Also, that among the many controversies she faced during her six years in the White House, nothing else so far had compared to her planned attendance at the American Youth Congress, an affiliation of organizations with alleged ties to communism.[14] It may have been no mere coincidence that she was using a public forum in the home state of Martin Dies to test out her defense of the Youth Congress. The following December, when its leaders were called before his committee on Un-American activities, the First Lady attended the two days of hearings. Though she did not testify and made no substantive remarks at that time, she made her allegiance clear by taking the young people to lunch and even boarding some of them at the White House.[15]

In that same manner, Mrs. Roosevelt's very presence in Sherman had an effect on the community. It's likely that some of the citizens listening to her that night had also been present the last time a Roosevelt came to town. President Teddy Roosevelt drew a crowd of more than 35,000 when he spoke at the town square in 1905. But the more recent big event, hard to blot from memory, was the lynching and subsequent weeks of bedlam. That was just nine years prior. The period of violence surely lingered in people's minds as they listened to Mrs. Roosevelt express caution and concern about harsh and reactionary attitudes to those deemed to be different, unknown, and unwelcome.

Mrs. Roosevelt's making that lengthy drive from Fort Worth in order to share dinner with the Ridings and speak at an event put together by Hope's mother was certainly a gift to the people of Sherman. The good feelings also rubbed off on Sam Rayburn, Sherman being the largest city in his district. But the whole affair was a colossal favor to Hope, and one more example of the extent to which the First Lady went in building alliances with the women of the press. Though Hope had remained in Washington, it was her ties to the First Lady that facilitated not just an extraordinary night for her mom but also a notable chapter, perhaps even a healing event, in the history of her little hometown.

Hope's relationship with Mrs. Roosevelt continued to result in favors toward her mother. The following year when the Dallas branch of the Pen Women held a luncheon in Mrs. Ridings's honor, the First Lady sent a congratulatory note at Hope's behest. A reading of it from the dais was a highlight of the event. Mrs. Ridings remained a regular visitor to Washington and was received at the White House when Mrs. Roosevelt hosted a tea for more than 300 women writers. It's curious that in a series of thank you notes and longer letters to the First Lady, Mrs. Ridings never once mentions her daughter, who interacted with Mrs. Roosevelt on a weekly basis.[16]

Grace Ridings died at Baylor Hospital in Dallas in August 1941 following an illness of several weeks. She was sixty-four years old.[17] Her creative legacy included plays, short stories, a bit of journalism, and two published volumes of poetry, *Shawl of Song*, and *By the Light of the Lone Star*. Hope received telegrams of sympathy from Mrs. Roosevelt and Secretary of State Cordell Hull, among others.

5

THE ROYAL VISIT

"The President and the First Lady made more news than anybody and they made it easy for the press to get news. You never called the White House that you didn't get an answer to whatever you asked, no matter how silly it was. They cooperated and that way they managed to manipulate the press."

That last phrase from Hope's recollections of the Roosevelt administration —"manipulate the press"—came from a viewpoint of admiration, not disdain. That's how things worked, and, more often than not, mutual cooperation was the result.

"Society editors are not usually overly critical. They're not supposed to be," said Hope. "They're supposed to put a good face on everything if they can."[1]

That became a difficult task during the period leading up to the June 1939 visit of King George VI and Queen Elizabeth. Shortly after the royal visit was confirmed, the First Lady said she would answer all questions as White House plans developed, but that details about the embassy arrangements would have to come from the British Embassy itself.[2] Therein began the troubles.

Sir Ronald Lindsay, a tall, hulking man with a walrus mustache and an aloof air, had been the British ambassador since 1930 and dean of the diplomatic corps for the last five years. Lady Lindsay was a native of Long Island and childhood friend of Eleanor Roosevelt. But after many years as the wife of a career diplomat, she had become "more English than Yorkshire pudding," according to Hope. She was a reliable presence on the social scene and each year gave two popular garden parties on the embassy grounds.[3]

Milady's press relations, though, were handled by her Canadian-born social secretary, the curt and withholding Irene Boyle. "We spelled it B-o-i-l," recalled Hope.[4] A regular dilemma came when lists of dinner guests released to the press contained only surnames, no first names. If a reporter inquired as to which Mr. Thompson this was, for example, she'd snap, "Lady Lindsay's guests are so well known they need no special identification."[5]

As interest in the royal visit grew, society editors were clamoring for information but Miss Boyle stonewalled more than ever. Hope's able assistant, Dudley Harmon, had been given the duty of phoning embassies because of her appealing speaking voice and gentle phone manner. But getting nowhere with Miss Boyle, she became insistent. Boyle hung up on her.[6] Hope's ears pricked up as Dudley summoned her courage, redialed the embassy, and managed to get Lady Lindsay herself on the phone. Trying to calmly explain the situation, Dudley's voice rose in exclamation, "We're desperate! Everybody in the country wants to know what the embassy is planning, and we can get nothing from Miss Boyle—as usual!"

Taken aback, Lady Lindsay asked for guidance and Dudley suggested a press conference as soon as possible. One was organized the following week for ten women reporters, primarily the society "editoresses," as the Lady referred to them, but definitely not the full complement that attended Mrs. Roosevelt's weekly gatherings.[7]

"So, we went to see her, and she was very courteous, very nice to us," recalled Hope. "She said it astounded her that Miss Boyle, who was her dear friend, had offended us and she wanted to handle it just as well as she could. Well, she handled it as well as she could, but it got to be the biggest mess that ever was."[8]

Just a week prior, Hope had begun the rollout of her royal coverage with a typical mix of optimism and curiosity. There would be a state dinner at the White House, which was where the King and Queen would also lodge for two nights. The British Embassy was planning two events, a relatively small dinner and a sizable afternoon garden party.

> Many a Washingtonian is pinning her social hopes on that party. A red-letter occasion on many accounts, it probably will be the one function on the royal calendar to which some guests will be invited without reference to protocol; but none yet knows how big the garden party will be or how inclusive. The whole thing rests now in Lady Lindsay's very capable hands, though Potomac Park wouldn't be large enough to accommodate all those hoping to be invited.[9]

At Lady Lindsay's press conference, the questions were many, but first was the matter of the guest list. She explained that it would number 1,300 and had been drawn from the social registers of a number of cities as well as from Lady Lindsay's personal records. "The list, which also includes a generous layer of top-flight government officials and diplomats, is closed, she said, and no additions or substitutions are to be made. She added that the 13,000 enemies probably resulting from invitation omissions are hers and hers alone—not England's and not any social secretary's."

To curtsy or not to curtsy, and to bow or not to bow, are decisions that Americans would have to decide for themselves, Lady Lindsay maintained. Likewise, floor-length or street-length dresses, either would be appropriate attire. And to add further clarity, she added, "Men should wear just what they would to any other formal garden party." For the dinner, the guests would number just over thirty, with Their Majesties serving as hosts and the President and Mrs. Roosevelt as guests of honor. "Lady Lindsay implied that she and Sir Ronald will be seated far below the salt."[10]

As if the social register weren't exclusive enough, Sir Ronald did that one better at his own press conference two days later. "The garden party is just like heaven, you know. Some are taken and some are not," he was quoted as saying.[11] Asked about why the King and Queen would not have occasion to meet more "average Americans," he smiled gently and replied, "There's such an awful lot of them."[12]

This was the first such exchange with the press in the ambassador's long career and it showed. Speaking from midway up a rounded staircase, he jolted each time a photographer's flashbulb went off. "I don't pretend to enjoy this," he said. The presence of women reporters among the gaggle also surprised him. "I didn't know any ladies were going to be here. The things that interest them I am really not competent to speak about."[13]

No, Sir. You're doing just fine.

A national hullabaloo followed this one-two punch from the Lindsays. Meanwhile, acute disappointment swept over every Washington woman who kept looking in her mailbox for an invitation but to no avail.

Mindful of the temperature of the city, Hope had already been preparing an expansive Sunday newspaper spread on the great Lady Lindsay. It ran just three days after the ambassador's encounter with the press and was the largest personality profile Hope had yet written.

> Her friends—and they are many—describe her as 'the wittiest woman in Washington' and sing her praises as a superb hostess, a stimulating companion, an excellent gardener whose artistic taste has never been questioned, and one of the best informed doyennes ever to rule the social wave in the Capital of the land in which she was born.

Her enemies—and there has been a mushroom growth of them recently—bandy about such adjectives as 'cold,' 'condescending' and 'smug' each time her name is mentioned. Calling her 'more British than the British,' they are complimenting neither her nor the empire upon which the sun never sets.

Casual acquaintances who haven't yet made up their minds whether they like her—or rather whether she likes them—just think she is 'indifferent' and let it go at that.

Probably somewhere between the best and the worst that is said of her is the real Lady Lindsay, who now faces the stiffest ordeal in a hitherto smooth and successful career—negotiating as her 'swan song' a garden party to be given by England's King and Queen on their first visit to the nation's capital.

This assignment would tax the diplomacy of an Eleanor Roosevelt and the patience of Griselda. Virtually everybody in Washington's social register, the congressional directory and the diplomatic blue book feels entitled to an invitation.[14]

Lady Lindsay did have some store of goodwill built up, thanks in large part to a self-deprecating sense of humor that was frequently on display. Speaking at one of Mrs. Roosevelt's annual Gridiron Widows parties, Lady Lindsay suggested her own epitaph: "Served by all, of service to none, died of the tea hour." She also read aloud a seed catalog's description of the hybrid rose that was named for her: "Thorny, inclined to ramble, sturdy, but in need of cultivation."[15]

After attending the Women's National Press Club stunt party in early March 1939, when the show poked so much fun at the British, Lady Lindsay wrote to Hope: "I cannot resist telling you once again how much I enjoyed the party last night. . . . I shall never forget the charm and ease with which you conducted the entire evening." A recent injury meant that Lady Lindsay had attended the event with her right arm in a sling. This also prevented her from writing her thank-you note by hand and she apologized for that before concluding: "I was so sorry not to go on to Mrs. Meyer's afterwards but I became very self-conscious about my sling and the fact that I was able to drink with only one arm."[16]

Maybe Lady Lindsay was able to properly tip back a drink by June. Whatever her physical capabilities, she kept to her schedule of weekly press conferences, opening the second session by stating, "My head is bloody but unbowed." News from that forum was mostly a listing, though incomplete, of the "representative Americans" to whom invitations had been sent. Among them were industrialists J. P. Morgan; John D. Rockefeller, Jr.; and Henry Ford; celebrity aviator Charles Lindbergh; Gen. John J. Pershing; the Episcopal Bishop and the papal delegate. Also, Mayor LaGuardia, the heads of the A.F.L. and the C.I.O., Lady Lindsay's close friend Alice Roosevelt Longworth, and the widows of Presidents Coolidge, Taft, Wilson, Roosevelt, Cleveland, and Harrison. A lone exception to the closed list was the addition of the Roosevelt children, who were coming to town to participate in the swirl of events. Probably the only people in the country to send regrets were former President and Mrs. Hoover.[17]

During Sir Lindsay's second and final outing with journalists, he was cool and collected. He wouldn't have achieved his status if he weren't a quick study. This time, he received "the newspaper men" in his oak-paneled office, where he wore a tan suit and leaned against his desk while smoking a cigarette in a long holder. Questions came fast, but answers were brief and guarded. No, the King and Queen would not need passports when they crossed the Canadian border. No, the King would not hold a press conference. As to how long Their Majesties might remain at the garden party, he replied, "I rather think they'll go away when they've had enough of it." How about the hot dogs that Mrs. Roosevelt planned to serve at the Hyde Park picnic, which was scheduled after the two days in Washington? Sir Lindsay remarked that it "would be the first time Their Majesties have eaten the thing under that name." After a moment, he paraphrased the Bard of Avon, "a rose by another name would taste as sweet."[18]

The next day, at Mrs. Roosevelt's own regularly scheduled meeting with the press, she announced that the royals would be given WPA guidebooks and that entertainment following the state dinner would come from "radio singer" Kate Smith and cowboy balladeer Alan Lomax. Opera singer Marion Anderson was later added to the bill. At the end of the session, the First Lady displayed her new dress made of lightweight British wool, which she'd wear to meet the King and Queen at Union Station the following week. Otherwise, when asked if she was excited about the coming festivities, Roosevelt replied, "No. I'm a calm person."[19]

The rest of Washington remained in a dither. At men's shops, there was a run on top hats, striped trousers, and cutaways. Among the ladies, whether they'd been invited to the garden party or not, skirt lengths were debated at length. As an arbiter of rectitude in the Capital, Hope fielded countless calls on the matter. Feigning a bit of fatigue at the topic, she wrote up a kind of fashion tote board, sampling which prominent women veered to which side of the hemline. "Mrs. John Nance Garner, wife of the Vice President, announced, 'I'll go short. I'm opposed to buying a long dress, for just one party.' Mrs. Claude Swanson, wife of the Secretary of the Navy, was among those holding out for a sweeping garb, saying, 'I have a long dress; I bought it for my son's wedding, and I certainly don't plan to cut it off.'"[20] Mrs. Cordell Hull, wife of the Secretary of State and one of Hope's most-mentioned ladies, was also going floor-length. "So, you see, it really makes no difference. My personal vote goes for the longer frock and the picture hat. Sweeping dresses are more graceful and more garden-partyish. But, of course, if there's a shower. . . ."[21]

Just five days before the garden fete, while the hedges were being trimmed and errant weeds yanked, the guest list was expanded one final time. Previously, the only Senators invited were the ranking members and chairmen of standing committees, but now the entire body was to be welcomed along with a larger portion of the House of Representatives. Fretful senate wives had complained to Mrs. Garner, who served as her husband's secretary. She prevailed on the Vice President to "do something."[22] Shortly thereafter, Sir Lindsay was seen emerging from a breakfast at the Senate dining room where he received a gentle but clear talking to. "Remember, every one of these Senators can vote against our going into war," was how the Vice President recounted the exchange to Hope.[23]

At 11:00 a.m. on Thursday June 8, President and Mrs. Roosevelt greeted the Royals at Union Station, after their overnight journey from Niagara Falls. Three-quarters of a million people lined the city streets to welcome them as the parade took a swing by the Capitol before heading west on Pennsylvania Avenue, cutting cross 15th Street in front of the Treasury and arriving at the southeast gate of the White House. Behind the tanks that led the procession, there were two open motorcades carrying the President and the King, the Queen and her hostess. Various dignitaries rode in another dozen vehicles, followed by caissons and cavalry. Overhead zoomed forty-two Army aircraft. The entire parade took thirteen minutes to pass any given point and arrived at the executive mansion by noon.[24]

At 4:00 p.m., the front doors of the British Embassy on Massachusetts Avenue opened to receive the first of the 1,500 hand-picked guests. Those arriving much after the hour would be ushered in through a garden gate. Expected at 5 o'clock, Their Majesties appeared on the portico at 5:20 p.m.[25]

As the King and Queen, accompanied by Ambassador and Lady Lindsay, made their separate tours around the greensward, some women bobbed with self-conscious speed, and some virtually prostrated themselves.[26]

While the King, who looks much younger than his photographs, and the Queen, who is twice as pretty as any of her pictures, mingled with their guests on the portico, others who had come to see them stood silently, hopefully, watching every move. Many a feminine eye weighed Her Majesty's gown in the balance and found it more than satisfactory. Flounced and full, it was fashioned of white net with embroidered panels, edged with ruffles, and horizontal tucks giving it a quaint, Victorian effect . . . one of the prettiest frocks ever seen in Washington. . . .

A few drops of rain, probably approximating what Lady Lindsay terms 'a nice Scotch mist,' sent Their Majesties back to the portico and the crowd after them. But members of their entourage and the British Embassy staff politely but firmly invited the throng to step back, shower or no shower, while the royal couple and a few notables had tea.

Their tea-time over, their meeting and mingling with the hundreds of garden party guests finished, and their chats with a select few having drawn to a close, Their Majesties stepped once more to the center of the portico. The Queen waved to the crowd; the King bowed; and, without further ceremony while the crowd cheered, they turned to leave the party by way of the embassy as the white-helmeted band played 'God Save the King.'

For half an hour longer, the crowd lingered in the garden, devoting attention for the first time to the 25,000 specially grown strawberries of uniform size that were ready to be served throughout the afternoon, and to the frappes, ice creams and fancy cakes featured on the tempting menu served up beneath the marquee at the foot of the sloping lawn. Over glasses of sauterne punch, many a story of what the King did and said, and of comments from the Queen went the rounds.[27]

Also in the talk among guests were accounts of two breaches of protocol witnessed amid the many passing exchanges. One was physical, one verbal, and both executed by Texans. The vice president, who was commonly known as "Cactus Jack" and usually avoided high society functions if at all possible, gave the King "a reassuring pat on the back." At least that's how it was described by Hope, who buried it deep in her account of the afternoon. But the front page headline proclaimed, "Garner Slaps King's Back at Garden Fete."[28]

Then there was Congressman Nat Patton from Crockett, Texas. He

bid for the headlines in the cow country by boldly stepping into the Queen's path and caroling, "Hi-ya, Cousin Elizabeth!" as he extended a plump palm.

Lady Lindsay froze. But Her Majesty, momentarily startled, quickly regained her composure, smiled warmly, and returned the handshake. The ecstatic congressman reenacted his role by approaching the King with a "Hi-ya, Cousin George!" and had a similar response.[29]

Hope left these down-home moments out of her news story entirely. Thirty years later, she couldn't resist recounting them in a book. But even then, she let the hapless legislator go unnamed.

6

CLOUDS OF WAR

Not long ago in a Washington beauty shop, an inveterate partygoer, who is one of Washington's numbered hostesses, breezed in and demanded the services of three operators. "I want the works," she said. "A facial, a hairdo, and a manicure." She added, archly, "I'm going to Japan, Mexico and Norway this evening, and I want to look my best." The girl at the desk, accustomed to the sometimes ambiguous vernacular of Capitalites, knew exactly what she meant. Within minutes, operators were in action to make Milady as pretty as possible for a routine round of parties on Embassy Row.[1]

A one-night world tour via the city's Northwest quadrant was still possible, but most of Washington took a collective sigh of relief after the whirlwind visit of the British monarchs came to an end. Though the rest period was brief, royal fatigue had set in. Only weeks after society saw the backs of George and Elizabeth, Norway's Crown Prince Olav and Crown Princess Martha came calling. They were greeted with considerably less hullabaloo, but a "round of brilliant parties" still ensued.[2] In early July, Hope noted that Prince and Princess Brancovan of Romania had slipped in and out of town "unheralded and unsung."[3]

After a late-summer lull, the fall season usually got underway. But Germany's invasion of Poland on September 1, 1939, shifted the tone of the social scene, as well as the nature of actual overseas travel. The items in social columns about overseas travels of important people became vital information. "Over current tea cups," wrote Hope, "talk revolves around only two subjects—when and whether persons who have been traveling in Europe will be safely home, and whether this country can stay strictly out of foreign entanglements."[4]

Hope also observed that it was no longer enough for ladies to have read a few books, know Emily Post by heart, and be able to throw out the occasional French phrase in conversation. The pressing matters of foreign affairs demanded that everyone stay informed. "One popular matron I know who has rarely concerned herself with anything more than bridge and plain and fancy gossip recently declared she had given up cards entirely so she could devote her time to 'studying up on the international situation.'"[5]

But being informed does lead to forming opinions. And that was raising the temperature at previously sedate occasions. "When ladies meet these days they have to watch themselves to keep from arguing about the arms embargo as hotly as a flock of Senators. At a small luncheon yesterday, for instance, the debate got under way with the cocktails and was still going strong by the time the last course went the rounds."[6]

World conflict and political posturing were also addressed to an unusual degree by the First Lady during an early October press conference. The Roosevelts' possible ties to Communist fronts were again raised during hearings of the Dies committee. The next day, Mrs. Roosevelt gave her response via the women's press corps.

> Asked whether she entertained Communists unawares several years ago when the American Youth Congress met here, the First Lady said she had no way then, or now, of determining political philosophies of her guests; that she had no intention then, or now, of having any censorship imposed on her guest lists; and that being a Communist did not necessarily bar a person from tossing off a cup of tea at the White House.

On the broader subject of war and peace, the First Lady even went on the record and at relative length.

> Peace, discussion of which has interlarded many of the First Lady's recent conferences and columns, was brought to the fore again yesterday. Answering accusations she is becoming a war monger, Mrs. Roosevelt said that she was as much a pacifist as she has ever been, but that she is convinced, "If there is war anywhere in the world, everybody must be concerned. A breach of peace anywhere is a menace to peace everywhere. The only way to keep peace is to keep the whole peace."[7]

If the unstable ground beneath the banquet tables wasn't already obvious, it became impossible to ignore upon the release of the almighty White House

social calendar. All state dinners were canceled, thus reducing the total functions during the winter season to just five receptions. Mrs. Roosevelt had been
hinting at the change, saying that the schedule was in the hands of the State
Department and pointing to "the President's heavy schedule."

Touches of both grief and defensiveness come through in Hope's news
story, which strains to explain it all away on account of appearances: "When
there's no telling which countries may be involved (in war) before the state
calendar gets under way, the safest way out seems to be to cut out entirely not
only the diplomatic dinner but all the others so omission of the diplomatic one
won't be so noticeable."[8]

By this point, Hope must have been longing for a big party to kick the
fall season into high gear. But her instincts were off when she predicted another
successful commemoration of the October Socialist Revolution, the most lavish annual event at the Soviet Embassy. "If you don't think it will be a mammoth affair, you don't know the U.S.S.R. Few indeed are members of
Washington's old guard who hold out against going to parties at 1119 Six-
teenth Street. Every time I've been there, the spacious rooms have been
crowded to the walls. Unless I miss my guess, this party will present a similar
picture."[9]

Communism itself hadn't kept the guests away since U.S.-Soviet relations
were established in 1934. That year, 1,200 had attended the grand affair where
the tables sagged under the weight of sturgeons and sterlets, caviar and pirosh-
kies, and forty waiters served 100 cases of champagne and thirty more of vodka.
Even the reigning president of the Daughters of the American Revolution
attended. As she explained it, "Since our government now recognizes the
Soviet Union, it is our duty to get better acquainted with Soviet representatives in our country. Besides, those don't *look* like Bolsheviks!"[10]

But in late 1938, the popular ambassador Alexander Antonovich Troya-
novsky had been summoned back to the motherland. In October, the Russians
and the Nazis had partitioned Poland. The following month—and after Hope
made her prediction about a fine affair to take place on the evening of November 7—Soviet troops assembled at the Finnish border. When Roosevelt
expressed strong sympathy for the threatened Finns, Vyacheslav Molotov, Sta-
lin's minister of foreign affairs, called the President a "meddler."[11] In sum, it
was enough to bring down a party.

"One of the grimmest soirees ever to take place in the capital. . . . It was
a disaster," wrote Hope. Some 1,400 invitations went out and 1,000 regrets
came back. Not one Supreme Court justice, Cabinet member, Senator or top-
ranking State Department official appeared. But the Russians took no chance

at having their spacious salons virtually bare and issued a raft of last minute invitations to Amtorg, a Soviet trade alliance in New York, which resulted in 800 out-of-towners showing up in a fleet of buses.

The British and French ambassadors claimed "previous appointments." But as according to protocol, at least one representative was sent by every embassy and legation with existing diplomatic relations to the Soviet Union. One of the only high-ranking diplomats to attend was Finland's Hjalmar Procope who stayed exactly five minutes. Reporters posted themselves at vantage points throughout the embassy and on its grounds, keeping a "death watch" until the end.[12]

The White House's Diplomatic Reception that December had more pulse but also its share of gloom. "Envoys Trade Nods Like Ice," read the front-page headline. Hope described it all as "brilliant but tension-shot." Members of the working press were initially corralled in the Green Room and only able to see a fraction of the receiving line in passing. But Hope was still able to convey again and at length the slow-moving grandeur and finery. "Beneath a seemingly smooth surface the entire political plight of Europe could be pieced together by noting frigid nods, stiff bows and the clever device more than one envoy employed of ignoring entirely diplomats from other countries unfriendly to his own."[13]

In her own postmortem two days after the fact, Hope's assistant Dudley Harmon was more frank. "People are still talking about the disappointment of not seeing any 'incidents' at the White House diplomatic reception, when all the envoys behaved like perfect little gentlemen."[14] Well-mannered or not, it would be the final such international gathering hosted by the Roosevelt administration.

December was also the time of year for Mrs. Roosevelt's "Gridiron Widows" party. Spirits there remained high, the humor campy and light. Looking ahead to the 1940 election, the show had a ranch-style roundup of possible new First Ladies.[15] "We took our playacting very seriously and would agonize to produce amusement and wit," recalled Oliver Clapper, wife of the *Post* columnist, who played the role of the ringmaster.[16]

That night may have been when Hope arrived at the idea of profiling each of the many potential First Ladies. The series ran for twelve consecutive Sundays in the winter and spring of 1940.

> Unless Eleanor Roosevelt succeeds herself, the chatelaine of the White House next year will have the toughest job ever cut out for the wife of a President. . . .

Probably her best course, as I heard someone suggest the other day, would be "to take to her bed and become an interesting invalid." Mrs. Roosevelt's indefatigable flair for negotiating a staggering schedule has made bridge tables hum from Maine to California for almost eight years. As a ceaseless newsmaker, she has proved herself an authentic American marvel, and her White House career might well be reviewed as The Halcyon Days of the Headline Writers. . . . It is almost too much to expect that the woman who follows her can chart a career as volatile and as newsworthy.[17]

The scaled-down expectations for any successor were all but acknowledged in a subhead to the series: "What about the next White House hostess?"—as if hostessing was the beginning and end of the job description. On the other hand, "hostess" was often the common synonym for "wife." For her part, Hope looked far beyond the women's abilities at entertaining and gave a thorough go at their histories, talents, and personality traits. In contrast to the sameness of so many contemporaneous columns on visiting dignitaries and the turnout at parties, these were unique, rich, and engaging life stories.

There was more than one Texan in the batch and first up was Frances Hutt Dewey, a fellow native of Sherman. The Hutt family departed Sherman for Oklahoma when Frances was just five and Hope still a toddler. "But her legend has lingered on through the years. It seems that any sewing bee or church social in Sherman wasn't quite what it should be unless 'that pretty little Hutt girl' who could sing like a lark and play the piano, too, had a part on the program." (Maybe young Hope filled the town's entertainment vacuum after Miss Hutt's departure.) Besides the hometown connection, also making the material fresh and memorable was Frances Hutt's short career in vaudeville under the stage name Eileen Hoyt and that her future husband, Thomas E. Dewey, was once an aspiring opera singer.[18]

Another standout in the series was the story on Elizabeth Farley, who explained that it was to keep her three children in their own schools that she chose to remain in New York while her husband's career took him to Washington. Hope gave Farley and her reasoning the benefit of the doubt, but not before a pretty loaded setup.

Truth is, Capitalites rarely understand nonconformists. And Elizabeth Finnegan Farley was consigned to that class the minute she made it clear that she did not intend to move to Washington and follow the routine prescribed for Cabinet hostesses. The town as a whole asked no further questions. If the wife of the Postmaster General did not choose to come here and negotiate the usual and endless round of calling, entertaining and being entertained, she must be a queer lot.[19]

It wasn't just Yankees that Hope had some fun with. When asked how she'd cotton to being First Lady, Adelaide Eugenia Bankhead, wife of the Speaker of the House from Alabama, drawled: "Why I wouldn't even dahr think about it. I nevah have; I nevah expect to. It's all too far-fetched to bothah about. Let's talk about somethin' else."[20]

In a kind of cleanup and finale to the series, the wives of three dark-horse Republican candidates got some attention. Among them was the spouse of the eventual nominee, the former Edith Wilk. When she and Wendell Willkie met at a wedding, they were naturally amused by the similarity in their family names. But Hope didn't seem to get much more than that from Mrs. Wilk Willkie—it was her first interview ever. So Hope fell back on good looks and charm. "A glimpse of her explains why her husband and son sometimes play-fully refer to her as 'a bit of a fluff.' She is a pocket-sized person, slim as a debutante. Her graying hair swirls softly around a youngish face and her lips curve into a smile on the slightest provocation."[21] During the interview, Hope explained to Mrs. Willkie how she could be an asset to her husband's political career. "Do you really think so?" she replied. When Hope offered her assur-ances, Mrs. Willkie whispered, "I wonder if you would tell my husband that, sometime?"[22]

Hope covered both political conventions that summer, though remaining largely at the periphery of substance. That is to say, she stayed among the women. But so too did Christine Sadler, another reporter dispatched by the *Post*. When Sadler joined the paper's staff back in 1937, she was given Hope's old beat for the city desk. Their published assessments of the Republican con-vention in Philadelphia were strikingly similar.

"Purely social is the women's angle at this convention, so far as I can see," wrote Hope.

> It's merely a matter of smart dressing, ubiquitous badge-wearing, and a flair for tossing off stock comments. . . . As remote from the real business of the conven-tion as if they were in the middle of a Kansas cornfield rather than on the scene of action, the ladies nevertheless are all over the place. They shuttle from one candidate's headquarters to another and collect in earnest groups to talk it over, as if the business of ballots were theirs and theirs only. . . . They pass out badges, sing songs, whirl like dervishes from party to party and feel they have a finger

in every political pie that's being served. They keep their powder dry by changing it as often as their snappy hats.[23]

Here's some of Sadler's observations: "Although this convention demon-
strates that women still are no great shakes politically, it also proves that their
value as 'window dressing' has gone sky high. They're the candidates' answer
to 1940s demand for 'glamour.' They make the photographs look better and
they help keep the women's clubs happy."[24]

So much for any marked difference between the work of a society editor
and a hard news reporter, as long as they're both women assigned to cover
women.

Sadler has been remembered as the first female to cover a political convention for the *Post*, but Hope was there, too. At the Republican gathering
Sadler did file daily stories, many of them running on the front page, while
Hope showed up toward the end of the convention. Midway through, Sadler
reported that the party platform included a plank endorsing an equal rights
amendment to the Constitution. After Willkie secured the nomination, she
also wrote about Mrs. Willkie, offering observations—small framed, soft
voiced, photogenic—that read similar to what Hope filed two months prior.

At the Democratic convention the following month in Chicago, there
was plenty more happening on the distaff side. Though Hope was there from
start to finish, her stories focused on the parties, the demi-celebrities hanging
about, and rumors that quickly became stale, mostly about who might be
Roosevelt's new running mate. Sadler's coverage again got bigger play, and
this time she had some meat to chew on. Women accounted for half of the
membership of the platform committee.[25] The First Lady was also making
news, coming out against an equal rights amendment because of its possible
detriment to unions and industry.[26] She also gave a "precedent shattering
speech" to the entire convention. True to form for a story about a woman,
Sadler's account of the address included a description of the First Lady's attire
in the fifth paragraph.[27]

Hope also captured some news and perhaps even moved events forward
a bit. She seems to have been the one who informed Ilo Browne Wallace that
her husband, Secretary of Agriculture Henry A. Wallace, was to be the vice-
presidential nominee. Mrs. Wallace had remained behind in Des Moines, having no apparent reason for attending the party convention. From Hope's story:
" 'I can't believe it,' she said, when the news came to her over the telephone.
Then, after a long pause, she added, 'Well, I'm glad,' and that was all."

Even after receiving the news, Mrs. Wallace planned to remain at home and listen to the evening's balloting over the radio. But her phone kept ring-ing, so she hopped on an afternoon flight with one of her sons. She could be seen that evening sitting on the dais one row behind Mrs. Roosevelt.

Hope referred to Mrs. Wallace as "one of the most unassuming women in Washington," recalled her arrival in the Capital in the early days of the New Deal and recounted the dramatic transformation of her image over the ensuing years. "She has streamlined her figure, put away her spectacles and looks ten years younger." Yet a makeover seemed to be about as far as Mrs. Wallace planned to go in being a politician's wife. "She will not take an active part in the coming campaign. Her plans for the remainder of the summer are exactly the same now that they were in May, when she left Washington."[28]

7

POWER AND CELEBRITY

U p until the 1940 Democratic convention, Roosevelt sent mixed signals on whether he was seeking or would accept nomination for a third term. Nevertheless, speculation on a new running mate had long been under way and Sam Rayburn was known to be on the short list.[1] It was clear enough that the House Majority Leader was more than open to the idea, so Hope decided to give him some unsolicited advice.

"Mr. Sam, I'll tell you what I think you need to help you in this campaign," she said. "You need a wife."

She proceeded to make the case for Margaret Palmer, the widow of Wilson's third attorney general, A. Mitchell Palmer. Hope knew that Rayburn had been taking the woman to dinner once a week at Pierre's, a French restaurant on the ground floor of The Anchorage, the four-story brick apartment building at Connecticut Avenue and Q Street where Rayburn lived. The Speaker and Mrs. Palmer also shared occasional lunches in the House dining room. Hope insisted that it was a good match.

"I just adored her. She was a wonderful hostess. She didn't have very much money but she had marvelous friends, marvelous contacts, great charm and she liked him very much. A charming, politically astute wife might enhance his prospects."

He dismissed the notion out of hand, telling Hope, "Marriage is not in the cards for Sam Rayburn. The House is my life and love."[2]

Rayburn was widely considered a confirmed bachelor, a perception that he did not usually bother to refute. But he had once taken a wife, Metze Jones. She was twenty-seven and he was forty-five years old when they exchanged vows in Cook County, just outside his district, in October 1927. There's long been conjecture but never any definitive facts as to why the marriage failed after only two months and three weeks. Metze fled Washington and settled in Dallas where she took a job at Neiman Marcus.[3]

Rayburn pointed out to Hope that his attempt at marriage lasted the same length of time as did Sam Houston's first marriage. Beyond that, she had no more luck than anyone else did in getting him to discuss the topic of marriages, past or future.[4]

Metze Jones was the sister of Congressman Marvin Jones, a friend of Rayburn's since their college days in Austin. Jones was sent to Washington by Texas voters in 1917, four years after Rayburn arrived, and the gentlemen were roommates until Rayburn married Metze.[5] For most of the 1930s, Rayburn was chairman of the Committee on Interstate and Foreign Commerce. Jones led the Agriculture Committee from 1931 to 1941. During the war he served in the executive branch as Food Administrator and after that he became chief justice on the Court of Claims.

Throughout their years in the House, Rayburn and Jones would often end their days walking the Capitol grounds together, discussing the legislative affairs of the day. Jones, like Rayburn, was considered a lifelong bachelor. But he, too, had had a very brief marriage, though all records of both the union and of the divorce conveniently disappeared.[6]

Hope made at least one further inquiry about Mr. Sam's relationship history. "I knew Marvin Jones very well and I said something to him about it. He told me, 'Well, Sam won't discuss this and I won't discuss it, but the fact that we're close friends tells you something. We've been close friends ever since.'"

Rayburn may have dismissed Hope's matchmaking plans, but he continued to see Mrs. Palmer. When Hope wrote up parties that they both attended, she'd put a discreet distance between their names. Still, it was no secret that Rayburn had helped Palmer find employment.

"He got her a job of some sort," recalled Hope, "like Curator of the Monuments, or something like that."[7] Actually, Rayburn used his patronage to see that Mrs. Palmer was employed by the House Small Business Committee. It was the last of a long string of day jobs for the prominent socialite. Her previous positions included working as a travel agent, serving as a motion picture censor, and handling press for the U.S. Maritime Commission.[8]

Though Hope and the Speaker were confidants on a certain level, she never maintained illusions about having strong influence on him. She was only moderately successful in encouraging him to entertain more. Exceptions to his quiet routine were some Sunday evening dinners in his apartment. The Texas delegation would always be well represented and Hope and Lee were often included. Chili and tamales were served, though they had to be brought in, since there was no kitchen in the Speaker's three-room apartment.

"Like all unattached men who achieve high position in Washington, Mr. Sam was avalanched with social invitations. But he was one beachhead never captured by many Capital hostesses," Hope once wrote.[9]

A coup even greater than having Rayburn as a dinner guest was if he could be coaxed into making a batch of Texas-style fried chicken in the hosts' kitchen. According to Hope, Rayburn could never find a satisfactory version of the dish in Washington so he took to making it himself. "Besides, I'm a rancher and I'm pretty much home on the range," he said.

When the Women's National Press Club issued a cookbook (*Who Says We Can't Cook!*), Hope's contribution was Mr. Sam's recipe.

Fried Chicken a la Sam Rayburn

2 young chickens	4 (heaping) tablespoons lard
4 cups flour	Salt and pepper to taste

Cut chicken in pieces. Dredge in flour and sprinkle with salt and pepper. Heat lard in iron skillet. Drop in chicken pieces and cook in sizzling lard until golden brown on each side. Then lower fire, put lid on skillet, and let chicken steam until tender. Service on hot platter, accompanied by a bowl of gravy, prepared as follows.

After removing chicken from skillet, stir grease to loosen flour and chicken particles left in pan. Add two tablespoons flour and stir until mixture is smooth; then slowly add cold water (or, if you want a white gravy, add milk or cream) and continue stirring until mixture is consistency you like. Let boil up two or three times, stir again thoroughly, and then remove from fire.[10]

"Make sure it's good old hog lard, not any of this fancy stuff," Rayburn added, "and have it hot."

Given the great volume of Hope's writing and the concurrent power and importance of Rayburn, she put his name in print relatively few times. This may have been deliberate, but it's also a reflection of how the modest bachelor just wasn't on the social track that she covered. Rayburn seldom left the Capitol for a luncheon and was usually in bed by 10:00 p.m.[11] He once explained to Hope his social reticence, "Nobody can quote what I said at a dinner, or tie me up to any promises I might make at a dinner, unless I'm there."[12]

During one of their conversations leading up to the 1940 conventions,

Hope confided her mild distaste for the idea of a third term for President Roosevelt. "Maybe the time has come when you vote for the man and not the party," she said. That remark resulted in a visit to the Board of Education, the metaphorical woodshed where errant House Democrats were given lessons in loyalty.

"There is no man, there's only a party," Rayburn said sternly. "These people who vote this way and that and they call themselves independents, they are the worst because they have no responsibility."[13]

Hope voted straight Democratic for the rest of her life. Anytime she was questioned about her conservative views being in conflict with her voting, she referred back to the lesson learned from Mr. Sam.

As things turned out, it was fortuitous that Rayburn was not put on the 1940 Presidential ticket. His long-held ambition to run the House was soon at hand. On September 15, just as the fall campaign season was fully under way, Speaker William Bankhead, sixty-six, died of a stomach hemorrhage. The very next day, Rayburn was elected to the top post by a unanimous vote. He took his oath in the well of the House chamber while, nearby, Bankhead's casket lay in state.[14]

An editorial in the *Post* that week remarked at the diminished power of the Speakership and noted that Rayburn was the fourth man to hold the office since John Nance Garner vacated it to become Roosevelt's Vice President less than eight years prior.[15] But during Rayburn's long tenure—three nonconsecutive terms totaling seventeen years—he both strengthened and ennobled the office. Late in his career when asked how many Presidents he'd "served under," Rayburn harrumphed that he hadn't served "under" any. Rather, he served "with" eight Presidents.

One day after Bankhead's death, another sad occurrence elevated Hope's own stature. Following a couple months of illness, Ruth Jones died of a brain tumor at age fifty-one. An obituary cited her as "one of the nation's best newspaper women."[16] Writing for the *Herald*, she was unquestionably the reigning society editor in Washington. That distinction now shifted to Hope.

It didn't take long for Cissy Patterson to start an intense recruiting effort. Ten years prior, she'd successfully persuaded Jones to move from the *Post* to the *Herald*, and she still welcomed any chance to win a battle with Eugene Meyer. After she lost out in the auction for the *Post*, Patterson made a power grab for the most popular comic strips, which resulted in a legal battle that wore on for twenty months. Compared to that, a society editor should have been easy pickings. What's more, in 1939 with backing from her family of publishers, Patterson went from being editor to owner of the *Times* and the *Herald*, which she then merged. The new *Times-Herald* became the dominant leader in circulation with ten daily editions that provided constantly updated news throughout the day. This meant that if Hope left the *Post*, there would be an automatic uptick in her readership and influence.

"Cissy used to have me to all of her parties and she liked me very much," said Hope. This was despite the fact that Hope rarely mentioned Patterson's name in her *Post* columns. But that was surely a reflection of the fact that Patterson ran a competing newspaper, not to mention that her sworn enemy was Hope's top boss.

"One reason that I think she liked me was that I was independent of her," continued Hope, "I wasn't working for her."

Patterson was unaccustomed to hearing the word "no." Yet that's what Hope communicated, though she probably used gentler language. On Patterson's third attempt to sign Hope, she pressed in, saying, "Why won't you ever come to work for me? I'll pay you a great deal more than Gene Meyer pays you."

"I'd rather be your friend than work for you, Cissy," replied Hope.[17]

Besides the *Herald*'s fierce anti-New Deal and pro-isolationist editorial slant, it was also known for being "a woman's paper" because of the substantial amount of space devoted to society, fashion, cooking, and the like. The success it achieved in that arena was part of what inspired Meyer's buildup of the women's pages at the *Post*. "Cissy's hen house" was the common nickname for the sizeable female staff, which in large part consisted of former debutantes, full of gossip but short on journalistic skill. They were usually compensated accordingly and had short tenures. Kathleen Kennedy, daughter of the British ambassador, was brought on as a secretary in 1940 and in time got assigned to the column, "Did You Happen to See?" Jacqueline Bouvier served as the *Herald*'s "Inquiring Photographer," during the paper's waning years of the early 1950s and prior to her marriage to Senator John F. Kennedy.[18]

"When Cissy took over the paper, there were only two women on the staff, me and an alcoholic who was sleeping with someone in the sports department," recalled Marie McNair. "Then, suddenly, we had women all over the place."[19]

McNair had begun her journalism career in 1921 at the *Post*, where her late father had once been managing editor.[20] After a period in New York, she returned to D.C. in 1929 and joined the *Herald*. Her skill and experience didn't make her immune to Patterson's quixotic leadership. Twice, she fled to Hope, tearfully begging for a job. On each occasion Hope was able to oblige with an offer. The first time, Cissy upped McNair's salary and she stayed on. But the second time, McNair wised up and returned to the *Post*, where she remained in the society department until retiring in 1965.

"The women who worked for the *Herald* were always very nervous," said Hope. "Cissy was fascinating but she made them miserable."[21]

Another fledgling at the *Herald*, even more conflicted about escaping, was Betty Hynes. She'd begun working as Patterson's secretary in New York and came along to Washington when her boss took over as editor of the *Herald* in 1930. Patterson put her through her paces with a string of positions up and down the newsroom ladder. A few years into Hynes' tenure, Patterson made her a general assignment reporter and from there she held the positions of drama editor, staff reporter, society reporter, and then society editor. In 1945, she went back to being the drama editor, then a society columnist again, before advancing once more to society editor. At least once along the way, she, too, pleaded with Hope for a way out. But after being offered a job, she phoned back to say, "I know you must think I'm a perfect fool, but I just can't leave Cissy. . . . She couldn't be more wonderful."[22]

In July 1948, Patterson died of a heart attack at age sixty-six. Hynes committed suicide less than two months later. In the *Post*'s obituary, her brother explained that she'd become despondent because her late employer, Mrs. Patterson, failed to keep a promise to "clear the mortgage" on Hynes's modest home in Georgetown. Patterson left the newspaper to seven executives, causing a year of legal chaos, but Hynes' name appeared nowhere in the will.[23]

As the calendar page turned to 1941, Hope continued her regular practice of writing out some New Year's resolutions. This year she decided to share with readers her efforts at being a better and happier society editor.

> I have firmly resolved:
>
> To talk less and listen more, and to put practically everything I hear in the paper—knowing full well that if I don't some other columnist will.
>
> To cooperate whole heartedly with anybody who coyly observed, "But, my dear, I really don't like to have my name in the newspapers." Truth is, in all my life I have known only three persons who sincerely disliked seeing themselves in print.
>
> To cease describing three-year old dresses and last season's hats as if they were up-to-the minute creations, just because they happen to be worn by women whose names make news; and never, never again to mention an ensemble as "stunning," a hostess as "clever," a debutante as "pretty," or a bachelor-about-town as "entertaining" . . . unless he, she or it actually is.

To take it as a matter of course when I see items that I have carried months before played up elsewhere as "a scoop."

To stifle the impulse to toss verbal bouquets indiscriminately, and to pare my copy of as many adjectives as possible.

To refrain from working myself into a fine frenzy when I hear a society story referred to as "publicity."

To stop wondering, when a hostess declines to give me her entire dinner list, who among her guests are the ones she doesn't want the world to know she is entertaining.

And finally, to keep all the above named resolutions as long as practicable, but to have no compunction whatsoever about breaking any, or all, the moment personal, social, or domestic emergency arises.[24]

This was the first published example of a self-revealing sort of writing that Hope began to periodically allow herself. But on the matter of full disclosures, she was exaggerating with that second resolution, the one about printing everything she heard. Her level of discretion was high. It went hand in hand with a personal dignity and general respect for those she interacted with on a regular basis. "I never wrote one thing in my entire career that would hurt anybody, so far as I know," said Hope.[25]

She stood as a polar opposite to Drew Pearson, who in his syndicated column "Washington Merry-Go-Round," never flinched at muckraking and attacking. Muckraker is certainly not a word ever associated with Hope, though a common description of her work is "gossip." When her stories are referenced in biographies or other histories, it's often along the lines of: "In her gossip column for the *Washington Post*, Hope Ridings Miller said. . . ." Interesting that historians should call her reporting gossip and yet also deem it worthy of citation.

But there were distinct differences between a society editor and a gossip columnist. First, there's the terrain at hand—society is about covering parties and people, while gossip is about spreading rumors and seeking scandal. Of course, the grounds do overlap, since people at parties will talk and sometimes they'll do inappropriate things. Free-flowing alcohol helps. A second contrast is in the economic strata of subjects. Generally speaking, society editors deal with an upper echelon, while gossip columnists look for the highest name recognition and the lowest common denominator. Then there are the professions of their subjects, which are usually a result of the geographic setting. Society in New York is populated by leaders of industry and finance, often doubling as or mingling with philanthropists. In Washington, it's politicians and diplomats, along with the occasional bureaucrat reaching for status. In time, military brass became a regular part of this circle. Gossip can sprout from any and all of these, but the deeper well, the richer soil, is in the field of entertainment, which operates out of New York and Los Angeles.

The liveliest society reporting, as well as the juiciest gossip, comes when these disparate realms spill over each other. Maybe this explains why the annual stunt parties of the Women's National Press Club were such a feast—a stew of celebrity and culture, power and politics always seasoned with out-of-towners. Special guests at the 1941 outing included actress Mary Martin and novelist Margaret Mitchell, among many others. Plus Hedda Hopper, who was definitely a gossip columnist, though she was, at the time, only three years into her long syndicated run.

Spending just thirty hours in Washington, Hopper began her stay by going to three different hotels until she found a room that was spacious enough for her one night of rest. She also needed the extra space for a crate of California orange blossoms that she brought along to serve as decoration at the evening's party.[26]

Hopper wrote it all up in her column and concluded: "The most creative women in our national Capital can and do ridicule each other publicly, all in a spirit of good clean fun, without any ill-feeling, so that all can see, hear and gasp. I'm going to speak to our Hollywood stars and see if just once in our lives we can't do likewise."

Hopper also noted—call it gossip, news or history—how centered and sincere the First Lady was in person, and how unexpectedly funny were the remarks she gave at the traditional close of the program. With a reporter's eye, Hopper noticed that while Mrs. Roosevelt had everyone else doubled over in laughter, Mrs. Willkie never cracked a smile.[27]

The following morning, just before flying back to the west coast, Hopper attended a Presidential press conference and was again surprised by her reaction to a Roosevelt. "I'm a dyed-in-the-wool Republican, but I fell like a ton of bricks."[28]

Hard to tell whether Hope and Hedda recognized each other as kindred spirits or merely observed each other from distant orbits. The *Post* story about Hopper's whirlwind visit mostly just recounted the busy itinerary and was yet another effort by someone, presumably a woman, that ran with no byline.

Around this time *Vanity Fair* carried a story that opens with a comparison of the social scenes in Washington and Hollywood. Each city is devoted to a single industry and guests at most parties are there purely for business reasons.

"Wherever you go in either town, your dinner partner is likely to be a columnist. In Hollywood, it would be Hedda Hopper or Louella Parsons, and in Washington, Hope Ridings Miller."

According to the story, lots of Washington women have taken a stab at reporting, among them such institutions as Evalyn Walsh McLean and Alice Roosevelt Longworth, as well as sundry spouses of congressmen and senators. A legislator's wife will likely send stories back to her hometown paper, which keeps her husband's name before the public and also earns her credentials to attend Mrs. Roosevelt's press conferences, where she sits quietly and never asks questions. The average career for a Washington society columnist is about nine months.

The *Vanity Fair* story continues:

> The girls who cover all this for the Washington papers very often appear in the society news themselves. Several of them are in great demand as tea-pourers at official receptions, perhaps because they are the only ones who know the names of all the guests, or perhaps because they are a decorative group on the whole. Clothes and charm are part of their stock in trade. . . . Hope Ridings Miller of the *Post* is the beauty among them, and the only one to have come up from the ranks of cub reporters.[29]

As for her elegant wardrobe, Hope sometimes referred to it as "cocktail armor."

The best evidence of Hope being a circumspect reporter rather than a gossip-monger is her almost complete failure to ever quote Alice Roosevelt Longworth. Daughter of the twenty-sixth president of the United States and widow of Speaker of the House Nicholas Longworth, she was omnipresent on the social scene. Known as Princess Alice, she was a harsh critic of the New Deal, at once a stickler for protocol and a gleeful troublemaker, and perhaps the most quotable woman to ever grace the salons of Washington. She's credited with the line, "If you can't say something good about someone, sit right here by me," and was also the one who remarked that Calvin Coolidge looked "like the little man on the wedding cake."

"She'd say anything," Hope recalled. "She had shock appeal and was loyal unto herself. I liked her very much, thought she was just charming. The things she said didn't sound so mean as she said them. That's often the way. But you put them in cold print and it made her seem very cruel. She would also mimic Eleanor Roosevelt."[30]

Longworth appears in Hope's columns almost as a specter, watching from the gallery of the House or gliding through the crowds at a party. If she was holding court, it was at a safe distance. By the time Hope arrived on the Washington scene, Alice's ways were already well known. So Hope had no need to protect her. What Hope was safeguarding was her own reputation as a newspaperwoman who could be trusted not to broadcast every sly slip of the tongue or newsy tidbit traveling by word of mouth.

The biggest play that Longworth received from Hope was a column about an after-theater party that she hosted. "Drop by my house after the show. Somerset Maugham probably will be there," was the offhand invitation Princess Alice issued during intermission. It was opening night at the National Theater of Maugham's latest, a stage adaptation of his 1937 novel, *Theater.*

Of course, Maugham was at Longworth's supper party. So too was his coauthor Guy Bolton, even though they'd already been feted and fed at a pre-performance dinner hosted by Countess Eleanor Palffy. "As is usually the case when Mrs. Longworth plans 'a small party,' last night's fete turned out to be a large gathering. Washington's official and top-flight residential contingent, as well as a representative number from the diplomatic corps, were in the crowd that hurried to meet Mr. Maugham." Mrs. Longworth wore "a dashing frock of Tahitian print, featuring a floral pattern in orange and green." Also in attendance was actress Cornelia Otis Skinner, the play's star, who was accompanied by her father, actor Otis Skinner, known at the time as the dean of American theater. Hope included in the column names of other dignitaries in attendance as well as an announcement that the following day Mrs. Longworth would entertain at a dinner in honor of Elsa Maxwell.[31]

"Playgirl of the Western World and the Nation's Number One Party Giver" is how Hope trumpeted Maxwell in a story around that same time. Also a writer, speaker, and filmmaker, Maxwell is remembered as the creator of the scavenger hunt. She was flitting in and out of Washington regularly, all the while claiming to have toned down her carefree life, due to the war and all.

She and Hope got down to it. They compared notes on successful entertaining and quickly drew up the most ideal guest list, including Alice Longworth, Cole Porter, Winston Churchill, Dorothy Parker, and Gertrude Lawrence. Next they conferred on the most deadly gathering imaginable. But Maxwell had to put a stop to it, declaring, "The crowd's getting so dull, I'm already bored to death with it. I can't go on."

Of the two women, Maxwell was certainly the more unbuttoned, but she and Hope had a common spirit of kindness and generosity.

In Miss Maxwell's bacon of buffoonery there is a wide strip of philosophy. To
the latter she gives credit for much of her success. She knows what she is about,
does Elsa. . . . She believes that happiness is the average person's ultimate aim.
"And happiness," she went on, "is one thing you can't receive until you give it
to others. And the more you receive, the more you give. You see, it's a circle
. . . but not a vicious one."[32]

A possible facelift, coveted invitations, and hats galore: These were some of
the weighty matters that flowed, one on top of another, in Hope's coverage of
another visit from British royalty. This time, it was the Duke and Duchess
of Windsor. The couple, alone and together, made several appearances in
Washington during autumn 1941. Take their Britannic titles out of the narrative and it's the stuff of celebrity gossip.

"I've heard enough Windsor stories to fill a book," stated Hope, as she
graciously shared more than a few of them.[33]

Earlier in the year, rumors went about that the Duchess had had some
work done, to use a more recent euphemism for plastic surgery. But Hope laid
the story to rest, once she heard from Evie Robert that it just wasn't so. Seems
that Evie, the glamour girl of the New Deal, was old friends with the Duchess.
She also had a history with the Duke, ever since she was presented at the Court
of St. James's and caused a minor scandal by declining his request for a dance.
Her reason was that she was taller than the prince.[34] Anyway, Evie and her
husband Chip, the current secretary of the Democratic National Committee
and former Assistant U.S. Treasurer, were just back from Nassau. To their
surprise, an invitation came from Government House where the Duke and
Duchess holed up during the war. The two couples certainly had much to chat
about. After the Roberts had returned to Washington by way of Palm Springs,
Hope put it to Evie "point blank" about the facelift. Evie said heavens no, and
instead gushed about the Duchess' great—and natural—beauty.[35] And Evie
wasn't one to be circumspect. For a time, she, too, wrote her own gossip
column for the *Hearld*, titled "Eve's Rib." Even as one of Cissy Patterson's
closest friends, she wasn't exempt from the getting-fired-and-rehired cycle.
But she did make it into the will. She inherited Cissy's signature black pearls
as well as a string of valuable commercial properties on Connecticut Avenue.[36]

Back to the Windsors. They arrived in Washington on September 24 and
stayed for all of 24 hours. Their schedule would be full. From Union Station,
they were to make calls at the Departments of Commerce and State and then
attended an informal noontime reception at the White House. In the afternoon, the Duke was to speak at the National Press Club while the Duchess

headed across the street to the Willard, where she would be received by the Women's National Press Club. Dinner in the evening would be at the British Embassy. With no parades nor mammoth gatherings, admiring fans had to line the streets for a glimpse—unless they'd managed to finagle their way into one of the select gatherings.

A *bid* was the term Hope used for how people would make a request for an invitation to a specific function or to be included on a hostess's future guest list. Once the Women's National Press Club's event for the Duchess was announced, lots of ladies were bidding to be Hope's best friend and special guest. Yet in this case, the term *bid* seems too mild. Note in Hope's account the use of war imagery:

> The technique of trying to wangle an invitation is, by this time, known to every one of us. Briefly, it has followed these lines: A warm handclasp and an ingratiating smile. 'Isn't it wonderful that you press girls are going to meet the Duke and Duchess! I'm so *thrilled* for you! I'd give *anything* to see them myself!
>
> A pause. Another sweet smile. Press member smiles back and says nothing.
>
> Friend tries a second-flank attack. "I suppose you're taking somebody terribly important along as your guest!"
>
> Scribe says she isn't sure members are to bring any guests.
>
> Friend looks horrified. "Oh, surely you girls won't have such a rule as *that*. After all, you want the club to make a good show, don't you?"
>
> Press club member meekly avers she hadn't given that point much thought.
>
> Friend calls it a day with final front-line attack. "Well, if you *do* have guests, as you undoubtedly will, *don't* forget poor little *me*. I'm dying to see the Windsors!"

Ultimately, no guests were allowed, other than those invited by the ducal couple. Hope put this in print, just so her many dear friends would know.[37]

Her reporting about the afternoon was just a slice of the *Post's* extensive coverage of the visit. In another foreshadowing of what would become a trait of celebrity-hood later in the century, Hope led with the Duchess's "pencil-slim figure." Soon, of course, she got to a lengthy description of Wallis's outfit. "A smart jacket-effect blouse of 'Windsor blue' silk crepe, with buttons up the front and a short peplum and a slightly flared black skirt. . . ."[38]

Alongside Hope's story ran staff writer Scott Hart's account of the Duke's own comings and goings, as well as his wardrobe. The description of his ensemble was less detailed, but more poetic and practically fawning: "Washington generally will remember the Duke of Windsor only as an indistinct impression of a hurrying well-tailed gray suit, a bare head, an appreciative smile and a frantic waving of the hand. . . . They couldn't know that tailors molded the coat collar on his neck in delicate triumph; that coat, trousers, socks, necktie, shoes were a blending such as composers have tried to express in music, or that he is possessed of an unbelievable languor."[39]

A third story—all of these were on the front page—also covered the style choices of each, noted that the Duchess changed clothes three times that day, the Duke two times, and that they were traveling with twenty-eight suitcases.[40]

Well before the Windsors had arrived, Mrs. Roosevelt departed Washington to be with her youngest brother Hall Roosevelt, who was ailing and actually died the day prior to the Windsors' arrival. That meant that there was no designated hostess during the couple's White House visit.

Almost exactly a month later, the Windsors made a return swing through town and there was much talk of whether this time the First Lady would receive them. But a long-scheduled appearance by Mrs. Roosevelt in Chicago conflicted with their October return. Just an unfortunate coincidence? The talk about town got so intense that the women of the press voiced their concern.

"Loyal as are the ladies of the press to the First Lady, a lot of them have been pretty perturbed that she hasn't made it a point to entertain the one American woman who managed to marry a former King of England. . . . So, at yesterday's conference Mrs. Roosevelt found herself facing a barrage of questions. Was there any foundation to the stories that she disliked the duchess? That she was dead set against having the Windsors entertained at the White House? That she had purposely arranged to be out of town while the couple was being feted?

"With more emotion than she usually displays, the First Lady made it clear that plans for the Windsor luncheon had been sprung on her at the last minute. She quashed rumors that she is prejudiced against the duke and duchess and does not wish to meet them at her own table. 'That's ridiculous,' she said. 'I should be delighted to see them here, but you can't cancel a contract made six months ago at the last minute.'"

The uproar remained so great that the White House made a midnight announcement. At 10 o'clock the following morning, the First Lady would receive the Windsors at the Office of Civilian Defense, a wartime agency based at Dupont Circle in which she'd taken an active role. From there, Mrs. Roosevelt was to proceed with her planned trip to Chicago.[41]

Lunch at the executive mansion was still on, but minor controversies continued. Hope was among the many watching at the White House gate as guests arrived. Conspicuously missing, the crowd observed, was Mrs. D. Buchanan Merryman, better known as the duchess's Aunt Bessie.

"No, she wasn't there," Hope told her readers. "But she had been invited. In fact, when the invitation went out to her on Monday and an answer wasn't forthcoming, there was a follow-up call from the White House. Then it was learned that Mrs. Merryman was visiting friends in New York and wouldn't be back in Washington in time for the party.

"So-o-o, although you'll probably hear on all sides that Aunt Bessie snubbed the White House—in retaliation for Mrs. Roosevelt's announcement that a lecture engagement would prevent her being on hand as hostess at the luncheon—the real story is the one I've just told you."[42]

Hope waded into many more matters of Winsoriana, skimming from the scuttlebutt and finding facts amidst the rumors whenever possible. One ongoing and convoluted story was about how some old-time Maryland friends of the Duchess were feuding and competing for her to be their guest. Meanwhile, there was related talk that the Court of St. James's was to recall Lord Halifax, the newish British ambassador who had become far more popular than Lord Lindsay ever was. Given the endless chatter, all the arrivals and departures, it's no wonder that when Hope wrote her book *Embassy Row*, she titled a chapter, "Always the British."

> One more word about the Duchess and then I'm really through—unless, of course, she has a return engagement. My special spy in New York called by telephone yesterday to say that despite any formal denials that the duchess had bought 15 hats, the story is true. "She hasn't actually bought them yet," said my informer, "because they aren't paid for. But she has selected 17 new hats, and is considering two others."
>
> "All beanies?" I asked breathlessly.
>
> "Seems most of them are, despite the fact that Mainbocher, her dressmaker, doesn't approve that type of lid for his best known customer."[43]

The Windsors did indeed make more appearances in Washington and Hope kept writing. In October 1943, she was among a select group of twenty guests at a private cocktail party given in their honor. She came away both effusive and circumspect.

"It was a party I shall never forget and I only wish I could divulge the name of the hostess. 'You mustn't do it,' she demanded. 'All the people I couldn't invite would never forgive me.' I'm sure she was right."[44]

Her name was Helen Essary. She was a fellow journalist who began her career under H. L. Mencken at the *Baltimore Sun*, where she covered society.

She later worked for the *Washington Times* and wrote a nationally syndicated political column. As a native of Baltimore, Essary had long family ties to the Duchess's forebears and was also good friends with Auntie Bessie.[45]

Some time after the event, Hope learned that Essary prepped the Duchess by giving her a biographical sketch of each guest in attendance. It worked. "I was so impressed with the way the Duchess of Windsor spoke to each of us and just seemed to know everything about our backgrounds," recalled Hope.[46]

On top of how well briefed the Duchess may have been, maybe there was a level of identification between the two women—both were kind, thoughtful, and genuine Southern ladies.

> I came away in a glow and with the feeling that at last I had discovered the secret of the Duchess' charm. I think it lies in her vivacity, her manner of looking at you so directly, and of acting the entire time she talks with you as if you are the one person in whom she is most interested. She has a disarming smile, an infectious laugh, and an attentive way of hanging on every word you speak as if your every statement were an epigram. If there was ever any snobbery in her make-up—which I doubt—it's entirely missing now; and she seems to be interested in everything. In short, she spread light and a certain sweetness all around her.[47]

8

TIMES BEING WHAT THEY ARE

Sunday December 7, 1941, was a clear and brisk day in Washington, D.C. News of the attack on Pearl Harbor interrupted the radio broadcast of the afternoon's football game, which pitted the Washington Redskins against the Philadelphia Eagles and drew a capacity crowd to D.C.'s Griffith Stadium. Hope and Lee lingered in their Columbia Heights apartment, keeping their ears glued to the ongoing reports. But there was no question about maintaining their commitments for the evening. They were expected for dinner at the home of Senator J. Lister Hill of Alabama and his wife. But first was a 5:30 p.m. reception.

The heavy traffic on Foxhall Road indicated that the Millers were not alone in their decision to make a showing. There would certainly be enough capacity at the venue known as Baker House, a thirty-room mansion modeled after the eighteenth-century Chateau de Villarceaux in France. It served as the current Washington home of the wealthy widow Mrs. Lucretia Bishop "Eva" Roberts Cromwell Stotesbury, a Washington native and reigning dowager of Palm Beach. Sharing in the hosting duties was Mrs. Stotesbury's son, James H. R. Cromwell, currently married to the 29-year-old Doris Duke. Another family member at the event was Mrs. Stotesbury's flamboyant daughter, Louise Cromwell Atwill, who was on her third husband, the British actor Lionel Atwill. Husband number two was General Douglas MacArthur. That association gave the stylish Mrs. Atwill the moxie to proclaim for all to hear, "I'm not afraid of the Japs. Douglas can hold them single-handed!"

The two-hour affair was one among a swirl of weekend events honoring the visit of former Secretary of the Navy and incumbent New Jersey Governor Charles Edison and his wife. The scores of guests included foreign emissaries, high State Department officials and a sufficient number of House and Senate members to pass a bill. They mingled in the richly furnished, oak-paneled salons in a common state of distress.

The governor's wife stepped away from the receiving line several times in order to take in the latest news broadcast. Emory Scott Land, the retired Vice Admiral and current Chairman of the U.S. Maritime Commission, spent as much time on the phone as he did with other guests. After greeting the Millers, he said, "Well, Hope, I expect your work is going to dwindle to nothing. Now that we're at war, nobody's going to be interested in society."

"Maybe so," she replied flatly. "Let's wait and see."

The imminent declaration of war wasn't putting off some. While strolling through the crowded parlors and drawing rooms, Gwen Cafritz invited folks to her Friday cocktail party.[1]

War had already been a sustained tremor running through the Capital for two years. Its effects on the social arteries were both constricting and expansive. The White House social calendar had now been completely scrubbed. On the other hand, the Soviet Embassy's commemoration of the October Revolution had rebounded to being a grand affair, now that high-level alliances had been smoothed over.

"Old-timers have told me time and again recently that Our Town today is a carbon copy of itself back in the days of World War I, only it's larger, of course, and noisier." For confirmation, Hope went into the morgues at the *Post* and found the following from July 1917: "The merry round of dinner parties, garden parties, evening receptions and other official affairs goes on in Washington as though it were not midsummer." She proceeded to quote numerous items, some with names that would ring familiar to her current readers, including Roosevelt, Longworth, Stotesbury, and Cromwell. "It's positive proof that this city never slackens in social speed during wartime."[2]

The President was consumed with putting the government on a war footing with all due haste. Yet even with entertainments erased from his calendar, he found the swirl about town more than a distraction and what's more a detriment to the war efforts. At least twice at press conferences, probably during moments of fatigue, he tried to put the brakes on the social scene and rid the Capital of those who were there merely out for a good time.

Besides the rounds of parties, another area of concern was that Washington's population was swelling at an alarming rate, as approximately 1,000 new government employees arrived each week. The housing shortage, in turn, led to a sudden inflation in prices.

"President Roosevelt yesterday suggested that overcrowding in the District of Columbia could be eased considerably if all the 'parasites' left town," wrote Christine Sadler. "Priorities of living space in the Federal area should go, he said, to persons essential to the war effort. There is no place under the Potomac sun, the Chief Executive indicated, for people here merely 'to watch the show,' participate in social events, or live with too much space around them in twenty-room homes on Massachusetts Avenue."[3]

"Parasites" immediately became the buzzword at parties, which were continuing full-speed ahead. And the pleasure seekers weren't put off. Hope was meeting legions of them who came to town for the social season. "So much more amusing than Florida this time of year," said one of them. "Palm Beach, you know, is cold and dreary and horribly dull. Hotels aren't half full, and nobody's in the mood to do anything. But here there's something doing every minute!"

"There is no doubt about it," declared Hope. "Wartime Washington is the most thrilling city that ever was."

> Everybody wants to be here. Hotels and restaurants may be crowded to the final space inch, transportation may be slow and difficult, but there is an air of exhilaration about the place. Parties are piling up as they never have before in the city's history. The town is thronged with famous folk from all over the world, with more scheduled for visits soon. So-o-o, despite the tension, despite the feeling of uneasiness beneath, the town apparently goes gaily along its crowded way. Old timers, who have gone south every winter for the past quarter of a century, are calling off their usual vacation (*'C'est la guerre,* you know') and newcomers are arriving by every plane, train and bus—with the intention of sticking around as long as possible.[4]

Just weeks after his jab at the "parasites," Roosevelt put another word into the Capital lexicon: "Cliveden."

The line of questions at this particular Presidential press conference started with whether the losses at Pearl Harbor had been underreported. That was "R-o-t," replied an unusually testy Roosevelt. He also defended the shipments of arms to Russia, saying their strategic value could be measured in dead Germans and smashed tanks.

Roosevelt then referenced an irksome political cartoon by Clifford K. Berryman that ran in the *Star.* It depicted a suspicious character whispering into the ear of John. Q. Public, "Why help the Russians? They'll turn on us later." The president said that was an apt depiction of the scene in Washington, a rumor factory that spreads lies across the country. He also claimed that the Capital has its own Cliveden Set, intent on undermining support for Russia.

Edward T. Folliard's news story in the *Post* included an explanation: "The term Cliveden Set was applied in England to a coterie of social and government leaders accused of being so fearful of bolshevism that they favored appeasement of the Nazis."[5] Yet that clarification was hardly enough to prevent days of bewilderment among Washingtonians as to the meaning of *Cliveden Set.*

Hope stepped up to offer some perspective. Rather than dashing off one of her well researched, historically informed feature stories, she reported on what she learned at a party. Not just another gathering over cocktails, either, but a "good-bye to a yacht party," given by Col. and Mrs. M. Robert Guggenheim, whose floating palace on the Potomac, the *Firenze*, would soon be given over to the Navy to further the war effort. The event also honored Hollywood actress Gene Tierney and her husband, the designer Oleg Cassini, who had been in Washington for a while already, but were still being feted left and right.

Amid a bountiful flow of names and chitchat in her "Capital Whirl" column, Hope shares the proper pronunciation of "Cliveden." Deep into the story she also reveals how the term came to be in the President's consciousness. That'll teach her readers to plow ahead through every last paragraph of her "Capital Whirl" columns.

> Are you a Cliveden setter?
>
> Well, maybe," was the answer, in effect, that I received from more than a score of Capitalites yesterday. But there was the invariable follow-up, "By the way, what *did* the President mean?" One Washingtonian had it confused with the Oxford Movement [a temperance program].
>
> So far as I could make out, nobody talked about anything except who was, or was not, a member of the Capital's Cliveden Set. . . . Only person who declined to discuss the subject at all was Mme. Maxim Litvinoff [wife of the Soviet ambassador]. She changed the topic, said she thought a farewell yacht party was fun. . . .
>
> Clarence Hewes was one guest who knew how to pronounce "Cliveden." First syllable rhymes with "give." And Mr. Hewes knows, because he once spent a weekend at the Astor home in the Thames Valley. . . .
>
> Mrs. George Barnett said she didn't know any Washingtonian who could be called a Cliveden setter. . . . Mrs. D. Buchanan Merryman declined to be quoted. . . . Harry Grant Meem: "Well, I guess I'm that, if I'm not a parasite. Everybody seems to have some kind of name these days. But I honestly don't know what the President meant."
>
> Meanwhile, as guests collected and lingered on the foredeck, an equally distinguished group continued to file down the receiving line in the drawing room. "Where's Gene Tierney?" asked more than one early arrival. . . .

Who else was there? Well, let me see. The Minister of Finland and Madame Procope . . . the Portuguese Minister and Madame Bianchi . . . Col. Stewart Roddie, slim, graying Britisher who gaily gave me a first-hand account of England's famous "Cliveden Set," and declared, "There was actually no such thing, you know. It was a catch phrase that somehow or another got attached to Viscountess Astor because, being a dynamic person, she liked to gather colorful political personalities around her so she could discuss affairs of the day. That was all."

Somebody else (who made me promise not to quote him) said Lord Halifax, the British Ambassador, lunched at the White House on Tuesday, the same day the President came out, in the afternoon, with his blast against the local Cliveden Set. "You know," said my informer, "perhaps that's the reason Mr. Roosevelt had the whole thing in his mind. Halifax, if you remember, was on the list of the prominent personalities originally associated with Britain's Cliveden set."

Who else was at the party? Quiet a crowd, and a lot of celebrities I didn't have a chance to see. . . . The Brazilian Ambassador greeted Mrs. Patrick Hurley and then bowed on through a group that included Senator and Mrs. Burnett Maybank. . . . The Egyptian Minister and Mme. Hassan chatted with George Abell. . . . Representative Katherine Byron and several dozen others made up the throng that stayed on, and on, enjoying the party, and trying to figure out the which, what and who of the local Cliveden set.[6]

There were other labels bandied about during the long lead up to America's entry into the war and in the months after Pearl Harbor. Those who publicly resisted U.S. involvement were often termed Isolationists or American Firsters. But a simple and personal kind of fear and reluctance was widespread, including among members of the press.

"I was very careful about anything I wrote in my columns before the war, not to let it reflect what I felt and my questions about going in," recalled Hope. "Looking back, you may wonder why anybody would feel that way, because it seems now the most logical thing that we could have done. But there were just differences then. I remember my husband, who was opposed to it, was one of the first to go."[7]

Lee had earned his M.D. from the University of Maryland in 1940 and joined the Army in March, 1942. He was thirty-six years old and received a commission as Captain in the Medical Corps, which stationed him at various bases in the South.[8] Hope's father had enlisted a quarter-century earlier, at the height of World War I. He also was thirty-six-years old and entered the Medical Corps at the rank of Captain. Hope became fond of recounting the parallel between the two doctor/soldiers in her life, but it was no mere coincidence. The influence of Sam Rayburn played a part in each of the high-level commissions.[9]

Within six months of when Lee shipped off, Hope closed their place on Harvard Street and moved downtown to the Mayflower Hotel. Given the crushing demand for lodging in the city, it could have been no easy feat for her to have landed the space. Located at 17th Street and Connecticut Avenue, the Mayflower opened in 1925 and was the largest and most elegant hotel in town. "Washington's second-best address," it was sometimes called. There were 440 guest rooms plus an additional 100 apartments, which were accessed from a separate entrance around the corner from the main lobby.[10] Hope's new home put her even more at the center of action and also allowed her to entertain more easily. Many congressmen, senators, and other establishment figures also resided at the Mayflower, and countless celebrities passed through either as short-term overnight guests or to appear at benefits and other glittery affairs held in the ballrooms.[11]

"It was the place to be," recalled Hope. "I could get a column any day by going to the Mayflower lounge, which we called the snake pit."[12]

Hope's columns continued to appear at a fast clip, a reflection of the unceasing pace of social life. What changed was how her coverage gave more focus to the shifting diplomatic set and the influx of those working in all aspects of defense. Naming names was still a vital part of her journalism, but slipping away was the habit of ending each column with a paragraph or two that simply listed those spotted at this or that event. There was simply more news to share.

About once a month, she'd step back from the day-to-day reporting to share broader observations of the changing scene. One development was that the social influence of the cave dwellers was on the wane. Newcomers were making their own social set: "A prominent New Yorker, down for the duration, got that point down pat when she hadn't been here more than a month. Said she to another New Yorker, 'It doesn't make a bit of difference whether we meet any Washingtonians while we're here. There are enough of us New Yorkers to have a good time together.'"

Mention of parties reminds me that the prophets who declared a social blackout was due to begin at once have had to eat their words the past six days. I've been around this town for years, but never before have I noted so many large and lavish parties in one week. Starting off with the Soviet Embassy celebration on Monday in honor of the Red Army, continuing on through the mammoth

Mexican Embassy reception on Tuesday, and the Brazilian Embassy fete for Artur de Souza Costa on Thursday, the diplomatic party calendar for the week concluded with the party yesterday afternoon at the Cuban Embassy in honor of the Mayor of Havana and Senora Raul Menocal. In addition to the four-star run of diplomatic receptions, there was also an embassy dinner, one of the largest of the season, given by the French Ambassador, Gaston Henry-Haye, on Thursday evening. And, of course, the usual number of informal cocktail fetes, luncheons, teas and dinners, to complete the brilliant but breath-taking current round.[13]

That paragraph was picked up by newspapers across the country. The public's reaction was not exactly pleasure or delight, but something closer to outrage. It manifested in piles of letters arriving on Hope's desk.

"If it would do any good, we'd send a delegation to the President to urge that he declare a complete blackout on all parties there for the duration!" wrote an acquaintance from Chicago.

"Doesn't Washington know we're having a war? And if so, why don't people there stop entertaining and give all their time and money to war work?" said one reader.

"Less tea-partying and more defense bond-buying around the Nation's Capital might speed up the war effort more than anything else," wrote another.[14]

After giving air to these grievances Hope became a one-women defense department—in defense of the serious business of society.

It's about time somebody cleared up this Great Misconception. It's about time, in other words, that the country at large gets wise to what makes the Washington party wheels go around. It's about time, finally, that everybody who might be interested realizes this: Society for society's sake died a natural death on the banks of the Potomac when the first bomb burst over Pearl Harbor.

Parties go on, yes. Celebrations-for-a-cause, rioting-with-a-reason, if you please. Even in peace times, Capital entertaining is generally a matter of promoting contacts, pulling political wires, grinding axes, partying-with-a-purpose; getting to know big shots at little dinner parties; brushing shoulders socially with Men of Importance by way of paving a path toward business dealings later. . . .

Today, the onslaught of defense officials and high-ranking Army and Navy officials—to say nothing of the continuous parade-to-town of visiting notables, both foreign and domestic—has given rise to a social life that on the surface seems merrier and madder than ever before.

Actually, however, two considerations have done more to foster an increase in the Capital's partying picture than all the others put together—the morale angle, and the growing conviction that life must go on normally as possible, as long as possible. There are more ways than one to help defeat Hitler and the minions of Hirohito.

In other words, partying-with-a-purpose, long the keynote of Washington's social calendar is spinning along its accustomed way. Peace times you'd call it a matter of grinding axes. Today, it's tied up with grinding the Axis.[15]

If only Hope could have coined another word for parties when they aren't meant for fun, it would have saved her a lot of explaining. The next best thing was "parties for a purpose," a phrase that she began to use regularly.

Yet, even to her own ears and heart, the argument for night after night of "going about" was feeling strained. Perhaps more so than with anyone else in town, to a society editor parties meant work. And putting on a pretense of cheerful interest became a forced labor once Lee had taken a uniform and gone to war.

"I was very blue," recalled Hope. "It made me sick to have to go cover parties."[16]

A few months after that last standing up for the value of society, she closed a column with a rare acknowledgment of exhaustion, not just at the continued misconceptions of Washington life, but also at the drudgery of an always-crowded datebook.

I'm worn out hearing Washington newcomers, and outlanders, rave and rant about "the social orgies" that are supposed to go on, endlessly, in this Nation's Capital. Social orgies, my eye. Never before have I seen so-called entertainment covered by such a thick layer of gloom, and so few persons really enjoying themselves.

The only good times anybody has around wartime Washington are at strictly informal parties, planned on the spur of the moment, and gathering in a group of guests with similar interests. I went to such a get-together the other evening . . . that was as much fun as any I've attended since before Pearl Harbor. Certainly, it was pleasant instead of purposeful, which is more than you can say for nine-tenths of the parties that accent the Washington calendar, even in peace time. But why try to explain the social workings of this town to anybody who doesn't already know them inside out. Just can't be done.[17]

When readers turned to Section IV of the *Washington Post* on Sunday July 19, 1942, they were greeted with large photos of enlisted men being served refreshments by pretty and smiling Red Cross volunteers. The single article on the page was the start of a lengthy column with the startling title, "Farewell to Society."

> Believing it is high time somebody steps out and puts Washington's prewar social picture where it belongs in a wartime Capital, the society staff of the *Post* today begins a new treatment of a scene that has been viewed from much the same perspective since the days of Dolley Madison. . . .
>
> If Americans at large understood the Washington picture, if every taxpayer from coast to coast realized that virtually every important party in this town is for a very definite purpose, it might be all right for those of us who cover the Capital scene to continue playing the social angle for all it is worth.
>
> But letters flooding my desk from all over the country shortly after a news service spread the alarm that the onset of war had increased the number of Washington parties convinced me that many Americans still feel that Capital society fiddled while Bataan burned. . . .
>
> Since nothing could be farther from the truth, obviously there is something wrong with the manner in which the Capital's social picture has been interpreted. Fact is, more emphasis has been placed on the parties than the people who gave them. Perhaps far too many paragraphs have been written about who was there (generally the same persons, time after time); what they wore; and the paper-thin sandwiches and cocktails they consumed.
>
> We propose to reverse the treatment—to play up people rather than parties; to throw the spotlight on personalities who are contributing to the war effort. . . .
>
> In other words, for the duration—and probably longer—we are finished with society-as-such. We are interested only in contributing our bit toward preservation of the only kind of world in which any of us would care to live.[18]

This new vision for society coverage in the *Post* is the most widely remembered story of Hope's career. It is cited in histories of American life during World War II and has been referenced over and over again when the United States engages in international conflict and is forced to reconsider its priorities on the home front—or at least before the years when overlapping combat missions, large and small, have numbed the nation to the very concept of "being at war." In the history of society reporting, "Farewell to Society" was a rare moment of brutal honesty.

But was it really at once a rebuke to the scores of dignitaries and hostesses that comprised Washington society, as well as a surrender to the distant perceptions of a war-weary nation? While not discounting the sincere desire to aid the war effort, it's hard to believe that there was a change in mindset so sweeping as to devalue decades of journalistic practice. What is clear, though, is that the story and the subsequent refocusing of reporting represented a savvy rebranding that was in tune with a new era. "It was a gimmick," Hope later admitted.[19]

The society and women's pages of the *Post* had already been featuring the good works going on in the Capital. Photos of smiling and earnest women rolling bandages or serving beer to men in uniform appeared frequently. What's more, Hope had been giving regular salutes to those who were organizing benefits for various war-related causes. For example, she reprinted a letter received from a young unmarried officer stationed in Washington. He pleaded that his lot not be overlooked while efforts were being given to cheer the enlisted. "All right, what about it?" Hope asked her readers. "A dance, or a series of dances, for young officers sounds as if it might be an interesting project for any number of Washington groups. Any suggestions?"[20]

Henceforth, this kind of focus—a mix of spotlighting, encouraging and prodding—would be underscored with new titles for the array of columns formerly considered society. Hope's own column, "Capital Whirl," would turn into "This Changing Whirl." "Top Hats and Tiaras" was renamed, "Now Is the Time." And "Society Notes," which mostly carried the itineraries of those with homes on the beach, the mountains, and the city, would now be titled, "Purely Personal." Of the five other writers on Hope's team, the two who were daughters of military officers would begin coverage of "women behind the men behind the guns."

All these changes were announced in the article. But also included were a number of caveats. "We shall continue to cover important parties because they have a definite connection with the war effort, but we shall try to keep our enthusiasm well within bounds." While brushing aside the socially ambitious, she acknowledged the value of members of the Cabinet, foreign envoys, and leaders of Congress, "all of whom naturally and rightfully supply a sizable share of the social spotlight." She also gave reassurance to families of those betrothed: "Brides and brides-elect we consider as important as ever. Still in the category of vital statistics, weddings shall be reported as fully as our space will permit."[21]

"Farewell to Society" grabbed attention like a flare shot into the night sky. Its message to America was, "We hear you." *Newsweek* called it a "social revolution" and quoted Hope as saying, "I couldn't stand the old formula of society reporting."[22]

Other periodicals that took note were the *New York Times, Time Magazine, Ad Age,* and *Editor & Publisher.* Highlights of the coverage were gathered together by the *Post* in a kind of ad for itself, with the headline, "The Nation Applauds."

The *Newark Evening News* offered a reply that waffled between support and concern: "It must be said that some of the solemn reporting of dinners and cocktail parties has been sometimes sickening. . . . (But) it just happens that 'society' people are among the most assiduous in serving on committees, organizing benefits and otherwise furthering more or less useful causes. So perhaps the new society page of the *Washington Post* won't be as belligerent as its publisher intends."[23]

The *News-Times* of Danbury, Connecticut, pointed out that society means fellowship and congenial company before concluding, "Probably only a handful of pretty stuffy persons will miss the society page of the *Washington Post*. It was beginning to look archaic."[24]

Despite such a ballyhooed change in course, Hope's columns carried on with a rather familiar array of subjects. In the weeks following "Farewell to Society," she covered a visit from Queen Wilhelmina of The Netherlands, the wedding of the top Presidential aid (and White House boarder) Harry Hopkins to Louise Macy, and an impromptu press conference for women reporters with industrialist Henry Kaiser, who was turning his attention to the mass production of ships.

As for parties, the sustained social fervor of the city wasn't ignored. Continuing on was coverage of the real stuff of life in the wartime Capital—who was talking to who about what. But there was less about the beauty and majesty of receptions, luncheons, and teas. And the straightforward listings of the guests at particular events, which previously filled multiple paragraphs, almost completely disappeared.

The more expansive coverage of war-related efforts by Washington women was largely the work of other writers in the *Post*'s women's department, plus the photographers whose halftones filled large spreads. For Hope, war was the overriding topic, yet there was still a distinct glamour to her beat, as she recounted cocktail or teatime rumors of which popular ambassadors and envoys might be reassigned. She also pursued interviews with the famous entertainers who poured into town.

On the steps of the Treasury, she grabbed a few moments with Irene Dunn. The star was on her way to a gala promoting the sale of war bonds and would speak of nothing else. "A film star who refused to talk about herself?" wrote Hope. "A woman bites dog story if ever there was one!"[25]

"I know war," declared Lillian Gish, who was appearing at the National

Theater. Though the actress had performed in numerous short promotional films during World War I, she took umbrage with the term *propaganda*. As she explained, "Its use simply kills the purpose of the whole thing and far too many people dismiss its effect, once they get the idea it's just another bill of goods."

Spencer Tracy snapped at Hope when she asked if he was in town seeking a military commission. That's what the rumor was. "I'm here for one thing only, to appear at this Community War Fair! That's all there is to it! This thing of thinking everybody who comes to Washington is out after something burns me up!"[26]

A testy interview subject was nothing new for Hope. While acknowledging the occasional difficult personality, in her writing she maintained a consistently positive viewpoint toward all humanity. Once war was being waged, she applied that same attitude to the nation's cause, emphasizing at every opportunity that the Allies were winning, people were pulling together, and the struggle wouldn't be long. When her even-keeled ladylike prose was truly interrupted, the effect was as unexpected as a high-heeled pump stepping on a landmine.

One explosion occurred in her home state. After a two-week vacation, she recounted to readers: "Every Texan I talked to expressed himself, violently, about the price administrator." The Roosevelt appointee, Leon Henderson, had recently given a speech in Dallas declaring that nationwide gasoline rationing was coming soon and the public must learn to like it. That's not a message Texans wanted to hear. During her vacation Hope was asked her impressions of this Mr. Henderson. Maybe she wanted her fellow Texans to see what a true Washington insider she'd become, but her honest answer was taken as a provocation. "Why, very able, and very personable, I answered innocently. Then the fireworks started." Fueling the sparks were complaints of ignorant Washington bureaucrats and proclamations that Texans were already doing more than their part to win the war.[27] Henderson, by the way, was out of his job by year's end.

Back in Washington, Hope found on her desk a review copy of the new book, *So Your Husband's Gone to War* by Ethel Gorham. Hope felt as if it had been written just for her and devoured it in hardly a night. A write-up gave her the chance to express the loneliness she was feeling in Lee's absence.

> You suddenly looked around your homey surroundings one dark morning, and came alive with a frantic realization that you were more alone than you had ever been in—oh, well, never you mind just how many years. . . . You might

be as hurt, as baffled, and as depressed as you pleased, but there was no getting around the fact you were on your own for the duration, you and thousands of other women just like you. And you decided you might as well show you were made of that stern stuff everybody talks about.[28]

One of the book's recommendations for "war widows" was work outside the home. Hope already had plenty of that. Some reporting outside Washington, though, proved to be more than just a good distraction. An assignment to the Deep South provided an opportunity to visit Lee and resulted in stories deeply immersed in the cold reality of war.

During a visit to Fort Croft in Spartanburg, South Carolina, one enlisted man after another boasted to Hope of his ambitions for officer-training school and expressed eagerness to cross the Atlantic or the Pacific "and get the job done!" Suspecting that homesickness lurked beneath all the bravado, Hope probed and questioned but to little avail. Then she met Mrs. D. B. "Ma" Fletcher, the senior hostess at the Service Club, which staged four parties a week.

"Many a draftee has looked up to meet as sympathetic a pair of eyes as you'll find anywhere in the world. She can tell in an instant, by a glimpse at a soldier's drooping shoulders and downcast eyes that he is despondent." In order to make direct contact with the soldiers, Fletcher kept the free stationary in her office.

"Half the time, a homesick boy is helped immeasurably by just talking to him about his home and his people," Mrs. Fletcher told Hope. "If you can get a boy out to even one of those parties, he has such a good time, blues vanish within an hour. He'll never be homesick again." Parties for a purpose, indeed.[29]

9

FOR THE DURATION

The Stage Door Canteen was one Washington party that needed no apology for carrying on nightly throughout World War II. Opening in late September 1942 at the Belasco Theater on Lafayette Square, the Canteen provided free dinner and entertainment to any man in uniform. Like its Manhattan prototype, and what would ultimately be six other canteens across the country, Washington's Stage Door Canteen was administered by the American Theater Wing, the organization that began presenting Tony Awards in 1947. Famous entertainers put on the shows and up to 2,500 military men visited every night of the week. In order to maintain a buoyant, upbeat spirit, singers had to avoid certain songs. "When the Lights Go on Again," "Dear Mom," "White Cliffs of Dover," and even "God Bless America" were on a no-play list.[1] Young women were brought in as junior hostesses to chat and dance with the boys while the senior hostesses, who cooked and served, were often ladies of the highest social strata. Senators and congressmen bused tables. Wives of ambassadors sometimes prepared exotic dishes from their native lands. Reporters were among the volunteers.

"If all else failed, you could go to the Stage Door Canteen and get a story," recalled Hope.[2] But before she could drop by to interview some soldiers or singers, she trumpeted the call for support to get the place up and running.

"Wanted: A flock of angels without wings for the Stage Door Canteen. No, they're not needed for background, atmosphere, or featured roles in the nightly show. They're wanted—at $100 a smack, or more—to help pay the overhead and underfoot of Washington's newest project to provide entertainment for men in uniform."

Prior to the war, it was rare that Hope would make such explicit appeals for any charitable cause. But in this story she practically knocks on the doors of individuals. Her insider tone suggests that she herself was a member of the Stage Door's original organizing team.[3]

Steering the ongoing operation was Armina Langner, a Broadway actress and wife of the playwright Lawrence Langner. Perle Mesta was another early contributor and faithful worker. She signed on at the urging of Mrs. Roosevelt.

"I was at the canteen almost every day," recalled Mesta in her memoir. "I helped organize the volunteer workers. I rolled up my sleeves and made salads and sandwiches to serve the boys. This was a different kind of party-giving for me, because I was part of a team of hostesses whose problem was to keep a party atmosphere going continuously."

A festive environment was not easily achieved or sustained, given that the guests could be either headed into or just returning from battle. Mesta remembered a certain dashing glamour about the soldiers in World War I, but now they seemed just young and scared.

"I went down to the Canteen on Christmas Day in 1942 and found a youngster sitting off by himself and looking lost. He told me that his two older brothers had already gone overseas and one of them had not been heard from for many months. Now he was going. The boy started to cry as he talked about his home and his folks and Christmas."[4]

It wasn't just to the well-off that Hope directed her printed appeals. "*The fighting men need nurses*" was a refrain she repeated in italics half a dozen times throughout a Sunday feature. The story wove together wartime statistics (2,500 new nurses needed every month by the Army), and job qualifications for nursing (women with judgment, training, and initiative), and the perspective of those already doing the work.

"Parents wondering if daughter should seek an appointment in the Navy Nurse Corps might well talk with Lt. Myrtle Carver, Chief Nurse at Naval Hospital. Her warm friendliness, the way the corpsmen say, 'Yes, Ma'am' to her—tells the story. Under the supervision of women like these anybody's daughter would grow in character and poise."[5] Word got back to Hope that after her story appeared twenty-five socialites signed up for training and duty.[6]

The Washington recruitment center of the Women's Army Auxiliary Corps, popularly known as WAACs, was a hive of activity by late fall 1942. In another story, Hope explained the enlistment process, from paperwork to interviews, plus the medical examinations, fingerprinting, and oath taking. She observed a team of eight civilian women conducting the interviews. Among them was Mrs. Herman Kiaer, daughter of the conductor Walter Damrosch.

The day I listened in, there was a pretty blonde from Oklahoma, daughter of a Methodist minister, who felt she "simply had to do something definite for the war effort." There was a switchboard operator who came to Washington from Maine some time ago and had wanted to be a WAAC ever since she first read about the organization. There was a young Negro girl, graduate of a teachers' college, who said she "wanted adventure." But what if you get a routine job in some out-of-the-way place where life is even less adventurous than in Washington?' she was asked. "Oh that would be all right," was the answer. "Any change would be an adventure.". . .

As would be expected in any organization where between 50 and 75 additional members are being taken in each week, a few amusing incidents and experiences are invariably indicated. There was the time, for example, when one new WAAC forgot to read carefully the instructions regarding the amount of luggage she could take with her (only two bags are allowed). She appeared at the train with seven bags, a violin case, a tennis racquet and golf clubs![7]

As women in uniform received ever-increasing attention in the *Post*, Hope got pushback from readers. But it didn't come from the society ladies who were used to seeing their names in print. Maybe they'd moved on to projects like the Stage Door Canteen. Or maybe they waited to express any displeasure to Hope in person. But one stay-at-home wife unleashed in a letter and Hope published it in full.

The fact is that no one in the wide world takes pains one minute to give us vanilla housewives even a little bit of encouragement, much less praise. . . . A great many of us have had plenty of domestic help through all our housekeeping days. Now the war has changed the picture. Some of us have husbands in service who, even if they have commissions, earn hardly more than half they did in civilian life. You might say we asked for it; 'cause when our men wanted to leap into service, we didn't discourage them.

With a tone of weary exhaustion, the letter slides into a list of chores, including dirty dishes, unmade beds, children's lunches that need fixing, and floors that need sweeping. And no maid to help out.

Hope began her response by recognizing that the term *Unsung Heroes* had become worn to the bone and that "there are times all of us feel pretty much in that category." She accepts the reader's points and admits that the *Post* may have gone a bit too far in focusing on women in uniform. "But there's more to the business of eulogizing the woman factory worker than meets the eye. More and more women are to be needed there, and the so-called 'glamorizing' of defense jobs is one way of persuading women with nothing but time on their hands to become part of the country's war-production power."[8]

Just a few months later, Hope added a new term to the wartime lexicon—WINS, the Women in National Service. An informal coalition for the 20 million women on active duty in the home, it was launched by the *Ladies Home Journal*. The magazine had begun orienting its household tips to the shortages and economies brought about by the war.[9] Wives of thirty-two governors were enlisted as state chairs of the WINS campaign, while in Washington, Mrs. William O. Douglas, wife of the Associate Justice of the Supreme Court, became the honorary chair. The effort was endorsed by James M. Landis, director of Civilian Defense.

Hope applauded that it required no new obligations and wrote: "The WINS program does not call for forming local organizations (thank goodness) nor for holding time-consuming meetings. Every housewife taking care of a home and family and devoting some time to usual community war activities is entitled to be a WINS."[10]

Women's work turned out to be a major part of Hope's interview with Walt Disney, who was staying at the Mayflower for a few days. After they sat down together in a booth at the hotel lounge, Disney dodged one question after another on just what kind of war-related business had brought him to town. He wouldn't reveal his social schedule, either. Despite the evasions, he succeeded in charming Hope. She saw a "boy next door" quality in him, noting that he smiles with his eyes as well as his dark-mustached lips.

Disney did open up about how things were going in his California studio. He'd seen about 170 of his staff artists go to war. As a result, he'd taken on more women, with about 300 female artists in his employ.

"Very few women are good cartoonists, you know," Disney observed.

"No, I didn't know, hadn't thought about it, in fact," replied Hope to her readers.

"Women artists are wonderful at putting on those delicate finishing touches that are so important to animated cartoons," continued Disney. "But the men handle the caricature part of the job much better."

Women artists gave Disney other troubles. Just as one starts showing talent, she'll catch the eye of a male artist. Soon came wedding bells. "And then my able women artist has her mind more on a home than on animated cartoons," said Disney.

From there the conversation turned to how Donald Duck was also doing his bit for the war effort.[11]

There were no more visits to bases in the South to see "my Captain," as she called him. Lee was headed overseas. As a surgeon, he served with the 137th General Hospital near the British battlefront.[12] Behind a surface anonymity, Hope wrote of her feelings with deep and raw immediacy:

> She wonders how it happens so many men in uniform manage to be assigned in Washington, while her husband's tour of duty is never less than a thousand miles away, and stands a chance momentarily of being a lot farther away than that.
>
> She envies every wife fortunate enough to have a husband at home, and she is deeply resentful that so many of her husband's contemporaries are still whipping around in civilian clothes.
>
> She accepts far more party invitations than she should; dashes about continually, even when she feels she will drop in her tracks any moment, and then keeps on going—all because she knows almost any pause may be filled with an engulfing loneliness.
>
> She notes that among her war-widow acquaintances, the ones who chirrup constantly about 'all the wolves in Washington' are those who have the greatest yen to be Little Red Ridinghoods.
>
> She gives an occasional dinner, by way of maintaining her own morale and paying back her obligations. In fact, she works pretty hard trying to be gay, or at least *seem* gay, and she smiles sweetly when friends say solemnly and in significant tones, "You're having a pretty good time these days, aren't you?"
>
> She feels her life is cut on a grim bias most of the time—but particularly when the kitchen sink stops up, or a door jams, or window refuses to budge, or a lamp cord won't work. All at once, she feels a manless existence is too much for her, and she simply can't bear it another minute.
>
> She knows she can't take any more of her troubles to her friends. Kind souls that they are, they've allowed their shoulders to be soaked in her tears too often already. Her best bet is to stop in the movies, where she can quietly weep it out among strangers in semi-darkness.
>
> In her most depressed moods, she tries to invoke all the comforting cliches that she has heard the past year. And she reminds herself, time and again, that her own particular man in uniform is in no more danger now than he might be at home. Besides, there's a fascinating postwar world to which she can look forward, she tells herself . . . and nothing can be worse than this. Well, nothing except the very worst. But that can't happen, she firmly believes. It mustn't happen. It won't.[13]

If the changing values and priorities of society ladies in Washington could be seen in one particular figure, it was with Evelyn Walsh McLean. Her Republican views had softened, she'd given her mansion on Massachusetts Avenue to the Red Cross and relocated to Georgetown where her new home was also dubbed Friendship.

"It doesn't make a bit of difference what guests wear to dinners these days, nor what they eat, or how they get there, whether by bus, streetcar or a-foot," McLean told Hope. "The thing about it is we've got to get together. We've got to keep in touch, discuss, argue, agree and disagree and thrash out our differences if we are to be ready to get together on the peace, and see that the right peace comes about this time."

That bit about transportation came after the Office of Price Administration issued a ban on so-called pleasure driving. No one was terribly sure what the definition of pleasure driving really was, but it did put the brakes on how party guests, from Supreme Court Justices on down, would be getting to social functions, or most anywhere else for that matter. With walking or riding street-cars suddenly the main options, and a rationing limit of three new pairs of shoes per year, the notion of proper evening attire was called into question, and the debate about hemlines renewed. At every party, the conversations began with how you and your fellow guests managed to get there. "Nobody remembers what else we used to talk about," said Hope.

Rationing of commodities also put a crimp in McLean's parties, which still continued most Sunday nights though in more modest scale—four courses, instead of ten, no coffee, and only artificial flowers. In addition, McLean instituted a donation box at the front door. Upon arrival, each guest would be expected to deposit at least $2. Toward the end of the night, there was a drawing. The person who pulls the card with "V" for Victory would win the kitty and be obliged to contribute it toward his or her favorite charity, the Stage Door Canteen being a popular choice.[14]

Such contributions to the war effort served as a counterbalance to McLean's famously lavish lifestyle. She once told Hope: "Honey, I'm not long for this life, and when I die, I hope somebody remembers me for something besides the Hope Diamond."[15]

McLean was among the angels who contributed to the Canteen and mingled there with the boys. She was known to show up sporting the Hope Diamond and would readily slip it off her neck like a trinket and pass it around for the soldiers to admire and fondle.

McLean also took to supplementing the guest lists for her house parties with soldiers and sailors. Joining the ranks of illustrious guests at her 1942 New Year's Eve gala were twenty uniformed young men, all winners of a lottery that same night at the Canteen. Hope tagged along behind a few of them as they went about shaking hands and ogling the crowd.

"Wish I'd brought my autograph book," one of the sailors whispered to a companion. "They'll never believe it back home when I tell 'em I've met all these people." These people included Vice President Henry A. Wallace, Mrs. Cornelius Vanderbilt, Manpower Chief Paul McNutt, Supreme Court Justice and Mrs. William O. Douglas, and Lieutenant General William S. Knudsen. "Pinch me, if I'm dreaming," said the sailor, "but I never thought this would happen to me."[16]

As 1942 drew to a close, Hope again published some New Year's resolutions. But this time, they appeared in two editions. First came a dozen or so resolutions that she wished others would make. The statements recall the gentle but firm admonitions about manners and decorum she wrote early in her career. They also live up to how one woman, the young daughter of a congressman, looked back on the era, saying: "The grown-ups were written about and apparently kept in line by the *Washington Post*'s society editor, Hope Ridings Miller, whom I always pictured as an optimistic woman in jodhpurs."[17]

Resolutions for 1943:

> Mrs. Roosevelt: I will not scoop other newspaper women in my own column, and at any time I am planning a trip out of the country I will see that members of my own press conference get the news first.
>
> I will invite Madame Chaing Kai-Shek to attend one of my conferences and will urge her to answer all questions that arise.
>
> I will continue, conscientiously as in the past, to answer in press conference all questions, no matter how stupid some of them seem; for I know editors frequently prompt reporters to ask questions as distasteful to them as they are to me.

> Clare Booth Luce: I shall surprise the Democrats, and please my Republican colleagues by not expressing my opinions on the House floor for at least a month after I take my seat in Congress, thus proving once more that beauty and brains can, and often do, go hand in hand.

> Oveta Culp Hobby, director of the Women's Army Auxiliary Corps: I shall smile for more newspaper snapshots during 1943 than I have during the past few months. No use in looking so grim about this thing. It may be a long war.

> Mildred Helen McAfee, director of Women Accepted for Volunteer Emergency Service: I shall not smile so broadly every time news cameras turn in my

direction. No use giving even a slight impression that I'm not taking this thing seriously enough.

MAJOR GENERAL ALLEN GULLION: I will break down and attend at least one big-league, late afternoon party during 1943. If General Marshall can manage to get out socially once in a while, why shouldn't I?

WENDELL WILLKIE: I will let at least two world-shaking events transpire during 1943 without issuing a statement as to how each should have been negotiated.

MRS. GEORGE MESTA: I shall begin to let credit fall where it should for the raising of money to underwrite the Stage Door Canteen. In other words, the next time a reporter wants to write a piece about what I have done, I won't put him off.[18]

And for society editor Hope Ridings Miller:

I resolve that for 1943 I shall: Manage to meet more newcomers to Washington, and not devote my entire time to those who have already been around, and written about, ever since the New Deal was really new, or even longer.

Quit making excuses to myself and to other members of the publicity committee of the Stage Door Canteen. I shall do my weekly stint there, no matter what else comes up. (You can count on it, Mrs. Langner, I'll be there next Wednesday.)

Refrain from taking issue with people who know a lot more about deciding factors in the war than I ever will; and I shall positively stop urging everybody I meet to speculate on when the war will end, who the next Presidential candidates may be, and the whys and wherefores of point rationing.[19]

A list can be a reliable device for any writer to get jogged into putting words on paper. It's especially helpful to a journalist like Hope, charged with filing multiple stories every week. When she used lists, they could become more than prompts for churning out the next story. As with the annual New Year's resolutions, they served to put some clarity, opinion, and hierarchy on the constant flow of people and parties.

Early in 1943, Hope stepped away from formal interviews and random teacup talk in order to respond to a national magazine's invitation that she compile a list of the ten most outstanding women in the world. Probably the information was wanted as background and Hope lets the magazine go unnamed. But she took up the assignment with typical gusto and turned it into a story for the *Post*. A stipulation in the request was that the list should only contain women she had met and also that she include at least three reasons for each choice.

"The most difficult task I have faced in a long time," Hope called it. First, she took heed of the word "outstanding," and interpreted it to mean of international importance and renown and contrasted it to women she most "admired." She claimed the latter would have been an easier assignment, though judging from the tone of appreciation and respect sown throughout her writing, the women Hope admired could fill most of the *Who's Who*.

She ended up hedging on the parameters a bit, since her list contained the names of only eight women and there was one whom she was yet to actually meet. After the obvious choices of First Lady Eleanor Roosevelt and Great Britain's Queen Elizabeth, there was Norwegian novelist Sigrid Undset ("because of her unerring search for intellectual and moral integrity"); anthropologist Margaret Mead ("one of the few women who have made their way brilliantly in a man's world"); writer Eve Curie, daughter of the pioneering scientists ("as intelligent as her last name and as intriguing as her first name"); the Arctic explorer Louise Boyd ("her wide background of experience is now being put to use in U.S. government capacity which comes under the head of military secrets"); and the Washington columnist Dorothy Thompson ("her voice, though in my opinion mighty strident for a woman, lifted itself in shrill accents of warning long before America as a whole realized the Nazi menace").[20]

Top of the list was the one outstanding woman who Hope had not yet met: Madame Chiang Kai-shek, the First Lady of China. Hope hardly bothered to give a thorough list of reasons for the choice, as she'd been dropping Chiang's name into columns on a regular basis for months. Madame Chiang was scheduled for a mid-February visit to Washington and as it drew near Hope joined her colleagues in another familiar buildup of anticipation for a foreign dignity poised to take the Capital by storm.

> I wonder why so many of us who see celebrities continuously somehow set our hearts on seeing one, especially, and aren't satisfied until we have followed that one around Washington for the duration of their visit. Is it curiosity, to see how a famous person conducts himself under the ordeal of meeting Washingtonians by the hundreds; making speeches; being gracious under circumstances that are sometimes trying? Is it because some of us fear that it is only distance that has lent enchantment? Or is it because so many of us gain inspiration from being in the presence of a truly great person? Whatever it is, for more than five years I have wanted to see Madame Chiang more than any other woman in the world.

Hope cites the countless stories she's read of Madame Chiang's selfless devotion to the less privileged people of her country, who accounted for almost one-quarter of the world's population. Also, the former Mei-ling Soong was educated in the United States and had written with passion of her Methodist faith.

Casting about for further explanation, Hope quotes an anonymous American who had not long prior spent a considerable amount of time with Madame Chiang and her husband, the Generalissimo, in their native land. The unnamed source told her: "Madame Chiang is positively the most charming woman I have ever seen. . . . I think it's probably because she talks so little and listens so well. . . . Thinking back over conversations I had with her, it seems I did all the talking, actually . . . but she talks with her eyes; apparently drinks in every word you say. She has a keen sense of humor, too. But you know that more because of her smile and twinkle than because of anything she says."[21]

The man who's doing all the talking here is likely to be the loquacious Wendell Willkie. Less than six months prior, the former Republican presidential candidate was sent by President Roosevelt on a weeks-long international tour, serving as an advocate of the Allies. He stayed for six days with the first family of China. Some who accompanied Willkie later recounted that he and Madame Chiang were alone together for extended periods, often late at night.[22]

Immediately after Willkie's return from the trip, Hope opened another column: "One of Madame Chiang Kai-shek's most enthusiastic admirers is our erstwhile roving ambassador of goodwill, Wendell Willkie. Everybody who has talked to him the past two days has come away with an off-the-record earful about China's First Lady. His praise of her and her work in a war-torn world transcend any paeans heard around these parts in a long time."[23]

If rumors were spreading of an affair between Willkie and Chiang, Hope would have heard them. But her discrete linking of names was about as close as she ever treaded to revealing the possibility of such carryings on.

Hope was always curious as to the secret or the essence to any woman's charisma. But she didn't buy wholesale into Willkie's declaration that the most gracious woman is the one who is seen but little heard. The lengthy Willkie quote ended, "I think the trouble with most smart women, most witty women, too, is that they talk too much to be charming." After that, Hope closed in a succinct and skeptical voice: "Well, we shall see."[24] The story appeared on the very day that Madame Chiang was to speak from the well of the House chamber.

Madame Chiang did indeed wow Washington. Her appearance refuted impressions of the Chinese as serfs and laundresses, but at the same time her petite presence conjured an image of China as a precious and fragile doll in need of protection.

Madame Chiang was the first private citizen and the first Asian to address the U.S. Congress and only the second woman, after Queen Wilhelmina who spoke there the prior August.[25] There was such demand for tickets to the speech that the Senate chamber held the overflow and Madame Chiang went there first to make a few extemporaneous remarks. Mrs. Roosevelt accompanied her from one side of the Capitol to the other and described the scene in the House: "A little, slim figure in Chinese dress, she made a dramatic entrance as she walked down the aisle, surrounded by tall men. She knew it, for she had a keen sense of the dramatic. Her speech, beautifully delivered, was a remarkable expression of her own conception of democracy."[26]

The ultimate goal of her visit was to garner American support for her country and to refocus Allied attention on Japan as the number one enemy. Madame Chiang reminded the legislators of what finally brought America into the war and painted the picture with grand literary allusions.

> When Japan thrust total war on China in 1937, military experts of every nation did not give China even a ghost of a chance. But when Japan failed to bring China cringing to her knees, the world took solace in this phenomenon by declaring that they had overestimated Japan's military might.
>
> Nevertheless, when the greedy flames of war inexorably spread to the Pacific following the perfidious attack on Pearl Harbor, the pendulum swung to the other extreme. Doubts and fears lifted their ugly heads and the world began to think that the Japanese were Nietzschean supermen, superior in intellect and physical prowess, a belief which the Gobineaus and the Houston Chamberlains and their apt pupils, the Nazi racists, had propounded about the Nordics.
>
> Again, now the prevailing opinion seems to consider the defeat of the Japanese as of relative unimportance and that Hitler is our first concern. This is not borne out by actual facts, nor is it to the interest of the United Nations as a whole to allow Japan to continue, not only as a vital potential threat but as a waiting sword of Damocles, ready to descend at a moment's notice.[27]

Given such literary command, it was no surprise that the male politicians were leery and confused. As Mrs. Roosevelt observed, "They found her charming, intelligent, and fascinating, but they were all a little afraid of her, because she could be a coolheaded statesmen."

Back at the White House Madame Chiang also showed a touch of cruelty. During a discussion over dinner, the president asked how a labor leader like

John L. Lewis would be handled in China. Her only response was a finger slicing across her neck. "Franklin looked across to make sure I had seen, and went right on talking," recalled the First Lady, who had given her husband an advanced briefing of Madame Chiang as being gentle and sweet.[28]

At a joint press conference with President and Mrs. Roosevelt, Hope observed Madame Chiang trying to sit in a large swivel chair and nearly topple over backwards. "She drew herself up quickly and pulled to the edge of the chair, trying to put her small feet firmly on the floor. They wouldn't reach. Mrs. Roosevelt took in Madame Chiang's plight at a glance. She put her hand firmly on the arm of the visitor's chair, and kept it from tilting backward for the remainder of the conference. Most gracious gesture I've seen lately."[29]

Just as she had during the royal visit of Elizabeth and George, Mrs. Roosevelt managed to deliver her illustrious guest to the faithful women of the press. Where the royals had merely made a ceremonial pass through the room filled with reporters, Madame Chiang took questions for nearly an hour. She reiterated her country's need for support, both military and humanitarian, and addressed women's changing roles in society and their contribution to finding peace. "I have never known brains to have any sex" was one of the takeaway quotes.

Madame Chiang's week in Washington not only satisfied Hope's curiosity but also lived up to her high expectations. While recognizing her as an outstanding world leader, Hope continued her tilt toward the women's angle by touching on charm, strength, and attire.

"Every time I see Madame Chiang I am more thoroughly impressed than before with her sincerity, intelligence, ability and warmth. A slip of a woman, who looks as if a mere breeze could blow her away, she is nevertheless—as her career has proved—a strong personality who can weather the fiercest storm."

Of course, Hope also reported on her attire:

> At her second meeting with American reporters since she has been a guest at the White House, Madame Chiang wore a satin embossed black Chinese robe, its side-slit skirt lined in turquoise to match the piping around the collar and yoke. Her earrings, ring, bracelet, and the buttons of her dress were carnelian, and her high-heeled black sandals were piped in gold. An aviation insignia, studded in diamonds, was on her left shoulder, adding a final stunning accent to her exquisite attire.[30]

Grace Deupree Ridings and Hope Deupree Ridings, c. 1910 Bonham, Texas.

Hope around age six.

Dr. Alfred Lafayette Ridings, Hope's father.

Hope c. 1925, Sherman, Texas.

Clarence Lee Miller,
c. 1930, Paris, Texas.

Hope c. 1930,
Sherman, Texas.

Hope's "headshot" for the Washington Post *(Library of Congress)*.

Hope as "Miss Lotta Business" and Esther Van Wagoner Tufty as "Franklin DeLayno" at the annual Stunt Party of the Women's National Press Club, March 5, 1938, Willard Hotel *(Library of Congress)*.

Hope serves tea to aviatrix Jacqueline Cochran during a meeting of the Women's National Press Club, September 13, 1938 (Library of Congress).

First Lady Eleanor Roosevelt's fifty-fourth Birthday, celebrated at a luncheon of the Women's National Press Club, October 11, 1938, Willard Hotel (Library of Congress).

*Hope with Mary Pickford at a luncheon meeting of the Women's National Press Club,
November 15, 1938, Willard Hotel.*

*With First Lady Eleanor
Roosevelt at the annual
Stunt Party of the Women's
National Press Club,
March 3, 1939, Willard
Hotel (Library of Congress).*

The Millers relaxing at a party in the late 1930s.

Members of the Women's National Press Club in a skit as part of the annual Stunt Party of the Women's National Press Club, March 9, 1940, Willard Hotel. From L: Mary Johnson (Time magazine); Emma "Bab" Lincoln (Washington Time-Herald); Corrine Frazier (independent correspondent); Elizabeth Craig (Portland Maine Press Herald); Bess Furman (independent correspondent); Malvina Lindsay (Washington Post) and Miller (Library of Congress).

After Hope christened the USS Aucilla, with Speaker of the House Sam Rayburn and Senator George Radcliffe of Maryland, November 20, 1943. Sparrows Point, Maryland.

Hope portrays Margaret Truman in a skit at the annual Stunt Party of the women's National Press Club, May 15, 1949, Statler Hotel.

With attorney Roy St. Lewis, prior to a hearing of the Ways and Means Subcommittee at the new House Office Building, March 20, 1953.

With Vice President Richard M. Nixon, mid-1950s.

With Lady Bird Johnson, early 1960s.

During a party celebrating the release of Embassy Row hosted by Perle Mesta, from left, Mrs. Strom Thurmand, Hope, Mesta, and Senator Strom Thurmond of South Carolina at the Sheraton Park's Cotillion Room. February 23, 1969.

With Perle Mesta, famed hostess and minister to Luxembourg, in the late 1960s.

With Guillermo Sevilla-Sacasa, Ambassador from Nicaragua and Dean of the Diplomatic Corps.

With President Johnson at a reception at the Embassy of Kuwait during a state visit of Emir of Kuwait, who is to the extreme left. To the right of Johnson is Tyler Abell, Chief of Protocol. At the Kuwait Embassy, December 1969.

Hope with journalist and author Ruth Montgomery, boarding the Queen Elizabeth II, 1982.

Author Joseph Dalton with Hope at a dinner party given in Dalton's honor at the Sulgrave Club, May 1985.

10

ROAD TO A BETTER MOUSETRAP

The opening of the 78th Congress on January 6, 1943 brought Hope back to Capitol Hill, keeping an eye on the women members and joining in the tributes to Mr. Sam. His reelection as Speaker took place on his sixty-first birthday and was celebrated by Republicans and Democrats alike, at least from Hope's point of view. "No sooner had Joe Martin announced that the Texas representative had been elected for the third time than the Republicans started singing, 'Happy Birthday, Sam Rayburn!' "[1]

Of the eight women who were sworn in, there was a new star, Clare Booth Luce, a Republican of Connecticut. A former magazine editor, sometime actress, author of successful Broadway plays, and the second wife of the wealthy *Time* magazine publisher, Henry Luce, she'd been a recurring subject in Hope's columns ever since she spoke to the Women's National Press Club during Hope's term as president of the organization. But Luce was masterful at the publicity game and thus earned occasional mention from Hedda Hopper, as well.

After being elected to Congress but before taking her seat, Luce darted out to Hollywood. At the request of her friend Madame Chiang Kai-shek, she was there to contribute some writing and ideas for the production of a film about China, *The 400 Million*. This, Hope explained, was the reason for the last-minute cancellation of a Capitol Hill luncheon in honor of Luce to be hosted by (of all people) the Democratic incumbent she defeated, Representative Joseph E. Talbot. "Guests were to have included other women in Congress, along with a hand-picked group from the male contingent. Everybody was looking forward to the event with special pleasure, and more than one lady legislator had purchased a new outfit for the occasion."[2]

A few weeks later and just days before the opening of Congress, Luce was scheduled to arrive in Washington by train. A contingent of reporters and photographers gathered at Union Station and awaited her arrival but she never showed. In fact, Luce was on the scheduled train but managed to elude the waiting throng. That evening, an enterprising scribe confirmed that she'd made it to town by calling the Wardman Park Hotel and asking to speak to Mrs. Henry Luce.[3]

Reporters finally got time with the Representative-elect at a press conference she called in her office the morning Rayburn would bring the House into session. *Post* staff writer Robert W. Harvey watched and recounted:

> The elusive Mrs. Luce, who left reporters waiting at the station gate when she came to town Monday night, slipped into the crowded anteroom of her suite in the new House Office Building only a few minutes late. She stood with her back to the wall and the female press closed in, flexing their fingernails.
>
> The male reportorial contingent mostly stood around and enjoyed the ensuing interview, which combined all the more interesting aspects of a Vassar homecoming weekend and the powder room scene from *The Women*.
>
> The girls started off with a little verbal scratching about Monday night's run around, which still rankled. Mrs. Luce parried, but was harried. She explained that her train was two hours late and she had appointments. One of the gals, who apparently had held a stopwatch on the train, said it was only 22 minutes late, and did Mrs. Luce instruct her secretary to slam the receiver in their ears when they telephoned?[4]

The following day's item in the *Post* ("First Slip Not Parliamentary") told how a Congressional Page alerted Congresswoman Luce, just before she strode onto the House floor, that her slip was showing.[5]

The papers carried on this way about Luce throughout the early weeks of the session, focusing especially on how the blond and glamorous playwright supposedly stirred up enmity from women of the press and women of the House.

For her part, Hope firmly rebutted such "Luce talk."

"Seemed a few of the newspaper men had made up their minds we women of the press didn't like La Luce, and were bent on fanning the flames of whatever feminine feud might be smoldering. Well, that's where they were on the wrong track for my money. I like her. I've admired her for years. I think she's pretty, personable, and knowing. I think she'll be an alert and able Representative."[6] An evening with the Women's National Press Club a week later solidified a bond between Luce and what Hope had taken to calling "the Petticoat press."[7]

Really, how could any reporter not appreciate someone who provided as much copy as the quotable, intelligent, and productive Clare Booth Luce? Sure, Hope complemented people for being smart and attractive all the time. But with Luce she went further. Hope took the rare step of advocating a piece of legislation, specifically a bill the conservative Congresswoman introduced about Army-Navy manpower that would limit the drafting of fathers, and institute a separate designation for men employed in industry. Luce told Hope its chances for passing were slim, since she was a freshman, a woman, and a Republican. Hope allowed that the proposals made good sense and wondered why no one else had yet thought of them.[8] Hope also slammed an unauthorized biography, titled *Au Clare de Luce*, calling it "acid toned."[9]

Yet for all of her normal circumspection, even Hope sometimes gave in to writing the tart item, including about Luce. She did, after all, make it a practice of passing along the well-turned phrase heard around town, such as this one from a couple years prior: "As Miss Booth and her husband Time-Life-Fortune publisher Henry Luce, who were recently in Washington, appeared in the door of the Mayflower dining room, somebody observed, 'There comes Arsenic and Old Luce.'"[10]

Tacky, perhaps, yet the term made the rounds for some time. If anyone remembered a decade hence, it would have a chilling resonance. While serving as Eisenhower's ambassador to Italy, Luce suffered from arsenic poisoning, caused by lead paint that fell from her bedroom ceiling. The debilitating condition ultimately led to her early resignation from the post.[11]

The argument for purposeful parties got tested in the late spring of 1943 with an incident that became known simply as The Big Red House on R Street. The passing scandal took wind in its sails when the House Military Affairs Subcommittee called two witnesses, a man and a woman, each of whom refused to even confirm their own names, let alone reveal what had been transpiring over cocktails at 2101 R Street NW. But money was exchanged —six checks to be exact—and introductions were made between potential contractors and some government officials authorized to cut lucrative deals.[12]

Though the F.B.I. had been monitoring and investigating for months, the scandal pretty much blew over within a couple of weeks after that first Congressional hearing. Still, the War Production Chairman, the Rubber Director, and the Undersecretary of War all found it necessary to say that they had never visited that particular house in the Embassy district. Conversely, the

Secretary of the Navy, a Senator from Vermont, and a Major General of the Army were among those who disclosed that they had indeed been to some social events there and that said gatherings were like most other Washington parties, sometimes delightful, often boring.[13]

Hope weighed in with a nonchalance attitude about the particulars, quickly launching into another formal and lengthy defense of the serious business of meeting and mingling.

> While newcomers to Washington gasp at each fresh rumor swirling around The Big Red House on R Street, old-timers sit back calmly and take the whole sensational story in their stride. Their so-what attitude indicates that they know this sort of thing has happened before. It will happen again. Fact is, it goes on all the time.
>
> As much a part of the Capital picture as the Washington Monument, the Lincoln Memorial and the Pan American Union is Our Town's type of purposeful party-giving that promotes causes, contracts and personal or political advancement. Little dinners for big men, where the ambitious managed to get on a first name basis with Nation's leaders somewhere between soup and dessert, have long made this 'Washington society business' just that, with emphasis on the business.
>
> In Washington, as nowhere else in the world, the people you meet at anybody's party may be your road to a better mouse trap.[14]

Even the First Lady had to respond to queries of whether she'd ever been to The Big Red House on R Street. No, she hadn't. Yes, she had met the notorious hostesses once when the woman attended a White House event. Discussing the affair at a press conference, Mrs. Roosevelt otherwise showed political skill in acknowledging both sides of the party line.

"I have never been quite able to understand why so many Washingtonians go to parties given by people they do not know; but one reason, of course, is that they are frequently asked to meet others whom they do know," said the First Lady. She further supposed that there was no other city where "such a thing" could happen. "But that is chiefly because there are so many strangers here, strangers eager to make friends," she concluded.

Another topic the First Lady took up at the same conference was proper attire for women with wartime duties. The session began with a guest speaker who described a newly designed uniform for the Women's Land Army, an agricultural training and labor effort. An overall of blue denim with roomy pockets and matching hat, it would be made available for purchase by any woman planning at least a month of farm work. Also, Mrs. Roosevelt said she took no issue with Mayor LaGuardia's recent order barring women from wearing slacks while serving in the Office of Civil Defense. Summarizing the First Lady's view, Hope wrote, "Unless there is a need, a war job should not be an excuse for any irregularity in feminine dress."[15]

Well, how about if the women were welders? Two such novelties were guests at the next press conference. Their names were Vera Anderson and Hermina "Billie" Strmiska. The assembled reporters were struck by their can-do attitude and tangible contribution to the war effort, plus the ladies' handsome weekly paychecks, which were reportedly equal to those of male welders.

Hope was ready to sign up.

> I wanna be a welder. I wanna feel important because I'm doing something to help win the war, and win a prize in a shipyard, be sent to Washington for the first time, and have the First Lady and the ladies of the press 'oh' and 'ah' over me as they ask question after question, eyeing me with admiration tinged with envy. That's the life, and to heck with columning; tearing around from conference, to interview, to reception, to tea, to dinner—dervish-whirl fashion, and always in a dither for fear you'll miss Something.[16]

There was considerable debate about how big of a something had occurred, or had been uttered, when Mrs. Roosevelt was the honored guest at the final spring party of the Women's National Press Club. The First Lady seemed to use her remarks to hint at what was ahead in her husband's administration. Not just policies though, but the duration of his tenure itself. Here's how it went: After indulging in a bit of reminiscing about her press conferences, Mrs. Roosevelt said she hoped that such gatherings would continue to prove beneficial in the "next few years." Or had she said "the next several years?" The club members had differing opinions about what they had heard, but a more important question was being raised. Did the statement suggest a fourth term in the offing? At that point, the President's already unprecedented third term was set to expire in eighteen months.

In the balance of her speech, the First Lady was complimentary to the women journalists. Of the 300 club members gathered that night at the Statler Hotel, about sixty were regular attendees of her press conferences. "I have never felt that those who come regularly have anything but a kindly feeling toward me," she said. "I have never looked on my press conference as a one-way street; I have always felt I should get as many ideas from reporters as they get from me; but I am not always sure I get what I want to get."

Hope replied in kind. "Well, if it's good publicity she wants, she has no complaint. None of the adverse criticism falling to her lot the past ten years has come from anybody who covers her conference regularly (note that *regularly*). Whether she is, as her fondest admirers will assure you, 'God's gift to newspaperwomen,' is a matter of opinion. Certainly, she has more loyal friends among women of the press than any other woman in the world."[17]

Sometimes without them even knowing it, prominent women writers at the *Post* were receiving a distinct and rather intimate honor from their publisher. On top of his duties in the newsroom, Mr. Meyer (as Hope always addressed him) maintained a New Jersey farm, Seven Springs, where he raised prize cattle. He named new heifers after his wife and four daughters. As the herd kept growing, he used the names of women at the paper. First there was Mary, for the star advice columnist Mary Hayworth, and then came Hope. It was only after Seven Springs Hope gave birth to twins that Meyer thought to inform Society Editor Hope that she had a namesake gazing out in the pasture. He let her name the progeny. She dubbed them Faith and Charity.[18]

That little item ran in Drew Pearson's column "Washington Merry-Go-Round" (of all places). Just a few months later came an episode that strained the good feelings between publisher and society editor. With her hackles raised, Hope strode into Meyer's office the morning that the paper's front page carried an editorial directed at the Speaker.

"Why did you attack Rayburn?" she asked her boss. "He's a candidate for vice president and this is designed to hurt his chances."

Though the next general election was still more than a year off, there was once again speculation, at least among certain Texans, of Rayburn being put on the Democratic ticket. Meanwhile, the Justice Department had been investigating Congressman Eugene E. Cox, a Georgia Democrat, for taking $2,500 from a constituent in exchange for a broadcast license. Cox chaired a select committee with oversight of the Federal Communications Commission. To get the matter off his desk, Rayburn referred it to the Judiciary Committee, which eventually claimed to have no jurisdiction. While things were stymied in the House, the Justice Department delayed filing an indictment.

In his open letter to Rayburn, Meyer outlined the situation and urged action. The tenth and final paragraph respectfully concluded:

> Mr. Speaker, you are known to us and to the country as a legislator of integrity and good will. The House is in the main composed of such legislators. The *Post* calls upon you and your colleagues to arouse yourself and to submerge whatever there may be of a personal loyalty to Mr. Cox to the far higher compulsions which derive from your proven loyalty to the integrity of the American legislative process.[19]

Maybe Hope never read the letter to completion. Maybe she feared no one else would, and that they'd only go by the headline, "A Public Letter to Speaker Rayburn."

After Hope confronted him, Meyer replied that he'd not attacked the Speaker at all. And besides, he'd never heard anything about VP possibilities for the Speaker and such a thing seemed unlikely anyway.[20]

Soon enough, Congressman Cox was removed from the committee relating to FCC matters and no further action was taken by the legislative or executive branches.

As for the VP talk, within the year Rayburn put it to rest, via Hope and the *Post*. Usually if Hope had a Rayburn item, she'd lead her column with it. But this was buried in a compilation of sundry "Round and About" quotes. She states that friends of the Speaker had been trying for a while to get him to establish himself as a candidate. He finally gave this reply: "I've been around this town a long, long time and have seen too many disappointed, aging men who yearned for higher positions that never came their way. I'm not going to entertain any ambition, lack of realization of which would make me an unhappy old man."[21]

Tears welled up in Hope's eyes and spilled down her cheeks the first time she witnessed the launching of a Navy crew ship in Baltimore's Bethlehem-Fairfield Shipyard. At the peak of the war effort, the Liberty ships—441 feet in length, and 14,000 tons in weight—were being produced at the astounding rate of one a day.

"I know only that the tenseness of the moment and the thought-in-a-flash, 'There goes another eloquent symbol of American power,' unleashed an emotional effluence that took me completely by surprise. Somewhat embarrassed, I glanced at others on the reviewing stand. I didn't see a dry eye anywhere."[22]

Five months later, on November 20, 1943, at Sparrows Point, Maryland, Hope herself was the designated sponsor of the USS *Aucilla*, an oil tanker produced by Bethlehem Steel. Speaker of the House Sam Rayburn and Senator George Radcliffe of Maryland were among the dignitaries at the launch and the celebration that followed in the Belvedere Hotel. The christening honor fell to Hope as a representative of the press and was witnessed by members of the Chesapeake Association of the Associated Press.

In front of the assembled crowd Hope made cautious steps toward the 16,000-ton *Aucilla*. The manager offered some advice:

"Just pretend that number is Jap and swing that bottle of champagne as if it's the only thing you've got to knock him out."

"Are the bottles pretty thin these days?" she asked nervously.

"No thinner than they used to be," he replied. "You'll have to give it all you've got."[23]

At the end of the countdown and as cameras flashed, she held the bottle tight in both hands and swung it over her shoulder like it was a baseball bat. Just after it smashed into a thousand pieces, Mr. Sam stepped toward her and whispered, "Well, Hope, right now we're a long piece from Coffee Mill Creek, aren't we?"[24]

Superstition holds that if the bottle is not crashed on the first swing, the ship is ill fated. But Hope's aim was strong and true, and the champagne foamed. The *Aucilla*, named for a river in Florida, served first in the North Atlantic and later provided fuel to the 3rd and 5th fleets during operations at Iwo Jima and Okinawa. She was decommissioned in 1970.[25]

Good feelings continued to flow as Hope shared a lyric view of life in Washington and some characteristic moments in the daily routine of its reigning society editor:

> I never heard two persons agree on any phase of Washington except that it is a state of mind, depressed and exhilarated by turns, its ups and downs depending largely on a thermometer that cavorts temperamentally through three unequivocal seasons—winter, summer and sinus trouble.
>
> In a word, this Nation's Capital is as many cities as there are persons who live in it, or visit it, or merely view it from afar. After 10 years here, the only Washington I really know is my own and this is it:
>
> It's five hours a day at the typewriter, five days a week, batting out three columns every seven days during the summer; five in the same period during the winter, and ever so many other stories, besides. And it's covering Mrs. Roosevelt's weekly 11 o'clock press conference and tearing back to the office to get the piece written before luncheon time.
>
> It's "covering" diplomatic receptions for visiting notables; getting sidelight stories on congressional openings; interviewing three or four celebrities a week; gathering news items, listening to political patter—and sometimes just plain gossip—over a luncheon table almost daily, and across dinner tables two or three times a week.
>
> It's being glad I live here, all over again, each time I glimpse the magnificent arches of the Taft Bridge, or the Lincoln Memorial by moonlight, or the rose-covered wall and the multicolored foundation and reflecting pool off the Shoreham Terrace, or Capitol Hill in a snowing setting, or any one of a dozen

tree-fringed driveways through Rock Creek Park, even though we have to walk them now.

It's seeing new faces everywhere, meeting most of them, and wondering along with everybody else what this wartime city is coming to. It's the thrill of feeling you have a ringside seat at the world's greatest show, an aisle seat to Adventure, a press pass to an endless parade of Important People from all over the world. And it's the satisfaction of knowing that beneath all the city's obvious glitter, and behind all the obnoxious movers and shakers that stand out from the crowd, Washington still has its share of worthwhile people, working earnestly and intelligently toward one end—to help win the war, as soon as possible.

Finally, it's "getting away from it all" occasionally—not by tearing out of town every time there's a chance, but by slipping over to the Mellon Art Gallery for a quiet, self-conducted tour and a few moments of meditation in the presence of great masters; or attending a Watergate concert; or dropping in at the Folger Library; or enjoying an air-conditioned, teatime interlude at the Mayflower lounge, or the Statler, or the Carlton.

All that is my Washington, and I love it. "Madhouse" or not I'd rather live here than anywhere else in the world.[26]

11

AFTER THE *POST*

H ope's writing for the *Post* came to an abrupt halt at the end of August
1944 when she left Washington to be with her 65-year-old father who
had suffered a heart attack. Sam Rayburn facilitated her quick transit to Texas
via military aircraft. An exchange of letters reveals a tender and rarely seen side
of the brusque and autocratic Speaker of the House.

The Grayson Hotel, Sherman, Texas
September 3, 1944

Dear Sam,

Daddy's condition is somewhat improved, but he is not yet out of danger.
The doctors seem to think he will get well, however. After that he will have to
take things easy for many months.

I can't begin to tell you how much both Daddy and I appreciate your
kindness in helping me get down here by plane. I don't know what I would do
without you.

Affectionately,
Hope Ridings Miller

The Speaker's Rooms
September 7, 1944

Dear Hope:

You were thoughtful to write as I have been terribly distressed about your
father's condition.

Being as sensible a man as he is and as good a doctor as he is, he should

125

know himself. I do trust and pray that he pulls out of this good and clean and that he may live so that you and I and his host of friends may have his association for many long years to come.

Please give him my affectionate regards.

With great love,

Sam Rayburn[1]

Hope remained in Texas for about six weeks. Before returning to Washington, she decided not to resume employment at the *Post*. But it was a move she was already planning and she'd been quietly grooming Elizabeth Ford to take the reigns of the society pages.

In the newspaper's archives, there's a single index card that served as her employment record. Written in cursive on the final line is the statement: "Discharge: Failed to report for work." The timing of her departure was precipitated by an inability to secure extended family leave, but the larger reason was a desire to pursue new writing outlets, both local and national.

Besides Cissy Patterson's repeated attempts to recruit Hope to the *Times-Herald*, other opportunities had been presenting themselves. After the initial burst of positive responses to "Farewell to Society" in summer 1942, a rebuttal appeared in *Town & Country* magazine. The oversized glossy was published monthly by Hearst and featured stars like Joan Crawford and Judy Garland in large fashion spreads. Hope described publisher Henry Bull's brief essay countering her observations on wartime society as "blistering." But in the days after it was published, Bull telephoned to make sure that he hadn't ruffled her feathers too much and also to offer her a job as the magazine's Washington correspondent. He insisted she could write for him while still working at the *Post*.[2]

"Our Washington Letter" in the December issue had no byline but bore all the hallmarks of an HRM column, with crisp writing, diverse viewpoints and a bounty of people and places. The same kind of content and style carried forward every other month in 1943 under the pen name Suzy Whitehouse. Hope's own byline ran for the first time in November 1944 and continued to appear regularly for the next two years. Also contributing to *Town & Country* during this period was Jack Anderson on politics, Lincoln Kirsten on dance, and Virgil Thomson on music, plus there were short stories, serialized pieces and such from Noel Coward, Roald Dahl, and Evelyn Waugh, among many others.

Other periodicals for which Hope wrote during the late 1940s were *The Argonaut*, a literary magazine out of California, and *Promenade*, a touristy kind of thing that bore the imprint of the various Washington hotels where it was distributed.

As for the newspaper trade, the best possibility for gaining a large readership plus a steady or even a substantive income was with a syndicated column. Many women of the Washington press corps had such an arrangement. Some, like May Craig and Esther Van Wagoner Tufty—both fixtures at the Eleanor Roosevelt press conferences—even had their own independent bureaus that fed stories to papers across the country. But neither of them focused on society and Hope had doubts as to how much appeal her material would carry outside Washington itself.

Nevertheless, the idea for syndication had been firmly planted in Hope's mind by Bascom Timmons. An experienced newspaperman and fellow Texan, Timmons surprised her one evening at a party by asking, "Are you just going to stay at the *Post* forever?"[3] After beginning his own career as a reporter at the *Fort Worth Record*, Timmons wrote for the *Dallas Times Herald* and the *Milwaukee Sentinel* and edited the *Amarillo News*. He also served for a time as president of the Press Club and was instrumental in getting FDR to sign a bill that saved its illustrious downtown building.[4] Good humored and well liked, Timmons was nominated as "a pin-up candidate" for vice president during both the 1940 and the 1944 Democratic conventions. He received one vote at each gathering. An editorial in the *Post* summarized the charade: "The name of Mr. Bascom Timmons as a possible nominee for the Vice Presidency was introduced into the Democratic National Convention for much the same reason that the porter scene was introduced into Macbeth—because the rest of the business was getting too painful to be endured without respite."[5]

The Timmons News Bureau operated out of Washington since the late teens. Hope did a variety of reporting for its various outlets in the year after leaving the *Post*. Among her assignments she was sent to cover the 1945 San Francisco Conference, a gathering of fifty allied countries that led to the signing of the United Nations Charter.

Another woman reporter that Timmons took on during the same period was Sarah McClendon, a native of Tyler, Texas. When she showed up at Timmons's office door with resume in hand, she was a single mother recently discharged from the WAACs. After the war ended and Timmons felt obliged to hire back his male reporters, McClendon established her own news service with some initial clients provided by Timmons. She went on to serve for four decades on the White House press corps.

Once Hope learned there was indeed a national market for her kind of work, she gained greater traction with the McNaught Syndicate, which was based in New York and had a more beefy lineup of columns and comics. Her "Just About Washington" column debuted on February 5, 1945 in *The Evening*

Star and within a few months was being carried by the *Chicago Daily News*, the *St. Louis Post Dispatch*, and *Newark Star Ledger*. Doing his part to help place the column, Sam Rayburn wrote a letter of introduction to Amon Carter, publisher of the *Fort Worth Star-Telegram*, although the paper decided against publication.

Hope produced the column three times a week for about three years. In contrast to her efforts at the *Post*, it was much shorter in length, never more than 700 words, and often ended up appearing in truncated form, especially in the *Star*, which was already full of Washington news. The insider's voice was still apparent, but it was no longer about Our Town, with the guest lists at parties and things like the incoming and outgoing diplomats. Instead, she gave to outsiders a glimpse of daily life in the nation's Capital. The columns relied heavily on the kind of folksy anecdotes that Hope previously appended at the end of her stories for the *Post*. She recalled that at its peak, the column was carried by more than 150 papers across the country.[6]

By war's end, Lee had attained the rank of Major in the Medical Corps. When he returned to Washington, Hope gave up her place in The Mayflower and the couple moved to 2500 Q Street NW. The low-rise, red-brick apartment house from 1942 was located just over the Dumbarton Bridge into Georgetown and provided a panoramic view of Rock Creek Park. Lee joined the medical staff of the U.S. Soldiers Home, a storied facility near the Maryland border on parklike grounds that had served as President Lincoln's summer getaway.

After being separated for the better part of four years, the couple's reunion was not smooth. Hope was still tending to her father from afar, while also coping once again with the pressures of being a freelancer. Out of professional responsibility and also personal allegiance, she continued to maintain an active presence on the social scene. Lee was also going about.

In most any other American city, a physician would hold high stature and certainly outrank his wife. In Washington, however, there was an ever-changing cast of elected officials, diplomats, and military brass. And on the cocktail and dinner party circuit, society editors had a distinct luster. Even apart from her professional standing, Hope was just popular. Lee himself was handsome and likeable. But long before the war came, he had tired of being the secondary spouse. Evenings when he wasn't accompanying his wife, he sometimes found other companionship.

By the end of the 1940s, the couple was divorced. Hope maintained the residence on Q Street and Lee moved into an apartment at the Soldiers Home.

Hope turned to what would always get her through periods of emotional hardship—hard work. Magazine writing continued, while the notion of authoring books beckoned from a distant horizon. And though the war was over, there were still plenty of civic causes that welcomed her organizing abilities, broad network of contacts, and strong work ethic.

On top of all that, Hope took the step that so many journalists consider at one point or another in their careers. She went from working as a writer to working in publicity. The term *publicist* often suggests pitching stories to media contacts with the goal of building up the reputation of a client. While that can be a part of the job, there's no evidence that Hope made cold calls or leaned on her newspaper colleagues to pay attention to an obscure or undeserving person or event. Instead, as a publicity consultant, she worked with selected clients, advising on strategy and managing the presentation and flow of information. When this kind of work is done well, it leaves little to no trace of the guiding hand.

In the long arc of Hope's career, publicity accounted for a relatively brief period. It supported her life as a single woman who was an occasional hostess and it brought her into the fields of entertainment and broadcasting. It also led to more opportunities than circumstances allowed her to accept and ended with a minor scandal.

A key advisor to Hope as she entered this new field was her friend Steve Hannagan who was also a former journalist. By the 1940s, Hannagan had become an influential, almost legendary press agent. At the height of the Great Depression, he was a behind-the-scenes aide to Samuel Insull, a notorious Chicago business magnate charged with mail fraud and antitrust. Hannagan engineered a shift in Insull's public persona from that of a rich renegade and expatriot into a haggard and put-upon old gentleman. Insull was ultimately acquitted. After that success, Steve Hannagan & Associates set up shop in New York and represented such major clients as Ford Motors and Coca-Cola. His promotional efforts helped establish Sun Valley and Miami Beach as destination resorts and auto racing as a national pastime for Memorial Day Weekend.[7]

If Hannagan was her model, then Hope had some big ambitions. She'd considered launching her practice with a group of partners, but Hannagan recommended she start out solo, adding that she could join a larger firm or expand as needed.[8] She consulted him regularly for guidance and began putting the word out to friends and associates that she was looking for business.

Parties, not surprisingly, were an initial focus. There were some fundraising galas and also a high-profile wedding that had a familiar ring to it. Though not the Duke and Duchess of Windsor, it was still a member of the

British royal family marrying an American divorcée named Simpson. The groom was David Michael Mountbatten, the Marquess of Milford Haven and a cousin of King George. The bride was Romaine Dahlgren Pierce Simpson of Washington. Members of the British royal family were among the 700 guests at the ceremony in the National Presbyterian Church. Recalling the difficulty she had as a reporter working with that obstinate press agent for the Roosevelt— du Pont wedding, Hope disseminated copious facts and "side lights" about the guest list, the family tree for each of the betrotheds, and the bride's trousseau. A few weeks before the big event, Hope's name did slip into one newspaper column: "Former Washington society editor Mrs. Hope Ridings Miller is the 'bomb shell' hired by Mrs. Simpson to manage the press until she says 'I do.' "[9]

Hope's principal ongoing client was the musician and television impresario Ted Mack. A successful clarinetist and bandleader, Mack had also served as a talent scout for the "Major Bowes Amateur Hour," a radio program that aired from 1934 to 1946. Two years later Mack created its successor with the "Ted Mack and the Original Amateur Hour," which was carried on the ABC television network. Mack was the emcee for the hour-long broadcast featuring real people with varying degrees of talent who sang and danced in hopes of earning cash prizes. It was the precursor to generations of talent shows, from "The Gong Show" to "American Idol."

Hope spent two years handling public relations for the show. It required her to spend several days each week in New York, where she prepared promotional materials and worked with media outlets in the hometowns of some of the more successful contestants.

The health of Hope's father continued to decline. After he suffered a stroke that resulted in partial paralysis, she persuaded him to move to Washington and live with her. Sam Rayburn had remained attentive to his old friend with regular phone calls and letters. Now he could visit in person. On weekends, Hope would sometimes leave the two gentlemen alone in her apartment watching baseball on television. Other times, the three of them relaxed together, sharing stories about Texas politics or discussing the condition of the cattle and crops on their respective properties back home.[10]

Tending to her ailing father prevented Hope from accepting a job offer from her close friend Perle Mesta, who'd become an important ally to Truman. The incumbent president's surprise defeat of Dewey in the 1948 election was aided in no small part by Mesta's fund-raising support. In her memoir, she recounts riding a train with the President as he campaigned across the western states. Mesta would telegraph ahead to wealthy oilmen and other millionaire friends, informing them she was coming to town with the president who would like to meet them. She then received the prospects in her own compartment of the president's railcar. If her appeal for support was being well received, she asked a porter to bring in Mr. Truman. If not, they got to shake the President's hand as they were being ushered out at the next station.[11]

After the headline "Dewey Defeats Truman" proved inaccurate, Mesta took an active hand with the inaugural ball, supervising everything from ticket sales to decorations. From there, with the Trumans securely in the White House for four more years, Mesta thought she could go back to her normal life of travel and entertaining. But Hope was among her intimates who anticipated that still more would be in store. Hope suggested that her friend start thinking of what kind of appointment she would like. "He will want to give you *something*," she said.[12]

Yet Mesta was still flummoxed when presidential aide India Edwards called to offer the position of Minister to Luxembourg. (Relations with the tiny nation did not warrant that the U.S. envoy hold the title of Ambassador.) Mesta pleaded for time to deliberate and consulted friends and family who were of differing opinions of whether she could be successful in the role and also content living abroad for four years. "Another friend of long standing, Hope Ridings Miller insisted that my experience in getting people together at parties was the best possible qualification for a diplomatic position where the chief requirement was to further friendly relations between two countries."[13]

After further soul searching, Mesta accepted the President's offer. Once she made it through an arduous Senate confirmation process, she asked Hope to work alongside her in Luxembourg City as press attaché. Hope had to decline in order to remain with her father in Washington. At Hope's suggestion, Mesta instead hired Dorothy Williams, a reporter for United Press who had just finished her term as president of the WNPC. But the job of the ambassador's top staffer went to a gentleman in *Call Me Madam*, the 1950 Irving Berlin musical in which Ethel Merman portrayed the "hostess with the mostest." In the film adaptation, the sprightly press agent was played by Donald O'Connor.

Despite her fondness for European travel, Hope never made it to Luxemburg during Mesta's tenure. But the pair maintained an active correspondence.

August 25, 1951

Hope Darling,
        Your letter of August 17th was just received with much pleasure and appreciation. I cannot begin to tell you how much I enjoyed reading all the

news of Washington you gave me. You write wonderful letters, so please let me continue to hear from you now and then.

You are a darling to tell me that Washington is not the same without me. I must admit I miss my dear friends, such as your charming self, but I must also admit that I do not miss the Washington life. It is much too interesting and stimulating here with new and unexpected things coming up almost every day. I couldn't help being perfectly happy under such an environment.

Thanks again for all the news of what's going on in Washington, and please do continue to write me. I'm looking forward already to getting another such letter.

Affectionately,

Perle Mesta

Hope continued to find outlets for her theatrical training and ambitions, sometimes as performer, sometimes as producer. A prime opportunity to have some fun onstage was still the annual stunt party of the Women's National Press Club. President and Mrs. Truman were present at the spring 1949 outing where the big skit focused on the most eligible woman in town, 25-year-old Margaret Truman, who was played by Hope. In the skit, Margaret is pestered by columnists desperate to cover a White House wedding, while also being hounded by bachelors eager for her hand. A photo from that night shows Margaret/Hope perched on a stool, wearing a full-skirted, ivory-colored dress and glowing beatifically, while completely ignoring a quartet of eager suitors, played by women in top hats and tails.[14]

Besides her prolonged status as a bachelorette, Miss Truman was making news pursuing a career as a singer, though with only middling success. The most famous negative review of her vocal talent came in December 1950 from Paul Hume of the *Post*. Infuriated by the harsh appraisal of his daughter, the President wrote to the critic: "Some day I hope to meet you. When that happens you'll need a new nose, a lot of beefsteak for black eyes, and perhaps a supporter below!"[15]

Just a few months later, as if in further response to Hume, Hope published a lengthy, flattering, and highly personal profile of Margaret Truman in *Promenade Magazine*. The style of the piece is unique in Hope's career. It seems to be based on an interview, yet is devoid of any quotations and, in fact, lacks any citations of direct contact with the subject. Yet it outlines not only Miss Truman's personal priorities and professional goals, but also what purports to be her most private thoughts, some presented in a manner bordering on psychological analysis.

If you were Margaret Truman, life at twenty-seven would be a prism, a multiple-mirror throwing back innumerable reflections of yourself: some flattering, others less so. Some as you appear to family and close friends, others as seen by casual acquaintances, and many by people who admire the Margaret Truman they never have met. Now and again, there's the reflection of a President's daughter, misunderstood and victimized by some who assume, mistakenly, that White House prestige is being used to further a singer's career. Undazzled by the light, not deterred by the shadows, Margaret Truman is, in fact, fortified by knowing that she would have aimed at the same career if her father had never been President.

The article is obviously written from a level of friendship with the subject. But sections of the story also suggest that Hope had levels of identification with Margaret Truman that went far beyond those few minutes of impersonating her onstage at the stunt party.

First off, both Margaret and Hope were each their parents' only child.

"Like most only children she assumed a responsibility that daughters and sons in larger families rarely assume, realizing that the hopes and ambitions of her father and mother were centered in her alone. Determined not to disappoint them, she dreamed of the day when they would be proud of her because of her own achievements."

Second, while still teens, both women were forced to put on hold their burning ambition to enter the performing arts.

"She made good grades, to please her parents; graduated high in her class with a prize in Spanish and her name on the English cup. She thought longingly of concentrating on voice study. Her father and mother were sympathetic but insisted she graduate from college first. Heated arguments and pouting didn't help."[16]

There's still another parallel that hadn't yet materialized—Truman's later success as a prolific writer.

Hope saved two handwritten letters that illustrate the personal connection she had with the Trumans:

March 30, 1951

Dear Hopie:

Just a note to say thanks for the nice article in Promenade. I am just leaving on tour and wanted to let you know I appreciate it.

My best wishes, most sincerely,

Margaret

May 2, 1951

The White House

Dear Mrs. Miller,

I am a bit embarrassed to be writing you so belatedly about the story you did on Margaret. The President and I thought it was very good and surely enjoyed it. I've been hoping I would see you somewhere so I could tell you this.

Thank you so much for being so nice to my Margaret.

Most sincerely,

Bess Truman

Under Hope's guidance, fund-raisers became lively productions that allowed dignitaries to contribute in unexpected ways. As a founding member of the Women's Board of the Washington Heart Association, Hope organized the entertainment for the 1950 gala, which included a chorus of forty senators and 160 congressmen.[17]

"Anything you asked her to do, she did it and them some." recalled Margaret Wimsatt, a fellow board member and friend. "She was great fun and had a great sense of humor."[18]

The following year, Hope was behind an even grander event for the Women's National Press Club. Its new president was Ruth Montgomery, Washington correspondent for the *New York Daily News* and one of Hope's closest friends. Club members had long fantasized of having their own head-quarters and Montgomery took that on as her mission. The first step would be bringing in some money.

The organization already knew how to throw parties and produce shows. Hope suggested roping in Ted Mack to host a "VIP Amateur Hour" with the contestants coming from every branch of government plus Embassy Row. Typical of volunteer efforts, if you have a good idea you usually get put in charge of making it happen. Sure enough, Montgomery named Hope as general chairman of the event.

Hope's first call was to none other than Sam Rayburn, who readily accepted the role of emcee. "With that, I could get anybody in the House," recalled Hope. Needing a Republican, she rang up Sen. Robert A. Taft who agreed to lead a chorus of Senators in a patriotic anthem.[19] The rest of Washington seemed to fall in line. The papers featured photos of congressmen ducking out of committee hearings to rehearse.[20]

But as plans progressed, so did the Korean War. The club decided it would be in the spirit of the times to instead raise funds for the U.S.O. Ticket prices were lowered, and all 3,700 seats in Constitution Hall were sold. Though President Truman had cancelled appearances at press parties such as the Gridiron, he and the First Lady agreed to attend because the event was in support of the war effort.

The three-hour show featured a cast of 150 and the first hour was broadcast on radio. In between each act, Rayburn rapped his heavy gavel. But the barrel-chested Speaker also drew hearty laughs each time he played a tingling little chime as part of a bell choir rendition of "The Bells of St. Mary's." A different gang of congressmen formed a ragtag band of washtubs and garbage cans, hoses, and horns. The wife of the French ambassador hosted a fashion show with wives of other foreign ministers, senators, and cabinet officers modeling Christian Dior gowns. Representative Albert Gore played a violin solo, Cuban ambassador Luis Machado gave a guitar solo, and Marjorie Merriweather Post led a square dance. Also onstage at one point or another were Secretary of State Dean Acheson, four other cabinet secretaries, and two Supreme Court Justices. For the grand finale, Second Lady Jane Barkley pushed onto the stage a wheelchair that carried a 25-year-old veteran who had lost both of his legs in Korea. He led the entire assembly in "The Battle Hymn of the Republic."[21]

Dwight D. Eisenhower's coattails in the 1952 general election brought a Republican majority into the House of Representatives, thus leading Sam Rayburn to surrender the speakership to Joseph W. Martin of Massachusetts. The top men in the House were already familiar with swapping positions. The Republicans had taken the majority in the 1946 general election but then lost it two years later. Here they were again. By most all accounts, Rayburn and Martin maintained a cordial relationship during their two decades of leading the opposing parties. Yet the Republican leadership in the 83rd Congress still sought ways to assert itself. One of its sharpest tools was investigation.

The Justice Department and Internal Revenue Service had already been targets of inquiry by separate panels during the prior Democratic-led Congress. Those efforts were scheduled to wrap up their business at the end of 1952, but instead were kept alive by the incoming Republicans and funded with new annual budgets of about $100,000 each.

The examination of the IRS was under the aegis of the powerful Ways and Means Committee, now chaired by Daniel Reed of New York. Like Speaker Martin, Reed was also on friendly terms with Rayburn. The two had lived for a time in the same Washington hotel and Rayburn kept on display in his ceremonial office an item that had been a gift from Reed. It was a shillelagh, a cudgel of rough-hewn wood that could be used as a walking stick or an instrument of power and torture depending upon one's particular needs.[22]

Heading the Ways and Means subcommittee in its search for graft and fraud in the realm of taxes would be seven-term Congressman Robert W. Kean of New Jersey. He was the grandson of industrialist Moses Taylor, an associate of Manhattan's notorious Tammany Hall political machine. His son Thomas Kean would one day become Governor of New Jersey.

Among a small parade of ne'er-do-wells called before the subcommittee during the early months of 1953 was 49-year-old Garry D. Iozia, of East Patterson, New Jersey who had been president and treasurer of the Housatonic Company, a printing and dyeing concern of Derby, Connecticut. In January, Iozia had pleaded guilty in a Manhattan court to a three-count indictment for evasion of $150,000 in Federal taxes owed on some $1.5 million in unreported income. He was fined an additional $20,000 and sentenced to two to four years in prison.[23]

On March 18, Iozia testified to the congressional body that starting several years prior to his eventual appearance in court he'd sought various remedies to his tax difficulties. In the course of such efforts, he shelled out more than $100,000 in payments to more than a dozen different attorneys and two public relations professionals, all claiming influence in high places. One of the latter was Hope Ridings Miller.

In his sworn testimony, Iozia made the following assertions: That when he was introduced to Miller in 1950 he was told she was a secretary to Speaker Rayburn. Only later did he find out "she was just a newspaper woman."[24] He had only one meeting with Miller, which took place in her Manhattan hotel room and was also attended by two attorneys, Wallace M. Cohen and Paul Arnold. At that meeting, Iozia said, he paid Miller $2,500 in cash. Another $2,500 was later paid to her through check that was made out to attorney Cohen and endorsed over to Miller.

One day after Iozia's appearance before the subcommittee, Cohen and Arnold also testified. In their separate interrogations, they agreed that there was no cash payment made to Miller. Otherwise, they differed on the reasons for her engagement by Iozia. Arnold said that Miller got the work because she was "very, very friendly with Sam Rayburn." Cohen said, "There was no mention of Rayburn or any other person in high office."

Most of the questioning came from the committee's counsel John E. Tobin, but Republican committee member John W. Byrnes asked how public relations entered into a criminal tax case. Cohen replied that Miller "could bring the force of public opinion to bear to prevent an injustice being done." Cohen also said that throughout the eighteen months he worked for Iozia, his client "maintained fervently that he was innocent of any wrongdoing." Cohen further said that he was "shocked" when Iozia pled guilty.[25]

Hope came before the subcommittee in the new House Office Building on Friday morning, March 20, 1953, to tell her side of the story. She was also there to address a further matter that had come up during a previous deposition—that she had failed to report Iozia's $2,500 retainer fee on her 1950 income tax returns. At her deposition and public testimomy, she was accompanied by her attorney, Roy St. Lewis. A native of Oklahoma and former Federal District Attorney there, St. Lewis was a Republican who had come to Washington to serve as an Assistant Attorney General under President Hoover. He was now in private practice.

Hope made an opening statement recounting her memory of an early August 1950 meeting with Iozia, Cohen, and Arnold, and a third attorney, Abba Schwartz.

> Mr. Garry Iozia was represented to me as a man who was a victim of grave injustice on the parts of former associates and Government employees. This representation was made to me by Mr. Iozia himself, in great and touching detail, for almost five hours. Mr. Iozia's representation was a pathetic recital of his persecution in the Department of Justice, in that he was an Italian and did not arrive in this country until 1913. . . . His persistence led me to believe, upon first impression, that he possibly was being victimized and that something could be done by bringing his plight to public attention.[26]

She was adamant that at that meeting there was no offer of employment, that no fee was discussed, and no funds changed hands. A few days later, Cohen met with her in Washington. The two agreed that she would do "a public relations job" for Iozia. "No promises were made by me, none were solicited. . . . The understanding was that I was to find out why Mr. Garry Iozia's case was not being given a full and fair hearing in the Department of Justice; to establish which person or persons were responsible for any discrimination and then to publicize the injustice, if any, to the best of my ability."[27] She was given a $2,500 retainer in form of a check endorsed by Cohen to her. After some investigation, she concluded that no injustice had occurred against Iozia and any publicity would be detrimental to his cause. She so informed Cohen and essentially stopped work on the case.

During subsequent questioning by counsel, it was clear that researchers for the committee had obtained the guest registry of the Lombardy Hotel at 56th and Park Avenue where Hope was staying when she met Iozia and the attorneys. They also secured and studied the phone logs of her room. Further questions dwelt on conflicting dates of the original meeting, of the endorsed check, and when it was deposited.

Hope explained that after the meeting between her and Cohen, her first step toward investigating the matter was an inquiry with her Congressman—Sam Rayburn. Within a few weeks, Rayburn informed her that there was nothing to the case and nothing to be done. When pressed on the Rayburn connection, Hope told the committee, "I don't think that any American citizen should have any compunction about asking his Congressman to look into the status of any case." At that, Louisiana Democrat Hale Boggs spoke up.

From the committee transcripts:

> Mr. Boggs: You simply represented the facts as you had them and simply asked him to get a report. You did not ask him to do anything?
> Mrs. Miller: I didn't dare ask him. Nobody would ask him who knows him.[28]

The Rayburn connection continued to come up in the questioning. Hope recalled that at some point in the meeting with Iozia, after he said he was from Italy, she said she was from Texas. Iozia then asked if she knew Speaker Rayburn and she replied that she'd known him for many years. But Kean laid to rest any possibility that the subcommittee was seeking a roundabout way of attacking Rayburn.

> Chairman Kean: Of course, the testimony of Mr. Iozia makes a pretty rotten attack on you because it would be a rotten thing for you to do to have used Mr. Rayburn's name or friendship to try to get money as Mr. Iozia claimed you did.
> Mrs. Miller: Mr. Chairman, it certainly was a rotten attack.
> Chairman Kean: We all know that Mr. Rayburn certainly would not under any circumstances, I believe, ever do anything that was in the least improper.
> Mrs. Miller: I am sure he would not.[29]

As Hope's counsel, St. Lewis remained quiet until near the end of the questioning when he erupted with a similar attack on Iozia and defense Rayburn.

> Mr. St. Lewis: Under the circumstances, the way he has blasphemed everybody from one end of the country to the other, both Republican Party and Democratic Party, and Cardinal Spellman, and has

proved himself a liar. This woman's reputation has been hurt forever having gotten mixed up with a man like that. He has tried to hurt Sam Rayburn, whom we all know is as clean as a hound's tooth.[30]

At some point in the weeks after consulting with Rayburn, Hope had an unexpected opportunity to bring up the Iozia matter to Assistant Attorney General Peyton Ford. Though she'd never met Ford, they were seated beside each other at a dinner party. He was familiar with the case and indicated that no discrimination existed.

This seemingly modest effort—making an inquiry to a Congressman and putting out some feelers around town—in exchange for a $2,500 retainer led to more questions. There was the absence of what would be considered traditional public relations work and the intimation that Iozia had been expecting some kind of influence be brought to bear on his behalf.

Hope explained that during this period she was new to the public relations field and receiving regular guidance from a more experienced colleague, Steve Hannagan. About a month prior to her being summoned by the committee, Hannagan had actually died. He was just fifty-four and suffered a heart attack while traveling in Africa. Hope recounted Hannagan's instruction: "Anything is within the realm of public relations where you have the chance to enhance the value of a client or to correct an injustice." Probably recalling his own experience with the fugitive millionaire Samuel Insull, Hannagan also told her: "For getting into a case like that, which is very difficult and may be very smelly, you would take some chance, but if you are going to stick just to the public relations end of it, ask for at least $15,000."[31]

It was the "smelly" nature of it all that led Hope to refrain from declaring the income on her 1950 tax return, fearing that sooner or later Iozia might come around, asking for the fee to be returned. Hope said that at some point in 1951 she learned that the services she provided—some investigation and the advice to avoid bringing the matter before the public—were possibly not what Iozia had been seeking. "I found out that I had not performed the service he had hoped I would, and that is the first time it ever occurred to me that he might have had something else in mind when he hired me. I don't know what he thought he was hiring me for," she testified.[32]

Congressman Byrnes pointed out that two years of tax returns had gone by since she took the $2,500 retainer.

Hope replied: "The case was really finished when he was convicted. Up to that time, I had some hope that he might not be guilty in which case . . . I would have been glad to go back in his home community and try to build up a feeling of good will toward him there. That is public relations."[33]

After further questions, she said: "But I knew that there was nothing I could ever do for a man who had confessed that he was a criminal. Therefore, the case was ended, and it was then income. That was my thinking."[34]

At this point Kean interjected:

> CHAIRMAN KEAN: That is an extraordinary decision—but of course I am not a tax lawyer, though I have had some experience in the tax law—to say that if you received money from a bad character it is not taxable income because some day the character might ask you to give it back. It seems to me a most unusual decision, but if this competent lawyer says that is the fact, maybe that is part of the tax law.
>
> MR. ST. LEWIS: Mr. Chairman, she thought all along that he would ask for this money back.[35]

When the topic first turned to Hope's own taxes, she informed the committee that in the week after being deposed by counsel Tobin, she filed an amended return for 1950 that included the $2,500 retainer.

The morning-long session ended with Tobin reminding the witness that she had been served with a subpoena calling for the production of all pertinent financial records. St. Louis said that they had the documents with them. He then added: "She has her records here, as much as a woman keeps."[36]

No actions were taken against Hope by the subcommittee or the IRS and Iozia apparently served his time. But there were other people, from inside and outside of government, who also got caught up in the affair and were brought in to testify. One of them was Joseph T. Sherman, the other public relations consultant engaged by Iozia. Even more flamboyant claims came from Iozia regarding what he hired Sherman to do, including going to Independence, Missouri, to speak with President Truman's brother.[37] But the investigation turned to Sherman's own taxes, just as it had done with Hope's, and significant improprieties were discovered. In 1955, Sherman was sentenced to fifteen months in prison.[38]

The days of hearings regarding Iozia and his circle received significant attention in the press and Hope's stone-faced testimony served as a fine crescendo to the first week of coverage. "Mrs. Miller's $2,500 Fee Is Probe Topic" was the headline to the *Post*'s story, which ran on page two. In the

Chicago Daily Tribune, the headline proclaimed, "Society Writer Admits Dodging $2,500 on Taxes."

The official transcripts of the subcommittee proceedings include a sad coda to Hope's testimony—a lengthy, notarized letter she sent to Chairman Kean correcting her testimony on May 15, 1953. It reads in part:

> Dr. Miller, my former husband who had assisted me in preparing my 1950 income tax return, was confident that I had included this $2,500 fee in my return but without the copy of Schedule C he could not substantiate this. Therefore, we erroneously concluded that I had followed the suggestion of Mr. Hannagan and the advice of Mr. St. Lewis not to report it as income until I knew more about the outcome of the tax difficulties of Mr. Iozia and his corporation.

But further digging and some assistance from a tax professional led to the conclusion that the income had indeed been reported for the year in which it was received.

"It is a source of keen regret that my thinking on this subject became so garbled and resulted in exhaustive questioning by you and your colleagues, as well as by Mr. Tobin. The error was entirely the result of my confused memory and inadequate bookkeeping. Please accept this letter as an apology and correction of my testimony."[39]

Viewing the ordeal of the Iozia affair as a kind of omen, Hope began stepping away from PR work and looked for a return to journalism on a full-time basis. If the year 1953 had not been troubling enough, it ended with her father's death at age seventy-four on December 16 at Washington's Mount Alto Hospital. Dr. Ridings was laid to rest beside his late wife in the family crypt in Sherman, Texas.

12

DIPLOMAT MAGAZINE

Starting with its launch in 1949, the *Diplomat* magazine carried a variety of subtitles as indication of its editorial focus. It debuted as "A Society Review," but a few years down the road, the banner on its cover read "Travel—Fashion—Society." Still later, it proudly proclaimed itself as "Prestige Window on the World." However it was phrased, this was Hope's kind of territory. She became a contributor to the monthly in January 1954 with "Town Talk," a reoccurring column about the Washington social scene.

The *Diplomat* was founded by a cultured but daring figure, I. Monte Radlovic. A native of Montenegro and graduate of Cambridge University, he began his journalism career with Reuters and the *Daily Mail* in London and then became a staff writer for the *Balkan Herald* in Belgrade. During the Axis invasion of Yugoslavia he fled the country on a submarine, eventually arriving in Egypt where he enlisted in the British Army. He fought valiantly and was decorated by King George. After the war he wrote a book, *Tito's Republic*, and befriended such figures as Bertrand Russell, George Bernard Shaw, and Frank Lloyd Wright.[1]

Radlovic's magazine ran about sixty pages in a typical issue, but it was still a fledgling concern when Radlovic persuaded Hope to start writing. Within a year, he named her an associate editor. That kind of title is usually an honorific for steady contributors and sympathetic souls. Aware that Radlovic had modest funds and a sense of wanderlust ready to kick in, Hope suggested that her friend and attorney Roy St. Lewis consider the magazine as an investment. St. Lewis purchased the *Diplomat* and became its publisher in April 1955. Knowing little about the magazine trade, St. Lewis continued at lawyering. Ten months after taking on the magazine, he named Hope as editor in chief and placed the entire operation in her hands. Meanwhile Rodlovic headed to the West Coast for more adventures.

The position of a magazine editor was an ideal fit for Hope. First, it allowed her to put behind her once and for all the PR game, with the chase for clients and the behind-the-scenes maneuvering. The purview of the *Diplomat*—international society, plus fashion, culture, and travel—also allowed Hope to broaden her game. Yet at the same time, steering a monthly publication made for a more relaxed pace compared to the daily grind of newspaper reporting, which she already knew so well.

Stability was also returning to Hope's personal life, as she and Lee reconciled and remarried. "The divorce was short lived," said a friend who knew them both. "Lee did not understand her life and her writing. But he knew he had made a mistake."

Lee had resisted when Hope was offered the position of society editor at the *Post*, telling her, "You'll wear yourself out if you've got to go to all these nighttime things." But Hope recalled that when she could persuade him to come along to an event, he usually enjoyed himself immensely.

With Hope's father out of the picture there was more room for Lee to be the number-one man in her life, even if he might still feel like the number-two spouse at parties. Lee's professional stature was also rising. He was promoted to chief of medical services at the Soldiers Home and he also established a private practice with offices on Rhode Island Avenue NW near Logan Circle.

The couple moved again, this time to The Norwood at 1868 Columbia Road NW, three blocks off Connecticut Avenue and overlooking Kalorama Park. It was a large and attractive seven-story apartment building dating from 1916. With a façade of cream-colored brick, the building boasted a small circular front drive, marble portico and elevator lobby.[2] The Millers selected a corner unit on an upper floor that had once been entirely occupied by Speaker of the House William Bankhead and his family (including Tallulah).[3]

After Hope took the reigns of the *Diplomat*, its offices moved to the National Press Building where her staff consisted of a full-time assistant and a part-time designer. Operating out of the Press Building instead of a home office had a number of advantages. It placed her closer to downtown luncheons and meetings and allowed for daily interactions, whether in the elevator or on the street corner, with colleagues from other publications.

Many a memoir of Washington journalists begins with arriving in town and heading to the Press Building where walking the halls and knocking on doors served as the most efficient way of finding work. And the *Diplomat* did rely heavily on freelance contributors. Hope's team outside of Washington included correspondents in twelve American cities and eight foreign capitals.

Under her leadership, the magazine helped launch the careers of numerous women writers and media figures. Already contributing to the *Diplomat* in the mid-1950s were two of Hope's closest friends, Ruth Montgomery, the political reporter, and Deena Clark, who later became well known for her interview programs on NBC and CBS. Helen Thomas had been in Washington more than a decade when she, too, filed a couple of stories with Hope—a 1958 profile of Harold E. Fellows, president of the National Association of Broadcasters, and the following year a story on the new Korean ambassador You Chan Yang. Sarah Booth Conroy served as correspondent from Zurich, where her husband was a diplomat. In the 1960s Conroy joined the *Post* and over the next three decades she became an institution there, covering Washington personalities, history, and architecture. Still others contributing to the *Diplomat* in the late 1950s were the Texans Sarah McClendon, once Hope's peers at the Bascom Timmons News Bureau, and the lively Liz Carpenter, who joined the staff of Vice President Johnson in 1961 and became Lady Bird Johnson's staff director and press aid in 1964.

Hope continued to write the Washington society news for the magazine. She also instituted the "Editor's Notebook" as a forum to introduce the issue at hand and address current topics on her mind. On top of that, she wrote, as needed, pieces on food, fashion, or travel. So that the HRM byline didn't land on too many pages, she took to using a few different pennames. Among the busiest was travel writer "Keith Wandelohr," who took in a different U.S. city or foreign country almost every month.

"Salon diplomacy" was Hope's own succinct way of describing the *Diplomat*'s purview. Instead of charged negotiations and elaborate treaties, this was about the parties that bring people together, foster understanding and long-term alliances. Sometimes, though, a party is just a party and that was okay, too. Many of Hope's early columns in the *Diplomat* are light as air, stretched thin by anecdotes and clever sayings—a marked contrast to the urgent thrice weekly reports in the *Post* about wartime Washington. It was now the mid-1950s, the comparatively easygoing and prosperous Eisenhower era and the more casual and flowing nature of her writing reflects that.

Sam Rayburn, of course, appeared regularly in the *Diplomat*. If nothing else, each year there was always a paragraph or two about his January 6 birthday party. Lobbyist Dale Miller and his wife, Scooter, both Texans, had started hosting the event in 1949 and the affair grew steadily in size and importance.[4]

Rayburn was at the center of an episode that occurred in this period at a dinner party for Perle Mesta. La Mesta was always looking to foster dialogue (or ignite sparks) between Republicans and Democrats, so she seated Princess Alice beside Speaker Rayburn. The two spent most of the meal volleying back and forth about current politics. When the topic turned to the Dem's proposed $20 across-the-board tax cut, Longworth pulled a twenty out of her purse, waived it under Rayburn's nose, and taunted, "Just how much would a tax cut of this small amount help any of us, anyway?" Rayburn snatched the money out of her hand and refused to return it, claiming, "Everybody knows a Republican has no business carrying around a bill with Andrew Jackson's picture on the back!" He put the greenback in his wallet and only returned it at the end of the night.[5]

In Hope's early issues at the *Diplomat* she returned to a number of familiar topics. Another go at "Christmas Around the World" was probably a reflection of the constant need to fill space. Other repeats illustrate the cyclical nature of politics and the ever-busy social scene. Worth regular consideration was how innovative or tradition-bound was the new White House social calendar. And the question of whether to curtsy before royalty was once again timely as the 1957 visit of Queen Elizabeth II drew near.

Still, there were some fresh and juicy items in her reporting for the *Diplomat*, such as the passing storm between Elsa Maxwell and Perle Mesta. In a new memoir titled *RSVP*, Maxwell said she had refused to go to Mesta's ball at Londonderry House on the night of Elizabeth's coronation. The event is remembered as perhaps Mesta's greatest party of all, with a guest list that included royalty from Norway, the Netherlands, and Hollywood. Maxwell complained of overcrowded conditions and no place to sit down—at the party she didn't attend. Mesta responded that Maxwell hadn't even been invited. "I probably would have asked her," she added. "But I simply forgot she was in London at the time." As to all the people milling about that night, Hope had this to say: "How many men and women, dressed to the teeth on the evening of a Coronation, want to sit down anyway? Most of them, according to my own private eye, seemed more than content to keep dancing . . . and being seen."[6]

Another fun item began with sundry facts and observations about the most eligible bachelor on the international scene, Prince Rainier III of Monaco. Sturdy, handsome, and affable, he was only thirty-two years old and carried twenty-four titles. An unnamed European source said that actress Grace Kelly had recently "paid a courtesy call on him" (whatever that means). But as Hope saw it, any talk that the "pluperfect prince" took a liking to Kelly was probably just trumped-up publicity for the Oscar-winning actress. In fact, the very same month this story ran, December 1955, the Prince was on his way to the United States for a second face-to-face with Miss Kelly. Five months later, the couple exchanged vows in what was called the wedding of the century.[7]

As during the *Post* years, some of Hope's best and most valuable stories are when she steps back from recounting the day-to-day mingling and assesses the state of affairs. In fall 1955, she took stock of the top Washington hostesses. It was the only time in her career that she dared to line up the ladies, shoulder to shoulder. First, though, she reminisced about Evalyn Walsh McLean. Then, she paid tribute to Perle Mesta's reign during the early Truman years and added that Mesta, now back from Luxembourg, could easily reclaim her crown if she chose to do so. Yet there were plenty of other hostesses vying for stature.

A Washington old-timer once observed that "Every prominent woman here seems to be a hostess . . . unless she happens to be a perpetual guest." In the long-established group who entertain with distinctive elegance are Mrs. Dwight Davis, Mrs. Nicholas Longworth, Mrs. J. Borden Harriman, and the Three B's—Mrs. Robert Low Bacon, Mrs. Truxtun Beale, and Mrs. Robert Woods Bliss.

Pauline Davis, widow of the Secretary of War under Coolidge, has one of the loveliest homes in town; her dinner and balls approach perfection in every detail. A distinctive political tinge flavors the cozy dinners given by "Princess Alice" Roosevelt Longworth, and "Daisy" Harriman, and the buffet suppers given by Mrs. Robert Low Bacon. All three hostesses dote on inviting guests whose opposing opinions will stimulate conversation. Mrs. Longworth's rapier wit enlivens her beautifully appointed dinners, attended by social notables and politicos, along with anyone else to whom she has taken a fancy. Mrs. Harriman's Sunday night suppers are fascinating political forums. Administration officials, bigwigs in both political parties, residential notables and diplomats flock to Mrs. Bacon's suppers, at which conversation invariably focuses on politics.

Marie Beale's historic home, Decatur House, which was wired for electricity only three years ago, symbolizes gracious living of an era long past. Its chatelaine gives ultra smart dinners-for-twelve at frequent intervals, and occasionally an elegant tea to which both men and women are invited. But her social principality rests chiefly on the exclusive supper party which she gives each year following the Diplomatic Reception at the White House, just across Lafayette Square. Not all the envoys and their wives are invited to her home, naturally. As someone put it, "Just those whom Marie has personally accredited and recognized."

Mildred Bliss' dinners are models of formal correctness. Invitations to them are always delivered by hand. She is the wife of a former Ambassador. Her interests are more cosmopolitan and artistic than political; and conversation at her parties accentuates the cultural.

Compared with the Three Bs, Mrs. Merriweather Post is a newcomer to the Capital scene; but a sizeable number of party-goers insist that she gives the best parties in town and deserves acclaim as the leading hostess. Several times in recent years, Mrs. Morris Cafritz, socially enterprising wife of a wealthy Washington realtor, has hit the headlines as Number One hostess. She cultivates ranking diplomats and high officialdom; fetes them at a series of superlative dinners at which 'little speeches' are in order; and she rounds out her annual calendar with a number of largish receptions, including a hardy Easter Sunday annual.

Some years ago, a New Yorker quoted a hard-boiled Washingtonian as saying, "What I like about Gwen Cafritz is that she makes absolutely no pretense of *not* being elaborate." Certainly, the Classical murals in her vast drawing room survey their share of elaborate get-togethers each year.

Presiding over a sumptuous Tudor mansion is Mrs. M. Robert Guggenheim, wife of our former Ambassador to Portugal, a leading hostess in Washington for a number of years. Her spectacular pin, centered with the world's largest sapphire surrounded by diamonds, pulsates at some of the most elegantly appointed dinners in the nation's Capital. Polished productions for 22 guests, they are gastronomical achievements, superbly planned, and outlined on the menu formally printed on silver-edge cards. Music and dancing often follow dinner. Now and then, large cocktail parties throng the spacious salons and the sweeping terrace of the Guggenheim mansion. This past June, a glittering debutante ball drew hundreds of young and no-so-young guests to the chandeliered salons presided over by this prominent hostess, who is among the most popular women in Washington . . . who numbers of her friends by the hundreds, and apparently has no enemies. And, Brother, in capital S Society, that's something.[8]

Friends by the hundreds and no enemies: The same could be said of Hope. What other writer working from firsthand knowledge could compare and contrast the great hostesses of Washington and yet still give each of them such individual and elegant praise.

Speaking of chandeliers, Hope's columns began carrying the title, "Chandelier Washington," and a pen and ink drawing of a crystal-festooned light fixture started gracing the top of the *Diplomat's* table of contents.

At the same time though, her columns began not just reporting on the illustrious guests and elegant tone of gatherings but also contributed to the discussions that took place in the glow of the salons. She placed the affairs of dignitaries in the context of world events and trends, such as the rising anti-Americanism and the mounting winds of communism. She offered opinion on the appropriate qualifications for an envoy, discussed trade with the Mexican ambassador, and explained how the profile of England was shifting from empire to commonwealth.

She labeled as "the new diplomacy" the practice, taken up by various embassies, of trotting out at dinners and receptions the most prized celebrities who hailed from the homeland. For example, in just one season, the Italian embassy welcomed at separate affairs Gina Lollobrigida and Sophia Loren. "And what, some of our readers may ask, is so *new* about the trend? Hasn't our Nation's Capital given a big play to Hollywood before this? The answer is yes . . . but not to such a social extent as in the past year."[9]

World issues were sometimes addressed at greater length in the pages of the *Diplomat* thanks to guest contributors. In the wake of the Russian launch of Sputnik came an article titled, "Diplomacy in the Space Age." The writer was Robert L. Smith, retired Brigadier General of the U.S. Air Force, who flew 388 combat missions in World War II and wrote a best-selling memoir, *God Is My Co-Pilot*. He argued for greater engagement in "the space race" and cautioned that security matters must be placed under the charge of skilled airmen.[10]

Highbrow culture got a periodic share of attention, a reflection of the affinity between the wealthy and the classical arts. Within one issue were profiles of the young lions of literature and music, Gore Vidal and Leonard Bernstein. Another large spread examined architect Edward Durell Stone's plans for the National Cultural Center (later named Kennedy Center).

A constant in every issue were the up-to-the-minute reports on trends in fashion and travel, with Hope sometimes weighing in. She was perplexed by the latest couture, and she sent Keith Wandelohr to check out the latest new hotels on the Las Vegas strip. But the "Editor's Notebook" in two consecutive issues was required to encompass all the details of the Millers' European vacation in early autumn 1959.

Initially, Hope and Lee's itinerary called for little more than a relaxing spell at the beach on the Spanish island of Majorca. But word came from those in the know that the place was jammed with tourists. So, one week before setting off, their destination changed to Estoril, Portugal. En route, they spent a couple of nights in Lisbon at the spanking new Ritz, where Hope—ever the reporter—spotted in the lobby Fulgencio Batista, the recently overthrown President of Cuba, accompanied by his wife and a retinue of husky men. The lavish hotel was also aflutter because of the arrival the following day of Mme. Sarah Kubitschek, wife of the Brazilian President. But the beach in Estoril beckoned and was just a half hour away by electric train. Hope found that locale to be comfortably low-key, aristocratic, and conservative (no two-piece bathing suits for the ladies). "It's a gay place where you can enjoy yourself without half trying," she wrote.[11]

From there, it was on to six more cities across the continent, all in about ten days. A pleasurable stroll on Paris's Left Bank with its art and book vendors was followed by a stop at the American Express Office near the Opera, "where any American any time is sure to run into at least one old acquaintance." In Berlin, their hotel was situated on the Kurfürstendamnn and they found the city's theater scene alive with seven new playhouses opened just since the war. They also crossed through the Brandenburg Gate and into East Berlin where "the people you see on the streets are unsmiling, with lack-luster eyes and lagging feet." Next was Madrid and a drastic time shift, with lunch at 2:30 p.m., and dinner never before 10 p.m. "You'll quickly grow accustomed to going for dress fittings at 7:30 in the evening, and to theater at 11 p.m." Then it was on to Munich, Vienna, and Zurich. Hope concluded the travelogue with copious acknowledgments of the airline service and convenience. "Stewards and stewardesses cater to the traveller's every whim and comfort, and meals aloft are veritable banquets."[12]

In April 1960, Hope found it necessary to define for readers the aim and scope of the *Diplomat*. Her format for the column was to answer a series of questions that were continually arising. The exclusivity of the magazine certainly comes through, since the answer to every question was "No."

No, the *Diplomat* is not exclusively about the diplomatic corps, otherwise it would be called the *Diplomats*. "It is for, and about, Very Important Persons in government (and diplomacy), business, industry, society and the arts." No, it is not just about high officialdom in Washington, although as the seat of government, Washington has a higher percent of leaders than any other American metropolis. No, it is not devoted just to high society, "although persons of impeachable social distinction are covered regularly."[13]

More spontaneous and impudent rebuttals and defenses of the *Diplomat*'s mission and purpose appeared now and then in the Letters sections.

> Your magazine interests me tremendously . . . but I could do with a little less emphasis on the Social Notables whose faces appear so regularly in your pages. What about paying occasional attention to worthy but not necessarily well-known educators and welfare works?
>
> J. K., Cedar Rapids, Iowa

We are all for worthy individuals, whatever their status of distinction. But, as its subtitle indicates, the *Diplomat* is primarily about persons in prestige groups, at home and abroad. Numerous publications are angled toward mass audiences. Our is for, and about, persons of eminence around the globe.

—Editor[14]

I get a big bang out of reading page after page of your fascinating publication, but occasionally I grow hot under the collar at some of the Letters to the Editor. I refer to one of your readers who was annoyed because your magazine sometimes features people who spend as much as $50,000 on a single party.

I wonder if a person who makes such a criticism gives the matter fair consideration. The money is not "thrown away." It is used to employ waiters and waitresses, to purchase food and linens, and to take care of musicians, laundry, et cetera, required for such a gala. This money is put into circulation by way of employment and the people who spend it are entitled to their enjoyment.

J. C., New York City

That they are. And we happen to be all for it, and them. Furthermore, at the drop of an invitation, we will write up almost any party costing $50,000, provided it's given by somebody whose distinction does not stem entirely from a big bank account.

—Editor[15]

Edward Tomlinson's splendid article on Mexico was both informative and inspiring. Let's have more along that line, and less about the Social Who's Who. Who cares?

J. P. M, Cuernavaca, Mexico

We care.

—Editor.[16]

13

CROSSING THE NEW FRONTIER

Hope waited until midsummer 1960 to consider the latest batch of "First Ladies in Waiting." Of the small pool of candidates, she already knew one of them quite well, had observed another for many years, but held guarded concerns about the third.

The Johnsons had come to Washington just four years after the Millers arrived. As fellow Texans in Sam Rayburn's inner circle, the two couples were well acquainted. Hope predicted that Mrs. Johnson would take the role of first hostess in stride and apply to her new duties a well-proven skill at organizing and compartmentalizing. "There's a solid, sincere quality about her, and you feel that she is the same unassuming type of person she would have been if she had never left Texas."

As the wife of the sitting vice president, Mrs. Nixon had the advantage of eight years of practice at top-level meeting, greeting, and entertaining. Hope noted her conservative tastes in fashion, a tendency to use slang, and an ability to read other people's desires and motives. "You get the impression that she is doing her dead-level best every minute. You wonder if she ever relaxes, ever forgets for a moment the multiple cameras and eyes focused on her and her family and the endless challenge of trying to please everybody all the time. . . . If her ready smile appears fixed at times, it is understandable."[1]

One might assume that the youthful Mrs. Kennedy's social pedigree (she was a popular debutante in New York and Newport) and background in journalism (that stint as Inquiring Photographer at the *Herald-Tribune*) would have already brought Hope to her side. There was also the redoubtable education at Vassar, the Sorbonne, and George Washington University and her fluency in French and Italian. Hope enumerated all of these attributes and more, but still concluded her brief profile with unusual suspicion: "Some of her acquaintances call her 'beautiful,' others take a dim view of what they term 'her gamin look.' But she does have an enchanting smile, noticeable chic, an alert manner, and obvious admiration, as well as wifely love for her husband. As a First Lady, she would probably try hard to adapt herself to the demanding role."

Throughout her twenty-five years of covering Washington, Hope had unfailingly averred loyalty and praise for each First Family. And every four years during her tenure, the *Diplomat* produced a special inauguration issue consisting of lavish profiles and generous tributes to those in the new administration. That became so much easier to execute this time around, all because of one candid photo of President-elect Kennedy. It was shot in late November 1960 outside Georgetown University Hospital where Mrs. Kennedy was convalescing after giving birth to JFK, Jr. While stopping for a moment to speak with a nurse, Mr. Kennedy is seen clutching against his chest a bundle of mail. At the top of the stack is the December issue of the *Diplomat*. Its black on white banner faces the camera and reads sharp and clear. Naturally, the photo ran in the January issue.

In the following month's Inaugural Special, Hope gave greater consideration to the new First Lady: "The public image of Jacqueline Kennedy as a possible First Lady changed drastically in the course of her husband's campaign. Briefly publicized at the beginning as an avant-garde individualist, unlikely to capture the fancy of an American electorate accustomed to more conventional types, she blossomed under closer scrutiny into one of her husband's best assets; a charmer with whimsical attraction almost as strong as JFK's boyish-but-no-nonsense appeal. And she revealed a refreshing sense of humor: 'I couldn't spend that much on clothes a year . . . unless I wore sable underwear.' "[2]

Hope suggested in the same article that Mrs. Kennedy might take a page from Mrs. Roosevelt and start holding press conferences. It was an off-the-cuff notion, offered as just one of many possibilities that might be ahead for the coming administration. But an assiduous courting of the press with frequent access and dialogue turned out to be very low on the list of priorities for the new First Lady.

Given the recent birth of her son, Kennedy was understandably slow to jump into official duties. Her first and only concerted outreach to the women of the press was a White House luncheon in the spring. Accustomed to being treated as guests, the ladies were shocked to find that the seating was pell-mell style. In other words, sit wherever you find a chair—except for the places closest to the First Lady, which were reserved for her friends. It was an un-orthodox scene that lingered in Hope's memory for decades. And yet she dutifully put a good face on the whole event and wrote, "Mrs. Kennedy delighted almost 200 women of the press when she entertained them in the East Room." Hope noted the lavish buffet, the remarks by the director of the National Gallery, and the First Lady's own brief comments expressing gratitude for the many recent stories about the White House and its history.[3]

Mrs. Kennedy certainly did give journalists plenty to write about, starting with her efforts to transform the White House decor from what she considered a cut-rate hotel into a museum of the finest American art and design. Where the Trumans usually entertained political pals and the Eisenhowers favored business leaders, the Kennedys hosted artists, composers, and intellectuals of all stripes.

As for innovations, Hope had nothing against them, per se. At the start of the Kennedy administration, she wrote: "Jacqueline Kennedy has described her interests as 'running to things of the spirit—art, literature, and the like.' She can be expected to follow admirably in the footsteps of some of her prede-cessors similarly inclined. But nobody will be surprised if, without defying cherished tradition, she establishes innovations. Every truly outstanding First Lady has."[4]

At state dinners and official receptions, the tedious receiving lines were abolished and seating was changed from banquet-style to round tables, a cus-tom that is still maintained. For the state dinner in honor of Ayub Khan, the President of Pakistan, guests were taken down the Potomac by a fleet of yachts to have dinner at Mount Vernon. Other events featured classical music and scenes from Shakespeare. Hope reported much of it and even put cellist Pablo Casals on the *Diplomat*'s cover.

The *Diplomat*'s coverage of Sam Rayburn during the first year of the Kennedy administration gave him even greater honor than usual, an indication of the change in his ranking instituted by the new President. While seated on the inaugural platform with the Vice President-elect and the Speaker, Kennedy leaned forward to tell the latter, "I'm going to see that you're put where you belong in protocol—second only to the Vice President."[5] Kennedy made good on his promise, elevating the Speaker one rung above the Chief Justice, an appropriate shift, given that the Speaker is second in the line of succession to the Presidency. Protocol rankings apply through the city, not just at the White House. They determine the prized order in which guests are received at events and where they are seated at meals, not to mention how an informed journalist reports on a Washington gathering. Eisenhower also made a modification, promoting the Secretary of State's rank above the Dean of the Diplomatic Corps. But such changes are made rarely and only with the greatest deliberation.

Despite Hope's constant efforts to present Rayburn in the best possible light, the pages of the *Diplomat* from this era have photos of him with his eyes downcast or his head turned in a curious direction. This was the result of his dramatic loss in vision that occurred in 1956, due to hemorrhaging of blood vessels in his eyes. Rayburn lost the ability to read and to distinguish faces that were more than a few feet away. Yet little to nothing was ever said about his handicap, as the high wall that cordoned off Rayburn's personal life from any discussion remained in place. Staff members and close allies made the habit of greeting by name those who were approaching the Speaker at social or business functions. Parliamentarians whispered to him which members were seeking recognition from the House floor.[6]

In 1961, when Rayburn was seventy-nine, he began having severe back pain. He became disoriented while walking on the Capitol grounds and twice had to be assisted out of the Speaker's chair while the House was in session. In late August, he returned to Texas, explaining to Congressman Jim Wright of Fort Worth, "Bonham is a place where people know it when you're sick and where they care when you die."[7]

At Baylor University Medical Center in Dallas, Rayburn was finally diagnosed with pancreatic cancer. President Kennedy, former President Truman, and Vice President Johnson paid calls on him there, as he lingered weeks longer than doctors had expected. He was taken by ambulance back to Bonham where he died in a clinic on November 16.[8]

Rayburn's funeral in Bonham was attended by Presidents Kennedy, Truman, and Eisenhower, a delegation of 128 members of Congress, and some 20,000 citizens. Due to publishing deadlines as well as an abhorrence of funerals, Hope remained in Washington. She spent the day writing a tribute to her late friend, confidant, and patron. The piece ran in the February issue of the *Diplomat* and was reprinted in the *Congressional Record*. It begins:

> "I feel as though a part of the Capitol has fallen down," said a tearful Washington cave dweller on the afternoon they laid Speaker Rayburn to rest in the sandy land of Willow Wild Cemetery near his Texas home.
>
> She was expressing the thought of many mourners for the veteran legislator who served 48 years in Congress and was Speaker twice as long as any other man.
>
> He had no instinct for personal publicity, no flair for projecting to strangers the kind of man he really was. Casual acquaintances often considered him

just another conscientious public servant who lacked color and reached high rank through luck and seniority, a rather shy bachelor who sidestepped society as such because he felt out of place in it, an innately cautious politician with a mulish devotion to the Democratic Party; and a sometimes cantankerous character who barked and balked at photographers.

To those of us who really knew him, none of these labels were apt in the least. We understood him, we loved him, and we admired his complete lack of side, his level head, Texas whang, and homey turn of phrase—in a city seething with subterfuge and pretense. We knew something of the startling contrasts and vivid facets in the background to which he was true all the days of his life.[9]

Prior to the burial, the Speaker's body laid in state in the marble lobby of the Sam Rayburn Library for a full twenty-four hours. Nearby stood a statue of him by Felix de Weldon, the Austrian-born sculptor whose most iconic work is the Iwo Jima Memorial in Arlington, Virginia. Resting on a large granite base, the bronze sculpture of the Speaker has him wielding the gavel. His demeanor is authoritative, as if surveying the vast chamber of the House. Hope had much to do with that sculpture's completion. She spearheaded the fundraising committee that commissioned it in 1956, served as a liaison between the Texas benefactors and de Weldon and even observed one of the sessions when Mr. Sam sat for the sculptor in his Capitol office.

The public's thirst for information about the Kennedy family seemed to be unquenchable. Tensions between reporters and White House staff were one result. Press secretary Pierre Salinger's initial plan was that he would handle the flow of all information pertinent to both the East and West wings of the White House. "News is news," he said.

When Betty Beale, the *Star*'s society editor and typically a night owl, made the effort to show up for one of Salinger's morning press conferences, she expected at least some morsel of information pertinent to her beat. At first, Salinger had nothing for her. But it did occur to him that the new cat would be arriving in a few days.

"What cat?
"Caroline's cat."
"What's its name?"
"Tom Kitten."
"What color is it?"
"I don't know."
"Is it a Maltese cat?"

"No, it's an alley cat—kitten."

"Is it a cat or a kitten?"

Soon the entire press pool was badgering Salinger about the little feline, asking its age, what door it would use, and if it would be allowed to go out at night unescorted. The public had a right to know, Beale insisted, only half facetiously.[10]

From there, the relationship between her and Salinger only went downhill. Soon, it was decreed that a pool of twelve press people, six men and six women, would cover the major social events. None of them would be society reporters. It didn't take long before Beale found an opportunity to appeal that ruling directly to the President, whom she'd known since his days as a Congressman. After that, the strictures on access to events were eased but frictions remained. "The harpies" became the not-so-secret code word that the First Lady and some staff used to describe women of the press.

At the start of the 1962 season, Letitia Baldrige, the social secretary, and Pamela Turnure, the novice press secretary to Mrs. Kennedy, summoned the society writers to the White House for a dressing-down, or as Ruth Montgomery described it "a course in how to seem invisible." Baldrige complained that at a recent White House function she had wanted to meet astronaut John Glenn but found it impossible because he was surrounded by newswomen all evening. She declared that reporters were to consider themselves working people and not guests, never mind that they were in long gowns. Henceforth, they should not monopolize invitees, eavesdrop on them, or even speak with the President.

"Well," one scribe asked, "what if the President speaks to me?"

"Why don't you get behind a pillar and stay there?" snapped Baldrige.[11]

Hope never ceased tossing laurels of praise at Mrs. Kennedy and even compared her to Dolley Madison. She was giving readers what they wanted—a glowing depiction of the young and glamorous First Lady. And the pictures of her in sleek Oleg Cassini gowns were dramatic additions to every issue of the *Diplomat*. Nevertheless, shortly after that session with Baldrige, Hope offered a roundabout rebuttal, defending her profession and explaining that there really was no such thing as a private party, or hardly even a confidential conversation, not when it occurred at the White House.

Alert Washington society reporters—and you won't find any better in the entire country—can always contact guests who are dying to tell all . . . and they do. Thus, within a few days of any soiree, no matter how private, the public can read in the daily press a full account of who was there, what was worn, eaten, and said. And a careful scanning of the guest list can give the perceptive reader a fair idea of who peeped to the reporter.

Fortunately for Washington social scribes, however, relatively few parties of wide interest require much, if any, extracurricular digging and quizzing. In most instances, reporters happily mingle as guests and carry on from there; or at the White House, they cover the story either first-hand or by briefing from reporters in the coverage pool. Thus, the public gets a prompt report on most Presidential parties, including some of those tabbed "private."[12]

The newswomen were again invited to the White House in December 1962. Since the appointed time was 12:30 p.m. to 2 p.m., they anticipated that it was a luncheon. After Baldrige and Turnure welcomed them, guides led a staid tour of the public rooms on the first floor, which most of the ladies had already seen hundreds of times. Wine was served, nothing more. When someone spoke up and asked when Mrs. Kennedy would be appearing, Baldrige said that the First Lady was too busy packing for a trip to Palm Beach the next day. Hungry and huffy, the reporters departed en mass for a late lunch at the Press Club.[13]

The Palm Beach trip was just one of many that Mrs. Kennedy took, often without her husband. There were some official trips, including a solo visit to India. But her travels were so extensive that it could seem as if she was making an effort to stay away from the White House as much as possible. She toured the Greek Islands with her sister Lee Radziwill, summered at Cape Cod and Newport, and spent long weekends at Glen Ora, the family's Virginia getaway where she did vigorous horseback riding.

Helen Thomas of United Press and Frances Lewine of the Associated Press were the most dogged pursuers of the First Lady. To Baldrige, it felt like they'd moved in. During one of the Florida visits when Mrs. Kennedy was walking into church for Sunday Mass, she saw Thomas and Lewine watching. She then alerted her secret service agents to the "two strange Spanish-looking women" who were following her. The journalists were briefly arrested.[14]

At the 1962 stunt party of the Women's National Press Club, Thomas got some playful revenge. Dressed in a pink evening gown and with her hair done up in a Jackie-style bouffant, Thomas sang in a breathy little voice:

> If I want to give a ball
> For just me and Charles DeGaulle,
> I have absolutely all the gall I need
> I'm . . . Jahh-keeee!

If I like to water-ski
And maintain my privacy
Am I to blame?
You would do the same
If you were me
I'm Jahh-keeee!

If I want to fly away, without taking JFK
Or if I'm fond of French champagne
And I'd rather not campaign
That's me . . . Jahh-keeee![15]

With the death of Eleanor Roosevelt in November 1962, Hope temporarily put aside the *Diplomat*'s monthly dispatch on current Washington society. Instead, she took a trip down memory lane and considered all four of the First Ladies that she'd covered over the last quarter century.

> Mrs. Roosevelt shattered social, and other precedents, steadily for years. She was to become the despair of the die-hards, the darling of the liberals, the most talked-about woman in the world. She was to be a focus for venomous criticism and the recipient of more honors than any of her White House predecessors. Throughout her tenure, she was to be lambasted for making money from newspaper and magazine writing and from her lectures, even though much of her earnings went to philanthropy. She was neither a very good writer not an excellent public speaker, but the fact that she found time to do both while handling White House hostessing was remarkable, indeed.[16]

The next two First Ladies, by contrast, entertained in a traditional and gracious fashion but only as much as duty demanded. Their political, civic, and cultural ambitions were minimal to nonexistent. Hope would later recall Mrs. Truman as "wonderful" and "genuine," but that she "wasn't trying to do anything except be a good wife." So, too, Mrs. Eisenhower was "likeable," but she'd already experienced "plenty of fanfare in her life." By the time her husband was elected to the highest office, "all she liked to do was play cards."[17] Thus, the interim between the Roosevelts and Kennedys was a fifteen-year period of debate and competition as to who was truly Washington's top hostess, because it probably wasn't the First Lady.

"There is no doubt today as to who is Washington's Number One Hostess. Mrs. Kennedy, charting her course in a distinct direction from any of her predecessors, has culture working for her, in addition to youth, good looks, and a flair for high fashion."[18]

But for all these assets and her headline-making White House parties, Mrs. Kennedy remained unpredictable. There was never anything resembling a White House social calendar of the sort that the Roosevelts issued in the years before the war. And it wasn't just the despised women of the press who might show up for a function, only to learn that the First Lady had decided to remain holed up in the family quarters.

By early 1963 Mrs. Kennedy had largely abdicated her position as First Hostess. She was pregnant again and determined to cut back on obligations. "No more ladies' luncheons!" she declared. She made good on that promise, declining to put in an appearance at the annual congressional wives' brunch in May, claiming the decision was doctor's orders. But the papers carried photos of her at the American Ballet Theater in Manhattan the night before.

That same month, Baldrige resigned as social secretary. The reasons were many, starting with complete exhaustion from the round-the-clock job. She also believed her credibility with the press to have dried up after making one excuse after another for the First Lady. And she'd had enough of telling her old college friend "You just have to do this" about duties at the White House,[19] or "You can't do that!" when the First Lady insisted on last-minute changes in foreign itineraries.[20]

Buried in the largely effusive coverage of the Kennedy family's every move, there was some notice given to the doldrums of traditional Washington society. Ruth Montgomery was well integrated into Washington circles though she focused her reporting more on politics than parties. But her syndicated column in late October 1963 carried the headline, "Capital Society in a Muddle."

> This fall, our society is rudderless and adrift. The First Lady, instead of decorously launching the traditional "season," has been tripping the light fantastic with the international jet set in the Aegean Sea, and slipping out the back door of royal palaces to go shopping in exotic Moroccan bazaars. Literally nothing is scheduled on the White House social calendar for the fall except a luncheon this week for the Bolivian President, and a cocktail party for the judiciary "sometime late in November."

Neither Perle Mesta nor Marjorie Post were stepping up to fill the void. But still doing her part with lavish parties and choice quips was Gwen Cafritz, the Hungarian-born wife of a Washington developer, whose ascent to the highest ranks of hostesses was launched by Cissy Patterson. She told Montgomery: "There are a lot of charming substitutes for Jackie. I sat next to Sarge the other day, and his wife isn't too bad," she told Montgomery, referring to Sargent Shriver, director of the Peace Corps, and his wife Eunice, JFK's sister.

Montgomery went on to call Cafritz "brave" for proceeding with her annual October party welcoming the Supreme Court back to town (an event that none of the justices ever attended).

"Operation hostess in the nation's capital is a great privilege," explained Cafritz. "Our policy is to avail ourselves of the best dynamic talent at all times, which includes men and women of great intellect. Our grand design is to entertain top experts in various fields, because we are conscious of our common responsibility for the survival of the West." Despite such high ideals, Cafritz had completely lost patience with Congress, which was staying in town much longer than normal and working so hard that none of the members were accepting invitations.

For the final word in diagnosing the ailments of society, Montgomery turned to the authority.

"Society? What society?" said Hope, with a rare dose of on-the-record candor. "Local Washington society has gone by the board. All we have now are high finance and hardy annuals. The annuals are those regular charity affairs like the Symphony, International and Navy League Balls, each of which tries to out do the other. The only parties have been for conventioneering bankers. There are so many ambassadors around now that a real, live senator at a party is considered a social coup."[21]

14

GREAT SOCIETY

On December 7, 1963, the day that the Johnson family took up residence in the White House, the single household item the new First Lady herself carried into the residence was a portrait of Sam Rayburn. In her diary, Mrs. Johnson said, "His is the only photograph of a person that we keep in our living room wherever we are and I wanted it with us at the White House. His face is comforting at this milestone, just as he was at so many happier ones."[1]

During private talks between Hope and Mr. Sam, a recurring topic had been the larger-than-life Lyndon Johnson, his modest roots on the Pedernales River in Central Texas, his steady rise to power, his legislative prowess as Senate Majority Leader, his further ambitions. Hope opened the "Editor's Notebook" in the January 1964 *Diplomat*, recalling one of her last conversations with Rayburn and how he spoke with fatherly admiration of Johnson, who'd recently become vice president. "It's not easy being second when you've tried to be first, but Lyndon's equal to anything," he told her. The balance of that issue of the magazine looked past the tragedy of Kennedy's assassination in order to focus on the prospects of the new President, his devoted wife, and their two daughters.[2]

Having studied journalism at the University of Texas, Lady Bird made it an early priority to establish good relations with the press. She requested that her press secretary Liz Carpenter solicit advice from the newspaperwomen. Carpenter hosted a series of small gatherings to field ideas and input. Her subsequent memo to the First Lady passed along two key points: The first was simply to be available. The second was to never lie in answering a question but instead just state if a matter couldn't be addressed. "I see no problem on either score," Lady Bird replied, again in her diary.

Nevertheless, she was anxious about a tea on the afternoon of January 10 for about sixty-five women of the press. Turns out that the event was less about getting acquainted than it was about setting a proper tone and a relaxed dynamic. Once the reporters began arriving, the First Lady was pleased to find that she already knew most of them by name. She even felt a fondness for many, including "my gardening friend Isabel Griffin . . . Helen Thomas, whom I feel I know best of all . . . and Dorothy McCardle, so sweet in face and manner, and Speaker Sam Rayburn's old friend Hope Ridings Miller." She added, "I hope the time never comes when I feel I have to be afraid of them."

Lady Bird was clear that the event was not to be considered a press conference, just an informal meeting. But borrowing a page from Mrs. Roosevelt's playbook, she took time to introduce a guest speaker, the consumer advocate Esther Peterson who'd just joined the new administration. After that, a tour of the second floor served as an opportunity for the reporters to see how the family was settling in. When the group made it to the Treaty Room, the First Lady noted that it was the site of Mrs. Roosevelt's press conferences. She then thought to ask how many present had attended those gatherings. Hope was among the dozen who raised their hands. In advance of the event, the First Lady had studied up on history and lore of the art and antiques in the residence, many of which were the result of Mrs. Kennedy's efforts. But she admitted, "I would much rather have listened to what (the reporters) had to say."

Once the black crepe of mourning had been removed from the White House and Christmas decorations put in place, the President wasted little time in launching a busy and often impromptu social schedule. Around lunchtime on December 22, after the month of official mourning had ended, he decided that the entire Congress should be invited over that very afternoon. While the announcement was being made from the floor of each chamber, Lady Bird and staff scrambled to prepare eggnog, coffee, and fruitcake for more than 500 guests. Benefits of the charm offensive were apparent soon enough, as the House passed a foreign aid bill before adjourning on Christmas Eve.

For all of his delight in the business of gabbing and backslapping, Johnson let it be known that he didn't want any of his staff "gallivanting around the cocktail circuit." That brief remark sent fear and disquiet through a variety of Washington channels, including diplomats and bureaucrats, caterers, and society reporters. Hope stepped up to save the day.

"If *cocktail party* is doomed to go by the board as a name, a substitute will have to be hauled into quick action," she wrote. "*Reception* is the key word on invitations. And if a White House staffer turns up occasionally at a late afternoon diplomatic to-do, who can say he's gallivanting on the deplorable circuit?"

For good measure, she also examined the origin of the term *cocktail*. According to one theory, it comes from a tonic made to enliven gamecocks ("cock ale"), which was sampled by trainers and found to be appetizing.

"Whatever the etymology, the word has flourished in Washington because it has labeled the most workable and least expensive way of entertaining and being entertained, of getting around, getting acquainted, and getting ahead. Our opinion is that our President, being a gregarious man himself and one wise to the ways of Washington, had no intention of liquidating this oftentimes pleasant and useful capital institution."[3]

Within months, Hope was declaring the White House social calendar the most active and inclusive in history and she provided evidence in each issue of the *Diplomat*. At a gay soiree for envoys to the Organization of American States, the President danced with at least half of the ladies in attendance, which caused the affair to carry on a full hour longer than scheduled. A brilliant dinner honoring King Hussein of Jordan was followed by a concert of the Dave Brubeck Quartet. The young monarch was a jazz buff and the President told him, "I strive to please."

Alongside Johnson's outgoing nature, there was also the depression and self pity that caused him to struggle under the burdens of the highest office. Hints of this come through in a few letters to Hope. After complimenting her on a particular magazine spread, he added, "It is reassuring and strengthening to know that there are Americans like you who understand the difficulties that our country faces and who are willing to help me bear my responsibilities."[4]

Even when Hope wasn't on the society beat, she seemed to carry in her mind the tall and handsome president. During a visit to Turkey with the American Travel Writers Association, she found a coin with a profile of Mustafa Kemal Atatürk, that nation's first elected leader, who she thought bore a striking resemblance to Johnson. She sent it to him along with a flattering letter that concluded, "You do not need me, but America needs you. And I am one of many who appreciate and admire the manner in which you are handling multiple, heart-breaking problems at a most trying time."

Johnson replied: "I may have to study that Turkish coin to find my likeness in it, but I can recognize instantly a thoughtful and generous friend."[5]

It follows that the Johnsons regularly put Hope on their guest lists for various White House functions. She visited the executive mansion more frequently under LBJ than during any other administration except that of FDR. President Johnson also honored her with an appointment to the Board of Governors of the U.S.O. In an internal memo to the President recommending the appointment, Civil Service chair John Macy wrote: "Mrs. Miller is a Johnson Lady of substantial reputation."[6]

Hope's allegiances notwithstanding, the *Diplomat* covered both sides of the 1964 campaign, though with a pace and focus appropriate to a monthly society magazine. At their convention, the Republicans tried something new, roping thirty-five foreign envoys into attending the week-long gathering at the Cow Palace in Daly City, California. The Democrats followed suit a month later in Atlantic City, where 135 diplomats were on hand as guests. Hope had no success in getting a one of them to go on record with observations about all the American-style politicking. Suffice it to say they weren't too enthralled with the proceedings.

Back in the political game was Perle Mesta, who borrowed a mansion just ten minutes from the site of the Democrat's convention headquarters. By day, she attended the rounds of luncheons and receptions and, by night, she hosted a couple hundred dignitaries for dinners. Mesta capped the week with a big affair at the Claridge, where Eddie Fisher was the headline entertainer and two orchestras alternated sets for four hours.[7]

At midsummer, Hope wrote a lengthy profile of the Republican nominee Sen. Barry Goldwater of Arizona. Over the years the two had chatted at plenty of Washington gatherings, but the piece was mostly a recollection of their first exchange, which took place about a decade prior. They'd been seated together for dinner at the exclusive 1925 F Street Club and somehow conversation turned to the passing trends of women's fashion. Given that the 44-year-old Senator came from a family of department store owners, he had plenty to say on the subject and generally shared Hope's conservative tastes. "Inspired, I burbled on for a moment or two, until I sensed I had lost my audience. The Senator was looking toward the next table, where his wife Margaret was seated. He caught her her eye and winked. . . . 'Now, there's a rather well dressed woman,' I said. Immediately, the Senator was back with me, and beaming. 'Yes, she is,' he purred."[8]

Less than a week after Johnson's landslide victory over Goldwater, Hope made a personal appeal to Lady Bird for an exclusive photo shoot with the *Diplomat's* photographer. The resulting portrait of the President and First Lady graced the cover of the 1965 Inaugural Special, which was available in time for the citywide festivities that began on January 18. According to Hope's interview with inaugural chairman Dale Miller, the total budget for the ceremony and parade, the galas, concerts, and balls was $1.5 million, making it the most expensive inauguration to date.[9]

The morning of the swearing-in, an estimated 1.2 million people filled the grounds of the Capitol and lined Pennsylvania Avenue. There were fifty-two marching bands in the afternoon parade, which to everyone's relief lasted only two and a half hours. The first of the many school bands was from the President's alma mater, Southwest Texas State College of San Marcos. Each time the U.S. flag passed by, the dignitaries in the reviewing stands were obliged to stand. Johnson said that it made for more jumping up and down than an Episcopal Church service.[10]

There would be five inaugural balls that evening with some 50,000 people invited. The Millers had planned to attend the one at the Shoreham with Bob and Ruth Montgomery. But Lee felt a cold coming on and Bob also begged off, having already experienced such jam-packed events several times previously. Hope and Ruth were instead accompanied by an eager newcomer to Washington, Luther Holcomb. A native of Sherman, Holcomb had been a respected minister in Dallas when LBJ persuaded him to come east and serve as vice chairman of the recently established Equal Employment Opportunity Commission.

The trio of Hope, Ruth, and Luther were happy to find Texans well represented at the Shoreham. But the mass of humanity made it feel more like a ballgame than a ball, despite all the tuxedos and long dresses. Once the Johnsons finally appeared, Secret Service agents had to keep pushing the crowd back, making room for the couple to execute a few perfunctory dance turns. From the stage, the President spoke briefly to the crowd and joked, "Never have so many paid so much to dance so little!"[11]

Hope returned home late that night to find that Lee had grown worse. He stayed bedridden the next day and began to have numbness in his feet and legs. The symptoms increased and led to paralysis that steadily traveled up through his entire body. At George Washington University Hospital, he was diagnosed with acute polyneuritis, also known as Guillain-Barré syndrome. To aid his breathing, he was placed in an iron lung for two days. But his condition only worsened and pneumonia set in. He died on January 29 at age fifty-nine.

The memorial service was held four days later at a funeral home on Wisconsin Avenue. More than 200 people were in attendance. They represented all aspects of Washington life and included members of the House and Senate. From the Soldiers Home hospital where Lee had worked for twenty years came medical and military colleagues, plus more than a dozen Roman Catholic nuns. He was buried at Arlington National Cemetery.

In his eulogy, the pastor from First Baptist said, "Patients have spoken of Lee as 'the best friend I ever had,' and all testify that his thoughtfulness and concern went far beyond the call of duty." Hope would remember him as "the handsomest man that ever lived."[12]

Hope and Lee's second marriage had lasted ten years. Far more tragic than the divorce that ended their first union was his sudden death in middle age. Lee's passing came twelve years after that of Hope's father, the only other close relative that she had, and three years after the loss of her greatest ally Sam Rayburn. Hope had no children and no siblings. Ruth Montgomery, Deena Clark, and Dale and Scooter Miller were among the close friends who gathered round to give comfort and support. Perle Mesta called her on the telephone most every evening for months.[13]

Once again, work obligations provided distraction. "Fortunately, I had my hands full," Hope recalled. "I have always thought that the only way in life that you can get through anything traumatic is to work very hard, and I did."[14]

Understandably, the March issue of the *Diplomat* did not carry her byline. But there was no letup in the continual duties of assigning stories and photo shoots, editing copy, and supervising layouts. "Cherry Blossom Special" for the April issue marked her return to writing. Thankfully, that was an historical piece that required no reporting from the social front. In early May, she was back at the White House for the one annual event that could probably best rouse her enthusiasm, the Diplomatic Reception. She wrote another expansive account that detailed the spectacle of style and the evolving customs.

That, at least, is how the *Diplomat* charts Hope's activities in the winter and spring after her husband's death—a relatively quick return to her desk and a much more gradual emergence back onto the public scene. Actually though, by the end of February, hardly a month after Lee's passing, she was again going about to parties and with more purpose than just seeking material to fill another column. Whether by deliberate design or some combination of serendipity and sudden inspiration, she finessed another sale of the *Diplomat* and thereby earned herself a sizeable increase in salary.

The deal was set in motion at a reception in early March when Hope had a reunion with John Kluge, a native of Germany who was raised in Detroit.

The two first met during the war years when Kluge served in military intelligence. They'd bonded over being fellow alums of Columbia University. Since then, Kluge had become a shrewd and visionary entrepreneur. In 1959, he purchased Washington's WTTG Channel 5, the first in a series of television and radio acquisitions that collectively became known as Metromedia.

As the two party guests got reacquainted, Hope complimented Kluge on his success and proposed that he add a publishing enterprise to Metromedia's portfolio. She describe the *Diplomat*'s wealthy international readership and the dramatic increase in circulation that it enjoyed during her years at the helm. When Kluge admitted he wasn't even aware of the magazine, she promised he'd have an issue on his desk the next day. Within a week, Kluge purchased the *Diplomat* from Roy St. Lewis for 6,000 shares of Metromedia stock, a value of approximately $246,000.

On top of a substantial salary boost, Hope was also upgraded to a new office in the Sheraton-Park Hotel on upper Connecticut Avenue, not far from the National Zoo. Originally known as the Wardman Tower, it was an elegant Georgian revival complex built in the 1920s. The residential annex was home to the most celebrated and influential Washingtonians of the midcentury. The *Diplomat* was also given office space at the Metromedia headquarters on Park Avenue in Manhattan and Hope spent several days there every week. With elegant offices in two major cities plus financial security, Hope had arrived at a new level of professional comfort and stature.

Yet starting immediately after the sale, she began to lose control of the magazine. While the masthead still carried Hope as editor in chief and St. Lewis as publisher, there were new layers of oversight, including an associate publisher, and managing and associate editors. The art director changed every few issues. The result was a magazine with a drifting and unsettled identity. High society was downplayed in favor of more extensive coverage of foreign lands and international relations. An uninviting issue devoted to China ran for a daunting 150 pages—more than twice the typical size of the monthly. Arts coverage was also beefed up, but it, too, arrived in fits and starts. Along with more reviews and profiles, a couple of issues carried full-length scripts to plays. All the while, the graphic style kept changing, an obvious attempt to be in tune with the more colorful and casual look of the 1960s.

None of it came cheap. "I lost a million dollars before I ever knew I lost it," said Kluge. The magazine purchase was a rare misstep by the business magnate, who later pioneered the practice of leveraged buyouts and at one point was deemed the second richest man in America. By his own count, Kluge had acquired more than 200 companies during his career, including six additional television stations, always the second-rung type that carried old movies and sitcom reruns. In the mid-1980s Rupert Murdoch purchased the group of stations for more than $2 billion and made them the foundation for the Fox network.[15]

The *Diplomat* did seem a hot property in early 1965. The same week that Hope put a bug in Kluge's ear about buying it, Igor Cassini unveiled a competitor, *Status*. Younger brother to Jackie Kennedy's most favored designer, Cassini started his writing career in the 1930s at the Washington *Herald*. Outside a Virginia country club in 1939, he was assaulted—literally tarred and feathered—as retribution for a gossip item about a couple of old Southern families. He parlayed the widely reported incident into a job with Hearst writing a column under the byline Cholly Knickerbocker, a pen name that dated to the 1890s. That gig ended in 1963 when a tip he gave to the Kennedy State Department about a possible coup in Santo Domingo led to a scandal (presidents shouldn't be receiving intelligence from gossip columnists). Also a nightclub owner and publicist, Cassini claimed credit for coining the term *jet set* to describe the international elite, and he helped launch the career of the famed columnist Liz Smith.[16]

Metromedia's top-dollar purchase of the *Diplomat* at the same time as Cassini's launch of *Status* led to brief talk of a magazine war. But the prestige market couldn't sustain two magazines. Once Kluge realized his purchase was a mistake, he wasted little time in cutting his loses. In November 1966, he sold the *Diplomat* to Cassini for an undisclosed amount. Cassini merged the two magazines, which thereafter published under the name *Status & Diplomat*. The initial circulation of the combined magazines was reported at 145,000. But Cassini's venture lasted less than two years.[17]

Most of the *Diplomat's* covers over the years featured exotic locales or suave fashion shots. During its last year, there were gloomy illustrations of refugees and soldiers, immodestly clothed fashion models, and blurry collages of nature and machinery. Hope's final column appeared in the July 1966 issue, which at least had royalty on the cover—King Tut. Her "RSVP Washington" in that issue was a late and truncated report on the State Dinner for India's Prime Minister Indira Gandhi. Among the details, eight American women appeared in saris, "none so exquisite as Mrs. Gandhi's in midnight purple silk." The First Lady, though never partial to extreme fashion, showed up in a sleeveless and beltless dress made of apple green chiffon. Following the meal of flaked turbor and sliced pheasant, violinist Isaac Stern performed Vitali, Mozart, Dvorak, and Saint-Saëns until midnight. After the guest of honor departed from the North Portico, Mrs. Johnson took one swing around the dance floor with the President to "Hello Dolly" and then retired. The President kept dancing until 1:30 a.m.[18]

The issue carried only one other society report and it was not written by Hope. "Murder on Bleecker Street" depicted the blare of rock 'n' roll and the slouch of hippie culture. A benefit for *The Paris Review*, the event was held at the Village Gate nightclub and was hosted by George Plimpton. Girls wore zebra coats, pajamas, leather skirts, or granny dresses. Among the unshaven, long-haired men in attendance were poet Allen Ginsberg and his companion Peter Orlovsky. Also there were Sen. Robert Kennedy and his wife, Ethel. When Frank Sinatra finally showed, he was mobbed. "It's a great party," said producer Mike Nichols, "but the noise is terrific."[19]

15

AUTHOR, AUTHOR, AUTHOR

After it became obvious that the 1966 sale of the *Diplomat* would mean the end of her tenure as editor in chief, Hope's next project was readily at hand—fulfilling a book contract she'd signed three years prior. It had been a lifelong ideal, seeing her name appear on the spine of a book. After some thirty years in journalism, it was almost a fantasy. Making it a reality wouldn't be easy.

During her early days at the *Post*, Hope had been nonplussed when she'd hear another reporter referred to as "a great writer." Someone who just does articles isn't really a writer, she thought. But facing one deadline after another while also striving to maintain strict standards of style and accuracy, she came to understand and appreciate that producing a newspaper column was, indeed, writing.

Finally, during her late fifties, she would become a recognized author of three published books. *Embassy Row: The Life and Times of Diplomatic Washington* was the first. An enterprising agent named John MacCampbell thought up that title and then went searching for an author. Numerous contacts pointed him in the direction of Hope Ridings Miller. He was certain, he told her, that he could land the project with a reputable paperback publisher.

"Paperback?" she replied. "Oh, I'm not going to write a book that comes out in paperback. It's got to be a hardcover or I won't even consider it."[1]

MacCampbell said he'd see what he could do. In the meantime, would she please prepare a five-page outline? Hope worked herself to a frazzle for ten days before mailing the proposal off to the agent's Manhattan office. Mac-Campbell told her that it was the most detailed and thorough effort he'd received in years, and he wasted no time in getting the proposal into the field. In late summer 1963, Hope signed with Holt, Rinehart & Winston.

Both the outline and the contract were quickly laid aside. Hope remained consumed with running her monthly magazine. Then her husband died unexpectedly. Shortly after that came the sale of the *Diplomat* to Metromedia, which in turn led to a new conceptual framework for the magazine and the forging of new working relationships with an expanded editorial and design team spread out over two cities.

Once the *Diplomat* was resold to Cassini, John Kluge gave Hope a handsome four-year contract with Metromedia's weekend talk show *Panorama*. Her main task was to book important guests—senators, congressmen, cabinet secretaries, diplomats (the usual). They never required much persuading. She also prepared a pro forma biography of each guest, and drew up a list of ten suggested questions, which the onscreen interviewers usually ignored. "It was the easiest job I ever had," she said.

There were other distractions that kept the book on the back burner. "I went to every party I was asked to. After all, I told myself, they had to do with what I was supposed to be writing about." She decided to have her apartment redecorated. She took trips to Egypt, Japan, Germany, Canada, and Mexico.

"Finally, the publisher said 'fish or cut bait' and set a deadline," Hope recalled. "He should have done that in the first place for an old newspaper woman like me."

She knocked out three chapters in one month's time and then headed off on a trip to Turkey. In the back of her mind, she clung to the possibility that her efforts would be rejected and this business of writing a book would be over and done with. No such luck. The editor said the chapters were excellent and asked for the remainder of the book as soon as possible.

In the meantime, Hope was approached about a second book, a coffee table volume titled *Great Houses of Washington, D.C.* Photographer Charles Baptie was already at work on the project for Clarkson N. Potter, an imprint of Crown Publishers. Accepting that offer meant that *Embassy Row* finally had to be written and put to bed. But much of the research for the two books could be done simultaneously, since the topics of embassy life and D.C.'s top residential architecture were closely related.

The principal source was her past writing for newspapers and magazines, plus a file cabinet full of research materials on sundry D.C. topics that she'd been compiling and hanging onto since the 1930s. She also called on some previously unpublished observations about the thousands of parties she'd attended. Maybe now it would be okay to speak a bit more freely about some of the people who had either left town or died. After nine months of working "skirt to chair," she delivered a completed manuscript for *Embassy Row*. The 280-page hardcover was released in February 1969.

As with most of Hope's past writing, it hews closely to the social side of diplomacy and repeatedly justifies and defends all of the parties, receptions, and dinners as a vital, even essential part of doing business in the court of Washington. Yet the book doesn't overlook some of the sillier and more startling episodes of what Truman once called the "tragedy under the chandeliers."[2]

Embassy Row opens with Thomas Jefferson wearing slippers and pantaloons as he received the very proper Anthony Merry, the first British minister to the United States. A second affront came when they dined together: Jefferson ignored Mrs. Merry and instead escorted Dolley Madison into the dining room and seated her to his right. Rather than acting out of ignorance, Jefferson was communicating that he had no special respect or use for the Britannic Kingdom. That dinner is what eventually led to the great protocol dictating who sits where, which has been observed and debated ever since.

To the pronouncement, "The people who matter don't mind, and the people who mind don't matter," Hope gives the retort, "Important men expect to be accorded the place to which they are entitled."[3] She continues that prerogatives are owed to the seniority of one's office, they reflect the dignity of an envoy's country, and can strengthen or imperil international relations. But abuse of such privileges makes for fun reading.

To longtime residents of Washington, the term *diplomatic immunity* usually evokes the despised DPL license plate. That tag seems to be carried on every car that whizzes by at ninety miles per hour or that's double-parked amid rush hour traffic. According to Hope, during one six-month period the Russians alone accumulated 1,500 parking tickets. To assuage hurt feelings caused by local police forces, the State Department is repeatedly called in. "But it draws the line when a mission employee counts on the protective cloak to cover not only relatives and servants but also the animal kingdom. A Belgian Embassy secretary, living in Arlington, Virginia, made this discovery a few years ago, after neighbors asked the police to confiscate her pet ocelots Sabu and Elizabeth. She insisted that they had diplomatic immunity."[4]

Embassy Row became recommended reading for aspiring employees of the foreign service, since it contains a good amount of instruction delivered in a conversational voice. Hope explains the different types of visits by foreign leaders (a State Visit is the highest classification); defines the "representation fund" (a pot of foreign monies allocated for food, entertaining, and the like);

and illustrates the changing ways in which presidents have welcomed new envoys to town and received their credentials.

The book is structured more like a cocktail party than a classroom lesson. Topics of wars and politics, nations and personalities, real estate and rights, are addressed and dropped and then picked up again. Not for nothing is Washington called the city of unfinished conversations.

The best heroes and villains are the ones that Hope knew firsthand. Her model for an effective diplomat was Hjalmar Procope of Finland.

> He leased a house on fashionable Tracy Place and promptly opened his doors to hordes of guests. Not for him the formal dinners at which no more than forty could be entertained at a time. The Finnish minister gave receptions and buffet suppers for hundreds. Divorced shortly before assignment to Washington, he was the most sought-after "extra man" in the city; and, keenly aware that influential contacts may be made at almost any capital party, he went everywhere. He charmed every American he met; and Washingtonians, who before 1938 could hardly place his country on the map, by 1939 were well aware of Finland's location, size, history and precarious plight as a tasty morsel for the hungry Russian bear on its border.[5]

One of several spy stories in the book involves the wife of Hans Thomsen, the charge d'affaires dispatched by the Third Reich. A sympathetic but bewildering figure, Frau Thomsen became known around town as Bébé. She and Hope first met in the newsroom when she dropped by to tearfully request a column about her pet squirrel. It was lost again. (What is it about foreigners and strange pets?) Hope had no interest in the story but Thomsen made an impression, just as she did each time she started weeping at a tea party because of the atrocities occurring in "Hitler's Germany." Sometime later when the familiar lament for "poor Bébé" was voiced at yet another dinner party, a Rumanian minister exploded, "Poor nothing! Hitler has a Bébé Thomsen in every capital of the Western Hemisphere! She's using the oldest device in intrigue; she lambasts the Nazis to get a rise—to find out how you stand!" After the United States entered the war and an exchange of envoys was arranged, the Thomsens were seen happily returning to "Hitler's Germany," where their diplomatic careers continued apace.[6]

During the postwar era, the growing number of envoys from African and Caribbean nations were easily recognized at big events by their voluminous robes and elaborate headgear. But if these same men were to travel outside the District in street clothes, they faced repeated humiliations. Among the many incidents, an African minister, his wife, and child were denied a glass of water at a Maryland lunch stand. The diplomat wrote to Secretary of State Dean Rusk explaining that he'd served in the French army and that even under battle conditions he had shared water from his canteen with thirsty children of the enemy.[7]

Also an attention grabber at receptions were the traditional outfits worn by ministers from Arab nations. A photo used to promote *Embassy Row* was taken in 1968 at the Kuwaiti embassy during a state visit by that nation's second Emir. Amid Americans in dark suits and Kuwaitis in white headscarves, President Johnson is seen greeting Hope with a kiss on the cheek.

"Hope Miller's friends were on an 'Embassy Row' kick all week," said the *Evening Star* about the series of parties that launched the national publicity campaign. At Perle Mesta's fete in the Cotillion Room of the Sheraton-Park, there were "wall-to-wall ambassadors," among them Yitzhak Rabin, the future Prime Minister of Israel, plus Senators Strom Thurmond and Howard Baker, and Interior Secretary Walter Hickel of the new Nixon administration. There were also several dinners, including a black-tie affair hosted by the Blake Clarks, just after Hope appeared on Deena's interview show, *A Moment With.*[8]

The following week in New York, Hope was interviewed by Joan Rivers on her late-night program, *That Show.* Joan's other guest was Liz Carpenter, who was busy writing her memoir of the Johnson administration and played jealous at Hope, whose book was already in print. From there, Hope made television and radio appearances and gave print interviews in Detroit, San Francisco, Los Angeles, Fort Worth, Dallas, Houston, Chicago, and Denver.

Embassy Row received a substantial number of reviews, almost all of them positive. A critic for the *Orlando Sentinel* said, "It is a cram-jammed book of history, anecdotes, chit-chat and insight into the folkways of diplomacy. Her prose sparkles and gallops with the rhythm of embassy life."[9] The *Chicago Tribune* ran an extended excerpt in its weekend magazine, and the *Philadelphia Inquirer* serialized the book in six installments. In her review for the *Chicago Sun Times*, Letitia Baldrige said that Hope wrote with "a reporter's gift for observation and an academic zest for history." She also notes how Hope charitably overlooks the hungry freeloaders of the social circuit and how dreary and repetitive that the culinary fare often is. Baldrige concludes, "Embassy life is far from being all glitter. Mrs. Miller tells it compassionately, enthusiastically and well."[10]

Great Houses of Washington, D.C. followed in October 1969. "If you want to see where we in Washington play, get a copy," wrote Betty Beale in the *Star.*

Each of the thirty-four featured residences is vast and impressive and was surely made for entertaining. Yet there's not a buffet to be seen, nor a lampshade out of place in the 144 color and black-and-white photos. Hope's narrative likewise sticks to the facts about architects and owners, and gives detailed descriptions of all the artworks, furnishings, and effects.

It opens with The Lindens, built in 1754 in Danvers, Massachusetts and transferred, brick by brick, to 2401 Kalorama Road during the mid-1930s by Miriam Hubbard Morris. The book's chronological conclusion is the Kreeger House on Foxhall Road, designed in 1963 by Philip Johnson to showcase a private collection of twentieth-century sculpture and paintings. Hope's language is never inordinately effusive in describing such wonders though words like "opulent," "elegant," and "distinctive" do get a workout.

Amazingly, each of the houses was originally intended for use as a private home, but many were already converted to embassies when the book appeared. Since then, others have become museums, including Marjorie Merriweather Post's Hillwood, which remains filled with her collections of art and antiques. The only house that appears to be genuinely lived in during the time of publication is Worthington House, the home of Sen. and Mrs. Claiborne Pell. In the series of photos, a beige telephone seems conspicuously out of place on the library's oak coffee table, and the Senator's office is obviously a place of active business.

The lineages of home ownerships give way to some narrative asides. Samuel Davidson, a red-headed Scotsman, made a killing as a realtor and speculator in the 1790s, snatching up properties on what was soon to be designated the President's Square (today, Lafayette Square). The reader also meets Mary Foote Henderson, wife of a one-time Missouri senator, who early in the twentieth century sought to turn 16th Street into a showplace of grand homes. She engaged architect George Oakley Totten, Jr., to design mansions that she built for resale, many of which eventually became embassies. Totten's built legacy remains visible throughout the city, though by the late 1930s the unofficial designation of Embassy Row shifted from 16th Street to Massachusetts Avenue.

Some events in the book occurred during Hope's own years in the Capital, including Mrs. Stotesbury's party on the night of December 7, 1941. Her grand affair took place at Baker House, which she was renting at the time. The hostess continued to use it for vast entertainments during the war, after which it was sold to the Belgian government. There's also Firenze House, a rambling Tudor mansion set on twenty-two rolling acres at the edge of Rock Creek Park. It was purchased and given its name in 1941 by Colonel and Mrs. M.

Robert Guggenheim, just after they donated to wartime service their yacht, also named *Firenze*.

Packaged in an elegant slipcase, *Great Houses* is an appealing visual display, but not a particularly readable narrative. Being a writer, Hope took greater pride in *Embassy Row*, which she described as an interpretive and anecdotal history. But the books arrived almost like twins and Hope acknowledged them as her children. "I had them after great labor pains," she said. "And I refuse to favor the second child just because it's prettier."[11]

Shortly after *Embassy Row* arrived in stores, its editor Charlotte Mayerson left Holt, Rhinehart & Winston for Random House. She wanted to bring Hope along with her. Hope had long nursed a fascination with Thomas Jefferson which led the author and her editor to consider the personal life of the third president as the subject of the next book. But others were already plumbing that ground and so Hope expanded her focus to encompass the private lives of all of the Presidents. The new project took three years of intensive research, primarily at the Library of Congress.

Our Maligned Presidents was Hope's working title. "But maligned is one of those dim words," she later realized. Igor Cassini ran an item that the next book from Miller would be *Sex Scandals and Presidents*. Yet that was too salacious to bear the imprint of HRM. Instead, the manuscript was finally dubbed *Scandals in the Highest Office: Facts and Fictions in the Private Lives of Our Presidents*.

"It's not a dirty book, but it is a juicy one," Hope told Betty Beale.[12] The timing could hardly have been better, since the release in October 1973 came just months after the arrest of the Watergate "plumbers."

Hope's stated objective was to humanize the presidents. To achieve that, her text concentrates on "the groin rather than the coin," as the Kirkus review stated.[13] While the purported mistresses are many, so too are the sources and citations. The writing is dense with information and Hope floats out lofty synonyms for rumors, lies, and slander, including "calumnies" and "canards," also "traducements" and "invidious imputations."

She brings the deified George Washington back down to earth with facts about his eager courting of several rich heiresses. The second chapter, "Miscegenation and Mr. Jefferson," gives a thorough account of his relationship with the slave Sally Hemings. Lacking DNA evidence, which was not yet available, Hope ultimately refutes the charge that Hemings bore Jefferson's children.

Hope couldn't look the other way though with Andrew Jackson's marriage to the not officially divorced Rachel Donelson Robards. She also explains the song used against Grover Cleveland ("Ma, Ma, where's my pa? Gone to the White House. Ha! Ha! Ha!"), and the nickname for Woodrow Wilson ("Mrs. Peck's Bad Boy").

The only major scandal in the book that's financial, not amorous is Harding's Tea Pot Dome affair. "When I finished writing the Harding chapter, I felt so sorry for him I could have cried," Hope said. "There he was, an affable but weak man who couldn't say no."[14]

Hope saves for the final chapter, titled "The Capital's Gossip Mill," all six of the Presidents she knew personally. During the Roosevelt years, she and other reporters watched for any signals of displeasure from Mrs. Roosevelt regarding Lucy Rutherford and Missy LeHand, both known as possible lovers to the President. Later rumors circled around Crown Princess Martha of Norway.

Neither Truman nor Nixon offered much in the realm of romantic dalliances, but the talk about Eisenhower started well before he entered office. Kay Summersby was his civilian driver during the war and published a book, *Eisenhower Was My Boss*. "Reporters who rushed to interview her observed that the tall, rangy woman appeared to be the antithesis of a femme fatale," writes Hope.[15]

As for Kennedy, Hope cites the prediction made just before the 1960 election by aide Ted Sorenson: "This administration is going to do for sex what the last one did for golf."[16] Throughout Kennedy's thousand days in the White House, a constant stream of small scandals always seemed on the verge of breaking. Hope allows that the President's numerous affairs helped to explain Mrs. Kennedy's frequent travels. Also, the rumors of the President's virility in bed helped offset the concerns over his health.

Turning to Johnson, there was talk about undue attention to a "comely columnist" and also to a female TV personality. Also, the young Harvard grad student Doris Kearns Goodwin was frequently with the President during his final months in office. Then there was Johnson's habit of kissing female friends in public. "It brought adverse comments from some people, but certainly not from the women thus saluted—they loved it."[17] Hope would know. She was one of them.

An early promoter of *Scandals* was Barry Goldwater who received an advance proof from Hope. He started reading it while seated at his desk on the Senate floor, then took it home and stayed with it until after 1:00 a.m. His subsequent letter to Hope endorses the book's principal thesis. As Goldwater says it, "The American people are not too concerned about the morality of the man in office, they are concerned only with the job he does while in the office." A more lengthy endorsement from Goldwater appears on the dust jacket. Later, as the Watergate scandal drew toward its bitter conclusion, Goldwater cited the book while being interviewed on *Meet the Press*.

Once again, a publicity campaign kicked off with a party at the Sheraton-Park. Among the 400 guests was Senator James Allen of Alabama, whose wife Maryon told a reporter, "Why half the doors in Washington would fall off their hinges for Hope."

The *Post* reporter covering the event listened in as Hope offered a prying guest this tidbit: "If all the women who told me they had had affairs with John Kennedy were in this room, they would stretch from one end to the other." Another remark that night suggests that Hope knew far more than she put in print. When asked what's Washington's greatest untold secret, she replied, "If I told you, then it would be told."[18]

One afternoon during Hope's early teens, after the family had moved from Bonham to Sherman, her mother was out attending a women's circle for the Christian Church. Somehow, she knew that she had to return home at once. After dashing three blocks to the house and bounding through the front door, she found Hope lying in the bathtub, unconscious. The flame had gone out on the gas heater. Had she not arrived in time, her daughter might have died from asphyxiation or by drowning.[19]

This story appears in Ruth Montgomery's book, *A Search for the Truth*. Released in 1967, it is a compendium of sundry episodes, from the curious to the bizarre, that she collected from friends and acquaintances, many of high standing in Washington. All of the stories point to forces and realms beyond normal human awareness.

The paranormal didn't start out as Ruth's normal newspaper beat. She launched her career at the *Waco News Tribune* while still a student at Baylor University. Later working for the *Detroit News*, she landed an exclusive interview with Doris Duke by sneaking into the heiress's honeymoon suite underneath a breakfast cart. The sleuthing and the scoops continued after Ruth arrived in Washington in 1943 and began writing for the *New York Daily News*. Besides covering Capitol Hill and the White House, she reported from Cuba on Batista's rise to power, interviewed Juan Peron in Argentina, and observed the downfall of King Farouk in Egypt. She wrote for the Hearst and UPI syndicates throughout the 1960s. Also during that decade, she released six books, three of which focused on the supernatural and occult.

In a city obsessed with power and destiny, psychic predictions have always been a draw. Starting in the mid-1950s, Ruth began each calendar year with a column featuring the latest forecasts from Washington's number-one psychic, Jeane Dixon. In 1965, Ruth parlayed that material into the book, *A Gift of Prophecy: The Phenomenal Jeane Dixon*. Along with Dixon's life story, it includes snapshots of readings given to Rayburn and Churchill, among others. The volume isn't a completely accurate scorecard for Dixon's predictions, since Ruth's editors deleted most of the strikeouts and emphasized the hits. But one homerun—Dixon's 1956 prediction of Kennedy's assassination—made the book an instant success. It sold more than three million copies.

Ruth long maintained that she was not herself a psychic. Instead, she was a reporter on the psychic realm, applying her skills of investigation and a healthy dose of journalistic skepticism. But from the first time she touched a Ouija board in the mid-1950s, she was really more of a curious dabbler than a detached observer. By the mid-1970s she'd become renowned for channeling information from the spirit realms, and not just specific messages from the deceased to their survivors but also broader teachings meant to aid all of humanity. Her string of best-sellers addressed such arcane topics as past civilizations, reincarnation, and space aliens.

Throughout much of Ruth's explorations, her best friend Hope was a companion along the way (to paraphrase another of her book titles). Hope was an active participant in séances hosted by Ruth and led by various mediums, including Arthur Ford, who was Ruth's principal teacher. (After his death, Ford became one of Ruth's spirit guides, perhaps even a de facto coauthor.) When Ruth and Hope spent a week at an Elizabeth Arden spa in Arizona, they were the two ladies showing off their new skills at automatic writing, wherein a pen in hand is allowed to move on its own thus allowing messages to arrive from the other side. Back in Washington, they formed a spiritual study group that brought aid and counsel to friends and various referrals.

Over the years, writing became an increasingly arduous process for the ever-meticulous Hope, who looked on with wonder as her friend's tally of books just kept growing. As an author, Ruth's lifetime output was sixteen titles.

"Well, you're getting help from the other side," Hope told her friend. Ruth did not disagree and insisted that Hope could do likewise. "One world at a time is all I can handle," Hope replied, as Ruth continued on her divine path.[20]

In *Companions Along the Way*, Ruth's 1970 book on reincarnation, she learned of her past life in the Holy Land where she was a sister of Lazarus, the beloved friend of Jesus. Still looking for journalistic balance, she insisted on also hearing from her guides about her past lives that weren't in such radiant times, and not marked by entirely benevolent acts.

Ruth returns to the subject of past lives in "Other Palestinians," a chapter in *The World to Come*, her final book on the psychic realm, published in 1999. She writes: "The guides had said that good friends and relatives in previous lifetimes tend to reincarnate together, into circumstances where they will find one another. I therefore asked about my closest friend for the past half century, Hope Ridings Miller."

Yes, she was told, Hope was there in Palestine, as well. The two of them were favorite cousins. "You and Hope always preferred each other's company as playmates, and her name then was Anna."[21]

Apart from the dabblings in the occult and her continued devotion to the Baptist faith, Hope had a spiritual life that was rich and personal. Starting with her first scrapbook and continuing into her late years, she collected various inspirational texts, often writing out classic poems and favorite adages in her own hand. Fragments remain of diaries from throughout her life. She also maintained a small collection of spiritual pamphlets. They were an ecumenical mix, published by the Christian Scientists and the Quakers, and written by minister Norman Vincent Peale and mystic Edgar Cayce.

On the professional front, Hope wrote items about psychics and seers on a random but recurring basis starting during the Roosevelt administration. A couple of choice examples from that period: Palm readers appeared regularly on the social scene during the 1940s, among them was Jean MacArthur, wife of the general.[22] Also a passing fashion during the war years was jewelry that used particular crystals as protective or summoning charms.[23]

Then there was Mrs. McLean's cursed and woefully misnamed Hope Diamond. Some partygoers welcomed the opportunity to fondle the mighty stone while others studiously avoided even glancing at it. Late in life, Hope explained that she never had the opportunity to hold the famous gem. "But I was all prepared!" she said with a twinkle in her eye.[24]

As a skilled journalist, Hope recognized diverting bits when she came across them and maybe psychic matters just popped up now and then. On the other hand, her writing never betrays a scoffing attitude toward such topics, where a disbelieving or disinterested reporter might have just looked the other way and moved on.

On more than one occasion, Hope deliberately sought out a psychic, of one variety or another, in order to supplement a story. For example, in the 1961 inauguration issue of the *Diplomat*, she ends her editor's column with brief personality profiles of President and Mrs. Kennedy, based on their astrological charts.[25]

Astrology was a field of abiding fascination for Hope. She was friends with Linda Goodman, also a best-selling author (*Linda Goodman's Sun Signs*), and also with Carroll Righter, who for decades was Hollywood's favorite astrologer. Hope received Righter's monthly newsletters of predictions and sometimes attended his classes or had readings from him during his East Coast visits. They were also friendly correspondents. Righter's letters to her begin with the salutation, "Dear Capricornia."

At some point in her studies, Hope realized that she got along best with others who were born between late December and mid-January. They included Lee and Mr. Sam. Also, Lady Bird Johnson (born on December 22), who received for her birthday in 1967 a special package from Hope. The cover letter reads in part:

December 21, 1967

My dear First Lady,

Since you and I share the birth sign of Capricorn, I am herewith sending you an Astrological Forecast for January along with one for December. The latter may give you an idea as to whether Carroll Righter is on the beam about you. . . .

I set little store by predictions of any kind, but I find them interesting. . . . Believing that our fate is not in our stars, but in ourselves, I cannot seriously rely on the advice of any astrologer, but I find it diverting to read Righter's predictions, *when they are favorable*. And I thought you might enjoy the ones herewith, since prospects for Capricornians seem so auspicious just now.

I wish I could find some way to thank you for your many kindnesses to me through the years. Anyway, my very best wishes to you and the President for a blessed holiday season—and to you for a happy birthday. You deserve it!

Fondly and admiringly,

Hope

Only after the sun had moved into Pisces (late February) did Mrs. Johnson get around to responding.

The White House
February 20, 1968

Dear Hope,

Somehow or other, your birthday wish got buried under a mountain of mail and has just come to light today! I enjoyed reading Mr. Righter's predictions, but like you I do not rely on my stars. I have always found that common

sense and hard work usually accomplish more than celestial influences. Thank
you for remembering me.

Sincere and affectionately,

Lady Bird Johnson

Twenty years later, another First Lady was not so dismissive of the stars.
Long before they were married, Ronald Reagan and Nancy Davis were part
of Carroll Righter's vast network of followers. During their extended courtship, they together attended his lavish "Sign of the Month" parties.[26] They also
consulted Jeane Dixon around the time of the 1976 presidential campaign.[27]
After arriving in the White House in 1981, Mrs. Reagan's astrologer was Joan
Quigley, who was kept so busy as to be on a monthly retainer.

In her memoir, the First Lady acknowledged the previous involvement
with astrology and explained that after the assassination attempt on her husband, she didn't want to take any chances. Quigley's guidance was strictly on
the right timing for appearances and travel by the President, Mrs. Reagan
emphasized, and not on policy itself. But after Donald Regan wrote a tell-all
about his years as Chief of Staff, there were weeks of headlines about the
astrologer who was supposedly running the country.

To this day, the sun still shines on the Reagan administration, while a dark
cloud lingers over the legacy of Johnson. It's enough to make one ponder if
history might have turned out differently had Lady Bird Johnson acted on
Hope's casual introduction to astrology.

After the release of *Scandals in the Highest Office*, Hope's next major writing
project took her just steps away from the seat of the Presidency. Her task was
a history of Lafayette Square. The seven-acre expanse to the north of the
White House was intended as the front lawn to the executive mansion, but
the egalitarian Jefferson thought such a spread too pretentious and gave it to the
city. He also insisted that Pennsylvania Avenue cut if off from the mansion,
thus serving as a kind of traffic moat and assuring that the parcel was perma-
nently severed away. Yet during the Clinton years, the street was closed for
security reasons and the house and the square were essentially reunited.

Hope's "Circling Lafayette Square" was commissioned by the National
Trust for Historic Preservation in advance of the American Bicentennial. Written to serve as an audio tour, the narration was recorded by the Trust's then-
president James Biddle. Every day throughout the year 1976, tourists could
pick up cassette players at Decatur House (just across from the White House),
hang them on their shoulders and then crisscross the Square, while listening to
the lively history.

Within the first two pages of the script, Hope touches on familiar themes and images. A few excerpts:

> Lafayette Square for almost a century was the locale of private dwellings occupied by patriots with tremendous influence on national affairs. It was a microcosm of American life at the highest political and social level and a nerve center of developments affecting our country as whole. . . .
>
> Presidents and First Ladies were constantly criticized—and defended—over elegant, candle lighted dinner tables. Now and then, scandal rattled teacups around the square and reverberated across the nation. . . .
>
> Some years ago a noted psychic, after daytime and evening visits to the central park, vowed she had seen shades of Dolley Madison, Henry Clay, William Seward and John Calhoun floating all around the square. She went to the park, she added, to feed the albino squirrels that are seen nowhere else in Washington and to "wish" under the Wishing Tree, said to have been planted on the northwest corner before the Civil War.

There was brief talk of turning the narrative into another book. Those plans never progressed, but from then on the subjects of architecture, art, and antiques were Hope's primary focus. She remained productive throughout her seventies, usually writing several magazine feature stories each year.

In 1976 Hope was named Washington editor for *Antiques Monthly*, a thriving publication out of Tuscaloosa, Alabama, with an avid readership of collectors and dealers from the burgeoning field. She was given rather wide discretion to cover Washington exhibits of decorative and fine arts, with the understanding that anything more than 100 years old could fit under the designation of "antiques." It wasn't a field where she had expertise, but it wasn't a bad match either, since research had always appealed to her more than writing.

In 1978 *Antiques Monthly* publisher Gray D. Boone purchased the failing *Horizon* magazine from American Heritage. *Horizon* had been launched in 1958 as a general arts monthly and was published in a hardback binding. Boone reformatted it to a traditional softcover and replaced the Old Master paintings on the cover with photos of contemporary dancers and actors. Hope joined the advisory board and also became a contributor. Many of her features in the late 1970s relate to mammoth art shows on display in the National Gallery's new I. M. Pei-designed East Wing. Also for *Horizon*, she traveled to Venice to view the modern art collection of the recently deceased Peggy Guggenheim; to Greece, as an official guest of the government, in advance of the traveling exhibit "The Search for Alexander"; and to Madrid and Toledo to view and study the work of El Greco.

During her seventy-seventh year, Hope took on some entirely new material by writing a couple of stories about horsemanship for *Spur Magazine*. The first, a look at the international polo scene, did begin on familiar turf—royal gossip. The newly married Prince Charles, said to be one of Britain's top ten players in "the gentleman's game," was considering giving up the sport because it bored Princess Diana. Hope's second story for *Spur* didn't lack for glamour either. It was a survey of top resorts around the world that offered equestrian activities.

In 1982, forty-nine years after Hope first began covering Washington life she filed her last in-depth look at society. The story for *Dossier* magazine was a profile of Margaret Wimsatt, a veteran social secretary, or *social consultant* to use a term then coming into vogue. The chatty and engaging piece opens with a potential disaster averted by Wimsatt's last-minute shuffling of place cards to keep divorced spouses on opposite sides of a dinner party for fifty-two people. It ends with the biggest challenge of Wimsatt's career, choreographing the flow of 1,118 wealthy guests from twenty-eight countries during a four-day cruise aboard the *Queen Elizabeth II*. In between those and other anecdotes comes sundry advice on party giving. Picking up on a favorite theme, Hope includes a quote from a publicist working with the Reagans. Recalling the productive atmosphere at a recent reception hosted by a trade organization and attended by cabinet members, congressional leaders, and 150 others, the PR exec said, "You might call it just one more Washington party. But I call it Washington working overtime." Hope caught the remark while watching the *Today* show.[28]

Well into her eighties Hope kept on challenging herself with assignments. For the newsletter of the Sam Rayburn Library she wrote "A Long Piece from Coffee Mill Creek," a substantial and affectionate tribute to her patron and friend. After a trip to Russia, she contributed to *Washington International* a piece on diamonds displayed at the Kremlin's state museum.

There was another more personal travel piece, this one written on spec and sold to the *Sun Sentinel* of South Florida. It begins with a tinge of sadness as she acknowledges the difficulty of being a childless widow during the family-oriented season of Christmas. She quickly turns to having "found the escape I needed," thanks to a small travel agency specializing in deluxe overseas tours during the holidays. Her 1984 trip started with six days and nights in Paris, then on to Marrakech for six nights, and finally to Madrid, where a late-night floor show at the Ritz carried on until 4:00 a.m. The following year's tour of Italy had only one flaw, a bombing at the Rome airport. The year after that the tour took them to northern Europe, with Christmas at the Bavarian town of Rothenburg ob der Tauber and New Year's Eve in the chic setting of Copenhagen.[29]

Back home in Washington, Hope continued to go about and also do her share of hostessing. By this point her age and deeply planted roots in the city probably put her in the ranks of the cave dwellers. But Hope maintained both presence and stature, thanks to regular mentions in the *Post* by Sarah Booth Conroy, whose writing career was launched at *Diplomat*. When Conroy wrote about local architecture and history, Hope's prior research was a natural resource, especially when it came to embassies. Conroy also cited Hope's old-fashioned grace at entertaining:

> Time was—at least among diplomats—that hosts sent lists in advance to guests identifying all the invited to a dinner. Hope Ridings Miller, author of books about Washington places and personalities, does even better. In her frequent luncheons, Mrs. Miller, with total recall, tells fascinating stories of each of her guests.
>
> Mrs. Miller just last week evoked another splendid practice no longer observed—turning the table. Now, I don't mean she stood up and moved it; the phrase refers to the ancient and honorable practice of talking to people seated on either side of you.
>
> Upon strict observance, in times of yore, guests would watch the hostess, and see when she turned from the gentleman on her right (the male guest of honor) to talk to the one on her left. The other guests would do likewise. Customarily, the turn came with the serving of each course.[30]

Hope also gave the courtesy of time and attention to seemingly each and every one of the journalists and authors who came calling. She sat for numerous interviews in her apartment with those who were researching the early years of the *Post* or the lives of Sam Rayburn, Katherine Graham, Lady Bird Johnson, and others.

In broadcaster David Brinkley's 1988 bestseller, *Washington Goes to War*, Hope is a recurring character in the chapter about the busy social scene. Brinkley writes with an attitude of high pique at all the pretense and frivolity, in particular Cissy Patterson's vast and numerically catalogued wardrobe and Evalyn Walsh McLean's extravagant weekly affairs. He applies a tone of sarcasm when referencing Hope's columns. About the city's extreme housing crunch, caused by the influx of new government employees and made worse by the lingering, well-heeled pleasure seekers, Brinkley writes, "Hope Ridings Miller on the society page of the *Post* rose bravely to confront the grave issue." Later she "rode to the rescue" to explain the meaning of *Cliveden* and how to pronounce the term. And by coining the phrase, *parties for a purpose*, which Brinkley borrows for his chapter title, she "anointed with a patriotic purpose" the wartime parties that never ceased.[31]

Gore Vidal covers the same time period in his historical novel, *Washington, D.C.* released in 1967. A prolific writer, trenchant commentator, and twice-defeated political candidate, Vidal was raised in the political environment of the Capital. His maternal grandfather was the blind Senator Thomas Gore of Alabama. His mother, the socialite Nina Gore Vidal Auchincloss Olds, was a close friend to Hope.

In contrast to Brinkley, Vidal seems to like society editors. He gives his character a name with a familiar rhythm to it—Helen Ashley Barbour—and honors her with a few walk-ons in the fictional narrative.

Barbour's biggest scene takes place on the morning of the royal garden party in 1939. Wearing a large hat and white gloves, she blows through the newsroom in search of the city editor who she suspects has her invitation. She's on a mission but still not sure if she's got the assignment. "Am I supposed to be covering the garden party or not?" she says. "That is the question. It certainly comes under Society. But of course it also comes under News and heaven knows all the press is going to be there." After taking a moment to exchange pleasantries with Harold, the son of the publisher, she goes on her busy way. Harold turns to his companion and says, "If you were going to build a Washington society editor from scratch, you couldn't do better than that."[32]

16

THE SULGRAVE CLUB

Tucked behind trees and a dense flower garden on a wedge of Dupont Circle, the Sulgrave Club is a well maintained relic of the Gilded Age and a spot of calm and elegance amidst the busy commercial district. The three-story building occupies an entire city block and was completed just a few years after the turn of the twentieth century. Martha Blow Wadsworth, wife of the original owner, had no credentials in drafting but supervised the design of the home to such an extent that she was listed as architect on the original plans. In contrast to the heavy brown and red Colonial buildings that had dominated the neighborhood, the exterior is in the fresh and classical Beaux Arts style, with yellow Roman brick and cream-colored terracotta. It became a women's club in 1932 and Hope joined in 1945, around the time she moved out of The Mayflower.

A porter greets guests at the glass and iron double doors. Just ahead in the narrow but well-lighted foyer are a few stone steps with an iron railing that lead to the coatroom and elevator. The color palette of the peach-striped wallpaper and light avocado carpets continues into the parlors and dining rooms that are to the right. There are more drawing rooms on the second floor, which is lined with tall windows looking out onto Massachusetts Avenue. Also on that level is a breathtakingly ornate ballroom with a 30-foot ceiling. It was the site of many of Perle Mesta's finest affairs, including a lavish dinner dance in honor of Harry Truman after his election as Vice President.

"Best club in town and I got in with one phone call." Hope must have said that to this author at least half a dozen times over the years, as we'd settle in for the Sunday lunch buffet. There were so many other things that she didn't tell me about, like her private dinner with the Roosevelts, the time she gently prodded General Eisenhower about his presidential ambitions, or LBJ's fondness for kissing her on the cheek. But the status of her and the Sulgrave, she did not want me to forget that.

Our first time at the club, we were joined by Grace Halsell, a Lubbock native and one of Hope's closest friends. Hope believed that there was no braver reporter than Grace, who had disguised her identity and even dyed her skin to live immersed in African American poverty, on a Navajo reservation, and with Mexican immigrants. Hope and Grace both seemed amused by my budding case of Potomac fever. Being writers, they encouraged me to start a diary, "about your Washington," as they both put it.

I took their advice, though in fits and starts. That evening, I wrote about how I'd enjoyed the Sulgrave's food so much that even the silverware tasted good. Also, how Hope alerted me that if she hugged or kissed people as we passed through the club but failed to introduce me, not to take offense. It just meant that she couldn't remember their names.

The first entry of my terribly short Washington diary concludes with this line: "Hope is great, and she never has anything bad to say about anyone."

Ruth Montgomery was another of Hope's intimates that I met sometime in those early months of 1981. She, too, was a published writer and a kindly older woman. That's about all I knew about her. But Ruth's name came up again when I told Hope of my interest in ghosts of the Capitol. This was still during my term as a Congressional Page. I was excited to have gotten permission, from Speaker Tip O'Neill himself, actually, to stay in the building until midnight watching for spooks. "Well, you know Ruth Montgomery. She's the world's expert on that stuff," Hope said. She then turned her head and set her jaw in a way that forestalled further inquiry. Though I didn't have a clue what she meant, I'd been raised to not pester my elders. Decades later while browsing the occult section of some used bookstore, Ruth's name jumped out at me. This led to finally realizing that along with meeting many powerful men in Washington, I'd also dined a time or two with one of most famed psychic travelers of the era.

Though my time as a page lasted for only four months, it was long enough for Washington to put its grip on me. After graduation from Capitol Page School, I returned in the fall as a music major at Catholic University of America. Hope faithfully attended the majority of my concerts and shows over the next four years, usually with one of her friends in tow. After taking in a student production of the folk-rock musical, *Working*, a rather gritty and profane affair with me conducting the pit band, Hope's guest said she wanted to wash all our mouths out with soap. But Hope remained composed and said she'd always appreciated the work of Studs Terkel, who wrote the original book. I later learned that her favorite musical was significantly lighter and less consequential—Andrew Lloyd Webber's *Cats*. She'd seen it repeatedly as she traveled the world.

There was one spring season that the university chorus and orchestra performed under maestro Mstislav Rostropovich at Constitution Hall. I'd sold a batch of tickets and so all my friends were seated together. I heard from them later about these two old ladies who showed up and how one of them went on and on about her talented young cousin who was up there onstage.

I returned junior year with wheels and that increased the frequency of our outings. I'd pull into the steep and narrow little circular drive in front of her building. After waiting in the lobby, she'd come out and happily plop down in the bucket seat of my 1980 burnt orange Honda Civic hatchback. She made sure to give some gesture of a kindness my way, I made sure she buckled up, and off we'd go.

A couple of times I accompanied Hope to Sunday morning church. "I'm proselytizing!" she joked. At the First Baptist Church on 16th Street she was a well-established member. Truman had often attended the church and it was also the congregation where Jimmy Carter belonged during his four years in Washington. One time when we arrived, there was a buzz in the pews that the former president was back and had just finished teaching Sunday School. After the service of hymns and readings, Carter shook hands with everyone as they exited through the church foyer. "This is my cousin from Texas," Hope told the President, who nodded politely.

When we went to an art opening on the Georgetown campus, parking proved difficult. As I circled about, we saw an empty spot, but the "Reserved" sign looked pretty definitive to me. "Park there. I know Father Healy," Hope said, referring to the university president. I wasn't so sure that would keep us from getting towed, but we were fine. After speaking to the artist, we strolled the small exhibit and I proffered some observations on the works. "Keep talking, you sound so smart," Hope said.

There was only one time that Hope brought me along to an embassy. I can't recall the nation but do remember that the gathering started with a brief talk by one of the officials and was followed by a reception. There was a bit of wine and soft drinks and a few trays of cheese puff pastries. "That's nothing, *nothing*," Hope declared, with an unfamiliar tone that bordered on scorn. Again, it was years later that I got some perspective on what she was saying. In

Embassy Row, she describes heavily laden tables with yards and yards of pheasants, turkeys and hams, huge bowls of caviar, and cases of champagne and vodka, all common in her days as society editor.

Some years into our friendship and while dining again at the Sulgrave, I mustered the courage to bring up an obvious but mysterious matter.

"How old are you, Hope?"

"Well," she replied, "can you keep a secret?"

"Oh yes, yes," I said. "Definitely."

"So can I."

It was one of her best lines. Her other reply to the subject was borrowed from Deena Clark: "Age is just a number. And mine's unlisted."

Being in Washington, politics was a natural and frequent subject. During the lead up to the primaries for the 1984 general election, Hope asked if there was a candidate on the Democratic side that I favored. Alan Cranston, the liberal senator from California, was saying some good stuff, I thought. She scoffed at the notion, saying, "After the way he's treated his wife." But no further details were forthcoming. After that, I began to picture her chatting on the telephone or having whispered exchanges at parties, still a repository for all the scuttlebutt making its way through the city. But she remained a repository with no leaks.

We did share certain intimacies. Along with telling me of the books she wrote and the editorial positions she held, she also told me that she divorced and remarried the same man. (I didn't press for more details on that.) Maybe because I never talked of girlfriends or asked to bring along a date on an outing, she surmised that I was probably gay. (I was still figuring it out myself.) She said that people should be allowed to do anything they want, "as long as they don't do it in the street and frighten the horses." I gave a little chuckle at the adage, which dates from the eighteenth century, and still appreciate it as the gesture of acceptance it was meant to be.

Hope turned eighty in 1985, the year I graduated. On the night before my commencement exercises, she hosted a dinner party for ten in my honor in the Sulgrave's cozy, circular-shaped Boardman Dining Room. I was allowed to set the guest list. Along with my parents, I invited two of my professors and some fellow students. Hope's handwritten invitations said "Informal." When asked what that meant, I told my friends, "No black tie, but dress up."

As the guest of honor, I sat to the right of the hostess. It remains the only meal I've ever attended that began with fingerbowl service. Unfortunately, the entrée, shad roe, was unidentifiable and almost inedible. Hope later apologized, saying the dish was once the club's specialty, and told me that she called the management the next day.

"Well, Mrs. Miller, did your guests complain?"

"No. They were too polite!"

The day after graduation would be my folks' last full day in Washington and they suggested we get together again with Cousin Hope. I phoned and invited her to join us for dinner, with the caveat that this would be a casual evening. During the prior four years, Hope had been the one doing most of the inviting. But I got the sense that she was always up for an outing, even on just a couple hours' notice. It was a warm and clear afternoon when we picked her up. There was a spring in her step as she came out of her building. She wore a sun hat with a wide floppy brim, a colorful floral dress, and several strands of eye-catching costume jewelry around her neck.

Once the weekend was over, I took it as my duty to send Hope the best thank you note I possibly could. But she wrote to me as well:

> Entertaining you and Yvonne and LeRoy and your special friends at the dinner last Friday evening gave me much pleasure. And I thoroughly enjoyed the Sunday dinner in Alexandria, as well as the drive to Mount Vernon. On returning home, I relived the whole afternoon in my memory and couldn't recall when I'd had a more pleasant time.
>
> I look forward to seeing you before you leave in July. Meanwhile, all good wishes,
>
> > with much love,
> > Hope

After completing a brief graduate program back in Texas, I was once again on the East Coast and starting my career in Manhattan. I visited Washington periodically and always made an effort to reconnect with Hope. During these trips, we'd usually share a meal at a restaurant in Adams Morgan, her increasingly fashionable neighborhood.

The first Bush administration was under way and Hope told how she'd recently been to an event at the White House. As she reported it to me, her brief exchange with the First Lady went like this:

"Mrs. Bush, I think you're just *wonderful*," gushed Hope.

"Well. We're going to keep you around here," replied Mrs. Bush.

Raising her eyebrows and giving me a look, Hope continued, "How about that!" After living in Washington for fifty-five years, it was still important that she counted.

Another reoccurring topic for us over the years was the craft and business of writing. Though she had been a prolific journalist and was a proud author,

Hope continually insisted, "I just *hate* to write." After examining her few surviving manuscripts, it's obvious why. She was a tough editor and unrelenting reviser.

It was around this time that she told me she was at work on a memoir. Once again, she was tight-lipped about specifics. But at least this time she provided some explanation: "Don't talk too much about a writing project or you'll think you've already written it."

What Hope described as her memoir could refer to a couple of different projects. She sat for a series of five interviews with writer Kathleen Currie, as part of an oral history project on women journalists that was sponsored by the Washington Press Club Foundation. After Hope read the transcripts, which ran for more than 200 pages, she was unhappy with how she sounded and withheld release of the material. She set about rewriting the conversations, sometimes to clarify information but mostly to smooth out the language and delete the more candid passages. For example, she crossed out a few statements about the different styles and personalities of the First Ladies she'd known, replacing them with the vague and inoffensive statement: "Each first lady was successful in her own unique way."

Editing the interviews became an overwhelming project that was left unfinished. Decades earlier, Hope made substantial progress toward a genuine memoir. In her archives are two neatly typed chapters that seem to date from the late 1940s. "This Washington Society Business" charts the scene just after V-J Day and includes an admiring tribute to Evalyn Walsh McLean. "All Outs Among the Ins" recounts the battles for power and turf that raged within the Roosevelt administration and spilled over to the Truman years. The fact that these are headed chapters 5 and 10, respectively, suggests that there was much more besides. If the balance of the material was of a personal and revealing nature, then it's likely that Hope destroyed it. In keeping with the nature of our conversations and also the character of published writing, she was a circumspect gentlewoman. Of all the Washington secrets that she knew, none were more closely held than her own.

"Old age is not for the faint of heart," Hope once confided to me. This told me that there had been some health problems. In a composition book with Hope's handwritten notations of inspiring quotes from great writers and quips picked up around town, there is only one personal statement. It reads:

> I discovered in the course of my serious illness (December 14, 1987 through January 29, 1988) just how many friends I have and how much I love them and they love me. I also came to terms with the fact that every minute of life counts,

and the important thing is to appreciate more and more every waking second as it passes.

So from now on, I don't intend to worry, ever, about the future; but I'll do my best to love the present to its fullest. In other words, I intend to enjoy every moment of the rest of my life as long as possible.

H. R. M.

It was after this period of convalescence that Hope insisted her attorney make a solemn promise, to never allow her to be put in a nursing home. Old age itself would bring enough indignities. She wanted to enjoy the privacy and comfort of her home. The attorney was Sara Hammond McIntyre, a fellow member of First Baptist Church and one of Hope's oldest friends. The two had met in the late 1930s around the time McIntyre began work for the Social Security Administration.

Hope resumed making appearances now and then. As an elder in the newspaper business, she was a valued guest at sundry trade functions. She also faithfully attended the semiannual reunions of the E-Streeters, the journalists, pressmen, and staffers of the *Post* who had worked at the long-shuttered down-town headquarters.

Hope's final visit to the White House was a private luncheon in her honor one week before her eighty-seventh birthday in December 1993. By this point, it was the Clinton years, thus marking the eleventh Presidential adminis-tration since her arrival in Washington. The meal was in the White House Mess, a series of cozy basement-level rooms that are more elegant than their name implies. The gathering was a reunion of old girlfriends, most from the newspaper trade including Sarah Booth Conroy, Deena Clark, and Grace Halsell. Communications Director George Stephanopoulos, the handsome young star of the Clinton team, stopped by for a greeting.

A companion during these years was Maisie Gordon Wittman, yet another longtime friend from the publishing world. Wittman aided Hope in going to functions and also just made sure she got out of the apartment now and then. Wittman recalled once escorting Hope to a nearby park. It was the holiday season and some school children gathered around to sing carols. As the two women continued to sit on a bench and take in the surroundings, Witt-man pointed out a man who was alone and looking rather contemplative. "He must be a writer," Hope said.

When Hope's health and faculties declined to the point that she required full-time care, McIntyre hired two nurses who were sisters. They served as a team, alternating shifts of living in the apartment with Hope, cooking, and caring for her. "And I think they love her," McIntyre told me. Juanita, one of the caregivers, referred to McIntyre as "Hope's guardian angel." The individual attention and the familiar surroundings, perhaps also the view out the window of the Capitol dome on the southern horizon, all surely contributed to Hope's living to be ninety-nine years old.

Hope died of congestive heart failure on April 29, 2005. A modest service was held at First Baptist and among those who spoke there was a cousin from the Deupree family. Hope could have been buried beside Lee at Arlington National, but she had promised to return to her parents' side. Her ashes are in the mausoleum of West Hill Cemetery in Sherman.

In a substantial obituary for the *Post*, Matt Schudel wrote, "Mrs. Miller epitomized the genteel, white-glove style of society reporting that once prevailed at America's newspapers, in which reporters were observers of the social scene as well as participants. . . . She was known as a hostess who could bring together a glittering list of guests from the city's diplomatic, political and journalistic circles."[1]

For one of my final visits with Hope, the nurses dressed her in a maroon suit and applied a bit of makeup. We sat beside each other on her antique Victorian sofa. Still on the coffee table were the novels and memoirs written by her friends. In a nearby curio cabinet was a collection of folk artifacts that she'd gathered during her world travels.

I reminisced about the meals we shared at the Sulgrave and told her some family news. Turning to the latest developments in Washington, I said, "There's another Bush in the White House, you know."

"He's pretty good?" she inquired.

"Well, Hope, he's a Republican."

"Oh, they're awful," she said, as she waved her hand in dismissal. She'd been a friend to Barry Goldwater and countless other conservatives and always assumed the best about every resident of the White House. But Sam Rayburn's lessons on political loyalty still came to the fore.

Of the many little sayings that Hope liked to share at parties, the kind of banter that made her so charming and popular, the following was one of her favorites. Even in her very late years, she could recite it with only a little prompting.

> London is a man's town, there's power in the air.
> Paris is a woman's town, with flowers in her hair.
> It's sweet to dream in Venice, and it's great to study Rome.
> But when it comes to living, there is no place like home.[2]

ACKNOWLEDGMENTS

My thanks to Helen Thomas, in memoriam. When I started work in earnest on this book she was my first call. During two meetings in the Hearst newsroom in Washington, she gave me a unique picture of the woman I knew and of the atmosphere of Washington in the mid-century. Most important of all, she told me that I was reporting valuable history.

To Kathleen Currie, who in 1988 conducted five interviews with Hope for the National Press Club Foundation's Women in Journalism oral history project. Hope never authorized the publication of the full interviews, but one copy of the full transcripts survived in her archive. It proved to be a goldmine.

To Justin Banks, the head of special collections at Austin College in Sherman. Hope's archive gets the best of care and Justin was efficient and professional during my three visits and many subsequent contacts. Also to the staff of the special collections at the Library of Congress, where a smaller HRM archive resides.

To Daisy Harvell, archivist at Paris Junior College who provided valuable information on Hope's years as a faculty member and also on the history and lore of the region.

To the staff of the Sam Rayburn Museum, and the good people at the Fannin County Museum of History and the Fannin County Historical Commission. Special thanks to Suzie Henderson who found the 1900 census and helped me decipher it, which allowed me to locate the site where Hope was born.

To Anthony Champagne for sharing insights on Hope's relationship with Sam Rayburn, and for his helpful read of the manuscript. Also to filmmaker Reed Penney, another Rayburn devotee.

There were precious few people still alive who knew Hope during her reign in Washington. I'm grateful for the opportunity to speak with Margaret Wimsatt, Molly Kellogg, Ruthanna Weber, Charlotte Mayerson, and Maisie Gordon Wittman.

To cousin Mary Faith Hatley for her in-depth research on the Ridings family tree. Also to Joseph Deupree for his information and encouragement.

To Julia Schoo, in memoriam, of the National Press Club for early guidance and contacts. And to archivist Jeff Schlosberg.

To Maurine H. Beasley for reading an early draft of the manuscript and offering guidance. Also for her excellent body of research and writing on Washington newspaper women, especially on the Women's National Press Club.

To Robert K. St. Francis, Jr., general manager of the Sulgrave Club, who allowed me to revisit the glorious clubhouse on Massachusetts Avenue.

To Matt Schudel and Anne Midgette, valued colleagues at the *Washington Post*.

To The Book Doctors, Arielle Eckstut and David Henry Sterry, who provided crucial guidance in preparing the book proposal and shaping the manuscript.

To Diane Nine, my terrific agent.

To my many friends and colleagues who have supported me and this project over the years, including David and Mary Ellen Cohn, David Lindsey Griffin, Marion Roach Smith, Gloria Mazure, Lyrysa Smith, Joseph Young, John Frederick, Greg Anderson and William Tuthill, Stephen Cowart, Mary Jane Leach, Kelly Cresap, William Safford, Gabriel Clark, and Victor Wright. To Caryl Dalton, in memoriam. And to my siblings, Cathy Burling, Celia Youngren, and Pat Dalton.

NOTES

WP = WASHINGTON POST

Post bylines Hope Ridings Miller, unless otherwise indicated.

PRELUDE

1. "Roosevelts Give Dinner," WP, June 1, 1939.
2. Hope Ridings Miller oral history.
3. Ibid.

CHAPTER 1

1. Hope Ridings Miller oral history, and Allen, J. Taylor, *Early Pioneer Days in Texas*, 88–93.
2. Grace Dupree Ridings, *Shawl of Song*, 81.
3. Anthony Champagne, *Congressman Sam Rayburn*, 138.
4. Oral history.
5. Edward H. Phillips, "The Sherman Courthouse Riot of 1930," *East Texas Historical Journal*, vol. 25, issue 2, 1987; and Nolan Thompson, *Handbook of Texas Online*, "Sherman Riot of 1930," http://www.tshaonline.org/handbook/online/articles/jcs06.
6. Oral History.
7. Ibid.

CHAPTER 2

1. Charles Hurd, *When the New Deal Was Young and Gay: FDR and His Circle*, 32.
2. Anthony Champagne interview with HRM, 1986, Rayburn Library.

3. Katharine Graham, *Personal History*, 61.

4. "Women Need Not Grow Old, Author Asserts," WP, January 29, 1934.

5. "Christmas Around the World in Washington," WP, December 24, 1933.

6. "Christmas Legends and Stories of Many Lands," *Evening Star*, December 24, 1933.

7. "Real Martha Washington Now Revealed to World as Bustlingly Domestic and Not Highly Educated," WP, February 22, 1934.

8. "Woe Stalked Book Heroine of '70s," WP, March 6, 1934.

9. HRM, unpublished memoir.

10. HRM, unpublished memoir.

11. Letter from Lindsay, March 13, 1969.

12. "Written by Women for Women Is Slogan of Post Department," WP, June 13, 1934.

13. "Social Life Here Divided Into 3 Parts," WP, October 14, 1934.

14. "Seven Rules Cover Street Car Manners," WP, July 8, 1934.

15. "Calling Card Code Is Rigid in the Capital," WP, September 30, 1934.

16. Graham, *Personal History,* 69.

17. Ibid., 131.

18. HRM, unpublished memoir.

19. "Aristocracy Responding to Large Families Announces Italian Woman Leader," WP, April 17, 1934.

20. "Beauty Not Sesame to Stage, Maintains Miss Jane Cowl," WP, March 22, 1934.

21. "Repeal of Marriage Clause for Capital Teachers Revives Old Controversy Over Efficiency," WP, March 7, 1935.0

22. "Wives Shouldn't Work, Unanimous Opinion of Anthropologist, Club Women, Economist," WP, May 21, 1934.

23. "Modern Women Accused of Leading Double Life," WP, April 27, 1934.

24. "Results Worth the Fight, Margaret Sangers Says after 21-Year 'Birth Control' Campaign," WP, February 9, 1935.

25. Chalmers M. Roberts, the *Washington Post: The First 100 Years*, 400.

26. Peggy A. Simpson, "Covering the Women's Movement," *Nieman Reports*, summer 1979.

27. "Babies for Sale," WP, October 16, 1936.

28. Oral History.

29. Oral History.

30. "Women Members of Congress Who Today Will Take Up Their Share of the Affairs of State," WP, January 5, 1937.

31. "Anderson, 'Baby' Legislator, Gained Fame as Prosecutor," WP, March 29, 1937.

32. Champagne interview with HRM.

33. Oral history, and "End to Jim Crowism Is Plea of Colored Session Speaker," WP, January 8 1937; "Colored Race Congress Asks Police Inquiry," WP, January 9, 1937.

34. Perle Mesta, *Perle: My Story*, 8.

35. Sarah Booth Conroy, "E Street Club Still Tracking the News," WP, November 22, 1999.

36. Oral History.

CHAPTER 3

1. "First Lady's Hunt Mystifies Capitol Crowd," WP, January 21, 1937.

2. Judith Colp, "Scribes of Society Had Ringside Seats," *Washington Times*, August 24, 1990.

3. "Chandelier Washington," the *Diplomat*, December 1962, 25.

4. Maureen Beasley, *Women of the Washington Press*, 75.

5. "First Lady Is Planning Slower Summer Tempo," WP, May 18, 1937.

6. Maureen Beasley, *Eleanor Roosevelt and the Media*, 44.

7. Oral History.

8. Beasley, *Women of the Washington Press*, 39.

9. "Mrs. Roosevelt Is Honor Guest as Audience of 500 Sees 'Moving Picture' Satire of Politics and Society," WP, March 6, 1938.

10. "Mrs. Roosevelt Adopts Lipstick, Hint of Rouge," WP, February 15, 1938.

11. "Parties Held for Guests of Women's Press Club," WP, March 7, 1938.

12. "Ruth Eleanor Jones, 51, Washington Society editor, Dies," WP, September 18, 1940.

13. Beasley, *Eleanor Roosevelt and the Media,* 64.

14. Oral History.

15. "Wedding, Premier's Visit Hold Spotlight in Capital," WP, June 20, 1937.

16. "To Watch a Roosevelt Marry a DuPont," WP, June 27, 1937.

17. "Round of Outdoor Parties Leads Social Calendar as Capital Dares Heat," WP, June 6, 1937.

18. "Roosevelt-duPont Marriage Today," WP, June 30, 1937.

19. "President Sees Son Marry Ethel DuPont," WP, July 1, 1937.

20. "Dudley Harmon Is Dead; Head of CBS News Unit," WP, September 16, 1966.

21. Dudley Harmon, "Former Post Society Writer Survives Atlantic Torpedoing," WP, July 4, 1942.

22. Betty Beale, *Power at Play*, 27–28.

23. "White House Plans to Launch Official Season a Month Earlier This Year," WP, October 17, 1937.

24. "1,000 Attend State Reception for Diplomats at White House," WP, December 17, 1937.

25. Ibid.

26. Oral history.

27. Agnes Hooper Gottlieb, "Society Reporting," *Encyclopedia of American Journalism,* 2007.

28. Oral history.

29. Graham, *A Personal History*, 68.

30. "Women Flock to See Justice Black Seated," WP, October 5, 1937.

31. "Social Welfare Dominates Washington Table Talk as Society Aids Chest," WP, October 24, 1937.

32. Evalyn Walsh McLean, *Father Struck It Rich,* 1936.

33. "Evalyn Walsh McLean," WP, April 29, 1947.

34. "Washington Whirl," the *Diplomat*, October 1955.

35. *Treasure! The Hope Diamond*, Greystone Communications, Inc., A&E Television Network, 1998.

36. "330 Are Entertained at Dinner Preceding Dance," WP, January 1, 1938.

CHAPTER 4

1. "Two Afternoon 'At Homes' Attract Capital Society," WP, January 26, 1938.

2. "Tea Table Talk Turns to Bids for St. James's," WP, March 2, 1938.

3. "Boston Irish Kennedy Turns Down Back Bay Lodge's Plea," WP, April 10, 1938.
4. "Coed's Harsh 'Expose' Has Society Buzzing," WP, July 19, 1938.
5. "Sally Clark Blows Hot Again on Song Subject," WP, October 25, 1938.
6. Maurine H. Beasley, "The Women's National Press Club: Case Study in the Professionalization of Women Journalists."
7. Helen Essay, untitled story, *Country Gentlemen*, February 1, 1939.
8. "Mary Pickford to Talk in Capital," WP, November 15, 1938.
9. "Women's Press Club Host to Noted Writers," WP, May 31, 1939.
10. "Press Women Tell in Satire How D.C. Will Greet Royalty," WP, March 4, 1939.
11. Oral history.
12. Eleanor Roosevelt, "My Day," March 14, 1939.
13. *Sherman Daily Democrat*, March 13, 1939.
14. "1,500 Hear First Lady," *The Paris News* (Paris, Texas), March 12, 1939.
15. Eileen Eagan, "American Youth Congress," *Eleanor Roosevelt Encyclopedia*, 18.
16. Archives, Roosevelt Presidential Library.
17. "Sherman Poet, Club Leader Dies in Dallas," *Dallas Morning News*, September 1, 1941.

CHAPTER 5

1. Hope Ridings Miller oral history.
2. Hope Ridings Miller, *Embassy Row*, 193.
3. Ibid., 192.
4. Oral history.
5. *Embassy Row*, 193.
6. Oral history.
7. *Embassy Row*, 193.
8. Oral history.
9. "Society Pleased as Britain Names Bachelor Lord Lothian as Envoy," WP, April 25, 1939.
10. "Social Registers Combed for 1,300 Invited to Meet Sovereigns Here," WP, May 17, 1939.
11. "Press Advised on Royal Visit by Sir Ronald," WP, May 19, 1939.
12. *Embassy Row*, 195.
13. "Press Advised on Royal Visit by Sir Ronald," WP, May 19, 1939.
14. "Royalty's Visit Forces Publicity Shy Lady Lindsay into Spotlight," WP, May 21, 1939.
15. *Embassy Row*, 192–93.
16. Lindsay letter to HRM, March 4, 1939. Austin College archives.
17. "Royal Garden Party Guest List closed, Lady Lindsay Declares," WP, May 24, 1939.
18. "No Press Talk with King, Lindsay Says," WP, May 28, 1939.
19. "Mrs. Roosevelt Exhibits Ensemble She'll Wear to Greet King, Queen," WP, May 30, 1939.
20. *Embassy Row*, 194–95.
21. "Taste to Be Yardstick for Royal Party Gowns," WP, June 4, 1939.
22. *Embassy Row*, 196.
23. Oral history.
24. "The Roosevelts to Greet Rulers Before Parade," WP, June 8, 1939.

25. "Garner Slaps King's Back at Garden Fete," WP, June 9, 1939.

26. *Embassy Row,* 197.

27. "Garner Slaps King's Back at Garden Fete," WP, June 9, 1939.

28. Ibid.

29. *Embassy Row,* 197 and "Social Leaders Attend Lend-Lease Hearings," WP, February 6, 1941.

CHAPTER 6

1. Unpublished speech by HRM to Rose Festival, Tyler, TX, 1969(?).

2. "Norwegian Crown Prince and Princess Climax Round of Brilliant Parties with Dinner at Own Legation," WP, June 29, 193.

3. "Rumanian Nobility Here as Sightseers," WP, July 4, 1939.

4. "Arrivals from Europe Cheered by Capitalites," WP, September 6, 1939.

5. "Society's Table Talk Revolves Around War," WP, September 14, 1939.

6. "Embargo Issue Argued Whenever Ladies Meet," WP, October 4, 1939.

7. "Mrs. Roosevelt Plans to Keep 55th Birthday Party Today to Minimum," WP, October 11, 1939.

8. "White House Drops All State Dinners," WP, October 15, 1939.

9. "Diplomatic Fetes Add to Season's Calendar," WP, October 31, 1939.

10. *Embassy Row,* 163–64.

11. Ibid, 167.

12. *Embassy Row,* 167–68, and "Soviet Party Finds U.S. Officials Absent," WP, November 8, 1939.

13. "Envoys Trade Nods Like Ice at White House," WP, December 15, 1939.

14. "About the Town with Dudley Harmon," WP, December 16, 1939.

15. "Gridiron Widows Toast White House Hopefuls," WP, December 10, 1939.

16. Oliver Ewing Clapper, *Washington Tapestry,* 170.

17. "Next White House Chatelaine Will be Heiress to a Difficult Job,' WP, May 5, 1940.

18. "Frances Hutt Dewey Is Talented, Charming," WP, February 18, 1940.

19. "Elizabeth Farley Dares to Be Different," WP, March 31, 1940.

20. "Mrs. W. B. Bankhead Has Artistic Talent," WP, April 7, 1940.

21. "If Fate Picks Dark Horse, These Three Wives Are Good Bets," WP, April 28, 1940.

22. "Oddments of Interest," WP, September 26, 1943.

23. "Luncheon and Dinner Schedules Crowded," WP, June 28, 1940.

24. Christine Sadler, "Willkie's Wife Is 100% Help to Candidate," WP, June 26, 1940.

25. Christine Sadler, "Women Get in Their Word on Platform," WP, July 18, 1940.

26. Christine Sadler, "Equal Rights Plank Opposed by First Lady," WP, July 16, 1940.

27. Christine Sadler, "Mrs. Roosevelt Asks Democratic Party to Share President's Task," WP, July 19, 1940.

28. "Wife of Nominee Flies to Chicago Convention," WP, July 19, 1940.

CHAPTER 7

1. Henry N. Dorris, "Four Considered for Second Place," *New York Times,* July 16, 1940.

2. Anthony Champagne interview of HRM, 1986, Rayburn Library.

3. Alfred Steinburg, *Sam Rayburn, A Biography*, 80.

4. Oral History.

5. Steinberg, *Sam Rayburn: A Biography*, 80–81.

6. Champagne, *Congressman Sam Rayburn*, 57; May, *Marvin Jones: The Public Life of an Agrarian Advocate*, 62, 81.

7. Champagne interview.

8. "Mrs. Palmer Represents Travel Agency," WP, November 17, 1963 and "Socialite Margaret Palmer Dies at 89," WP, May 3, 1973.

9. "In Memoriam: Mr. Sam," *Diplomat*, December 1961, 20.

10. *Who Says We Can't Cook!* Washington: Mciver Art and Publications, Inc., 1955, 150.

11. Steinburg, *Sam Rayburn: A Biography*, 173.

12. "The Reasons for Washington Society," *Town & Country*, December 1944.

13. Ibid.

14. Steinburg, *Sam Rayburn: A Biography*, 164.

15. "The Speakership," WP, September 17, 1940.

16. "Ruth Eleanor Jones, 51, Washington Society Editor, Dies," WP, September 18, 1940.

17. Oral History.

18. Amanda Smith, *Newspaper Titan*, 377.

19. Ralph G. Martin, *Cissy*, 278.

20. "Former *Post* Society Editor Marie McNair Dies at Age 89," WP, September 3, 1989.

21. Oral History.

22. Martin, *Cissy*, 309.

23. "Betty Hynes, Society Editor Times-Herald, Found Dead," WP, September 15, 1948.

24. "Ye Editor Makes Some New Year's Resolutions," WP, January 1, 1941.

25. Oral history.

26. "Hedda Hopper Finds Space Here for Self, Orange Blooms," WP, April 2, 1941.

27. "In the National Capital," by Hedda Hopper, WP, April 5, 1941.

28. "Hedda Hopper Finds Space Here for Self, Orange Blooms," WP, April 2, 1941.

29. "Capital Chorus" by Henrietta Malkiel, *Vanity Fair*, date unknown c. 1941.

30. Oral history.

31. "Somerset Maugham, British Writer, Feted at Two Topflight Parties," WP, April 15, 1941.

32. "Elsa Maxwell Selects Ideal Dinner Guests," WP, March 19, 1941.

33. "Calendar Crowded Despite Predictions," WP, October 30, 1941.

34. Jean R. Hailey, "Evie Robert, Society Leader, Dies," WP, September 7, 1972.

35. "Evie Robert Refutes Face-Lifting Rumor after Visit to the Windsors," WP, February 25, 1941.

36. Smith, *Newspaper Titan*, 573.

37. "Capital Looks Forward to Visit of Duke and Duchess of Windsor," WP, September 21, 1941.

38. "Ladies of Press Look on Wallis' Figure and Resolve to Diet," WP, September 26, 1941.

39. Scott Hart, "Crowds Get Scant Glimpses of Man Who Quit Throne for Love," WP, September 26, 1941.

40. "Victory Certain, Windsor Says," by Edward T. Folliard, WP, September 26, 1941.

41. "Duke and Duchess to Dine with President," WP, October 28, 1941.

42. "Aunt Bessie Out of Town, Unable to See Windsors," WP, October 29, 1941.

43. Ibid.

44. "About Washington," WP, October 22, 1943.

45. "Helen Essary, 65, A News Columnist," *New York Times*, August 16, 1951.

46. Oral history.

47. "About Washington," WP, October 22, 1943.

CHAPTER 8

1. *Great Houses of Washington*, 137; Notes from an unpublished memoir; "Edisons are Honored at Two Parties Here, WP, December 8, 1941; Oral history.

2. "Summer Whirl Goes On, Even as It Did in 1917," WP, June 6, 1941.

3. Christine Sadler, "President Suggests 'Parasites' Quit DC," WP, January 31, 1942.

4. "Capital Whirl," WP, February 8, 1942.

5. Edward T. Folliard, "Washington a Rumor Factory Spreading Lies, President Says," WP, February 18, 1942.

6. "Capital Whirl," WP, February 19, 1942.

7. Oral history.

8. "Dr. Clarence Miller Is Captain in Army," *Paris News*, March 23, 1943.

9. Champagne interview.

10. James M Goode, *Best Addresses*, 208.

11. Judith R. Cohen, *The Mayflower Hotel, Grande Dame of Washington, D.C.*, 102.

12. Oral history.

13. Ibid.

14. "Capital Whirl," WP, March 18, 1942.

15. Ibid.

16. Sarah Booth Conroy "Once again, War, and a Farewell to Society," WP, January 20, 1991.

17. "Capital Whirl," WP, June 18, 1942.

18. "Farewell to Society," WP, July 19, 1942.

19. Judith Colp, "Scribes of Society Had Ringside Seats," *Washington Times*, August 24, 1990.

20. "Capital Whirl," WP, May 7, 1942.

21. "Farewell to Society," WP, July 19, 1942.

22. "Fourth Estate," *Newsweek*, August 3, 1942.

23. "The Nation Applauds!," WP, July 19, 1942.

24. Ibid.

25. "Irene Dunn Tells All, But Not About Herself," WP, September 1, 1942.

26. "The Term 'Propaganda,' Used Too Often," WP, October 29, 1942.

27. "Gasoline Rationing Gets Under Way in Texas," WP, December 10, 1942.

28. "If Your Husband Has Gone to War, or May Go Soon, You'll Need Some of Ethel Gorham's Advice," WP, September 24, 1942.

29. "Service Club Hostess Is Draftee's Last link to Homelife," WP, September 11, 1942.

CHAPTER 9

1. Maxene Andrews and Bill Gilbert, *Over Here, Over There: The Andrews Sisters and the USO Stars in World War II*, 84.

2. Oral history.

3. "Wanted—A Flock of Angels," WP, September 27, 1942.

4. Perle Mesta, *Perle: My Story*, 93–94.

5. "Uncle Sam Needs Nurses," WP, August 30, 1942.

6. Judith Colp, "Scribes of Society Had Ringside Seats," *Washington Star*, August 24, 1990.

7. "Washington WAAC Recruiting Center, Only One of Kind in Country," WP, February 14, 1943.

8. "Unsung Heroines on Un-Glamorous Front Watch," WP, September 20, 1942.

9. Emily Yellin, *Our Mothers' War*, 26.

10. "Wedding in Locust Valley Today," WP, February 21, 1943.

11. "Walt Disney, Cartoon Wizard, Comes to Capital on War Mission," WP, December 2, 1943.

12. "Capt. Clarence L. Miller Here for Christmas," *Macon Chronicle-Herald*, December 27, 1945.

13. "War Widow in Washington," WP, June 29, 1943.

14. "Ban on Pleasure Driving," WP, January 17, 1943; "Dinner at Friendship," WP, January 31, 1943; "How They Got There," WP, February 9, 1943.

15. Elizabeth Carpenter, "Gal From Texas: She Makes Congress Jump Through Hopes," *Dallas Morning News*, December 14, 1950.

16. "Brace of Widely Publicized Fetes," WP, January 3, 1943.

17. Constance Casey, "Mixed Blessings," WP, April 19, 1992.

18. "With only three more days in which to make those proverbial resolutions, here are a few suggestions," WP, December 29, 1942.

19. "Whether you keep them or not, why not make those New Year's Resolutions? Here are a few for the record," WP, December 30, 1942.

20. "Who Are the 10 Outstanding Women of the Modern World," WP, February 3, 1943.

21. "It's 'China Lady's Day' in Washington," WP, February 18, 1943.

22. Laura Tyson Li, *Madame Chiang Kai-shek: China's Eternal First Lady*, 185.

23. "Willkie Loud in Praise of Mme. Chiang," WP, October 16, 1942.

24. "It's 'China Lady's Day' in Washington," WP, February 18, 1943.

25. Li, *Madame Chiang Kai-shek,* 199.

26. Eleanor Roosevelt, *The Autobiography of Eleanor Roosevelt,* 249.

27. "Mme. Chiang's Address to Congress," WP, February 19, 1943.

28. Roosevelt, *The Autobiography,* 49–50.

29. "Change in Style of Soviet Uniforms Scheduled Soon," WP, February 23, 1943.

30. "Mme. Chiang Kai-shek Attends Mrs. Roosevelt's Press Conference," WP, February 25, 1943.

CHAPTER 10

1. "It's 'Happy Birthday, Sam Rayburn," WP, January 7, 1943.

2. "Here's the Real Story of Why Connecticut's Incoming Woman Legislator Is Now in Hollywood," WP, December 16, 1942.

3. Sylvia Jukes Morris, *Price of Fame: The Honorable Clare Boothe Luce,* 4.

4. Robert W. Harvey, "Elusive Mrs. Luce Fails to Let Down Her Hair," WP, January 6, 1943.

5. "First Slip Not Parliamentary," (no byline), WP, January 7, 1943.
6. "It's 'Happy Birthday, Sam Rayburn," WP, January 7, 1943.
7. "Random Notes," WP, January 14, 1943.
8. "About Washington," WP, October 28, 1943.
9. "Soviet Embassy Party," WP, November 3, 1943.
10. "Talking to Myself," WP, August 23, 1942.
11. Edward T. Folliard, "Envoy Luce Resigns Due to Health," WP, November 20, 1956.
12. Edward Ryan, "Witnesses Defy Congress in Investigation of War Contracts," WP, April 29, 1943.
13. Edward Ryan, "Knox Explains, Patterson, Jeffers and Nelson Deny R Street Visits," WP, May 4, 1943.
14. "Latest Sensational Investigation of Purposeful Partying," WP, May 7, 1943.
15. "First Lady One of Many Washington Celebrities Who Never Attended Parties at That 'Big Red House on R Street,'" WP, May 11, 1943.
16. "Two Women Welders Attend Mrs. Roosevelt's Press Conference," WP, June 2, 1943.
17. "A Word or Two in Passing About Those Weekly Conferences," WP, July 1, 1943.
18. Drew Pearson, "Merry-Go-Round," *Dallas Morning News*, June 6, 1943.
19. "A Public Letter to Speaker Rayburn," WP, September 27, 1943.
20. Oral history of Eugene Meyer, Columbia University Library, 761.
21. "Prediction Made by Envoy Comes True on Schedule," WP, August 3, 1944.
22. "Launching of S. S. Robert J. Collier at Bethlehem-Fairfield Shipyards," WP, June 15, 1943.
23. "Week-end Memories Swirled Around a Dinner for Noted Author," WP, November 23, 1943.
24. Hope Ridings Miller, "A Long Way From Coffee Mill Creek," *Speak, Mr. Speaker*, Rayburn Library Newsletter, September 1986.
25. USS Aucilla (AO-56) https://en.wikipedia.org/wiki/USS_Aucilla_(AO-56).
26. Hope Ridings Miller, WP, June 27, 1943.

CHAPTER 11

1. Letters from archives Sam Rayburn Museum, Bonham, Texas.
2. Oral history.
3. Oral history.
4. Richard Pearson, "Journalist and Biographer Bascom Timmons, 97, Dies," WP, June 8, 1987.
5. "The Timmons Boom," WP, July 20, 1940.
6. "Hope Ridings Miller," *The Georgetowner*, May 21, 1957.
7. Scott M. Cutlip, *The Unseen Power: Public Relations a History*, Hillsdale, NJ: Erlbaum Associates, 1994, 251.
8. Hearings of the Subcommittee of the Committee on Ways and Means, House of Representatives, Eighty-third Congress, March 17–21, June 24, 1953, 767.
9. Wallis Ballinger, "Washington Daybook," *Valley Morning Star* (Harlingen, Texas), January 27, 1950.
10. Hope Ridings Miller, "A Long Way From Coffee Mill Creek," *Speak, Mr. Speaker*.
11. Perle Mesta, *Perle: My Story*, 121.

12. "Socialite Editor Is Famed Among Famous," *The Register,* February 2, 1965.

13. Mesta, *Perle: My Story,* 131.

14. "Women's Press Club Awards Given by President at Party," WP, May 15, 1949.

15. Letter from Truman, December 6, 1950.

16. "The Girl Behind Margaret Truman," *Promenade Magazine,* April 1951.

17. Elizabeth Carpenter, "Gal from Texas: She Makes Congress Jump Through Hoops," *Dallas Morning News,* December 14, 1950.

18. Author interview with Margaret Wimsatt.

19. Oral history.

20. Lucia Brown, "Big Magnet Draws VIPs Before the Footlights," WP, January 21, 1951.

21. Ruth Montgomery, *Hail to the Chiefs,* 83–84.

22. Steinberg, *Sam Rayburn: A Biography,* 176.

23. "Admits Evasion of Federal Tax," *New York Times,* January 15, 1953.

24. "Tax Inquiry Hears of 'Fix' Payments, *New York Times,* March 18, 1953.

25. "Witnesses Clash in Tax Fraud Case," *New York Times,* March 20, 1953.

26. Hearings of the Subcommittee of the Committee on Ways and Means, House of Representatives, Eighty-third Congress, March 17–21, June 24, 1953, 748.

27. Ibid, 748.

28. Ibid, 755.

29. Ibid, 765.

30. Ibid, 771–72.

31. Ibid, 766–67.

32. Ibid, 771.

33. Ibid, 768.

34. Ibid, 770.

35. Ibid, 772.

36. Ibid, 779.

37. "Probers Told of Payments to Avoid Tax," WP, March 18, 1953.

38. "Sherman Gets 15 Months on Income Tax Charge," WP, September 9, 1955.

39. Hearings of the Subcommittee, 780.

CHAPTER 12

1. Ilija Monte Radlovic. https://en.wikipedia.org/w/index.php?title = Ilija_Monte_Radlovic&oldid = 683091710.

2. Goode, *Best Addresses,* 168.

3. Tallulah Bankhead, *My Autobiography,* 53.

4. "Longtime Lobbyist Dale Miller Dies at 87," WP, April 25, 1997.

5. Miller, "A Long Way From Coffee Mill Creek," *Speak, Mr. Speaker,* Rayburn Library Newsletter, September 1986.

6. "Town Talk," the *Diplomat,* December 1954.

7. "Washington Whirl," the *Diplomat,* December 1955.

8. "Washington Whirl," the *Diplomat,* October 1955, 47.

9. "Editor's Notebook," the *Diplomat,* December 1958, 5.

10. "Wanted: Effective Diplomacy Keyed to the Space Age," the *Diplomat,* March 1953, 16.

11. "Editor's Notebook," the *Diplomat,* October 1959, 16.

12. "Editor's Notebook," the *Diplomat,* November 1959, 20.
13. "Editor's Notebook," the *Diplomat,* April 1960, 12.
14. Letters to the Editor, the *Diplomat,* August 1960, 2.
15. "Our Readers Write," the *Diplomat,* June 1962, 2.
16. Letters to the Editor, the *Diplomat,* December 1960, 2.

CHAPTER 13

1. "First Ladies in Waiting. . . ." the *Diplomat,* July 1960, 10.
2. "The Many Sided Kennedys," the *Diplomat,* February 1961, 29.
3. "Washington Whirl," the *Diplomat,* May 1961, 29.
4. "The Many Sided Kennedys," the *Diplomat,* February 1961, 29.
5. Embassy Row, 29.
6. Champagne, *Congressman Sam Rayburn*, 60–63.
7. Steinberg, *Sam Rayburn: A Biography*, 344.
8. D. B. Hardeman, and Donald C. Bacon, *Rayburn: A Biography*, 472–73.
9. "In Memoriam: Mr. Sam," the *Diplomat,* December 1961, 20.
10. Beale, *Power at Play*, 57–59.
11. Montgomery, *Hail to the Chiefs*, 244.
12. "Chandelier Washington," the *Diplomat,* March 1960, 22.
13. Montgomery, *Hail to the Chiefs*, 244.
14. Helen Thomas, *Dateline White House*, 7.
15. Helen Thomas, *Front Row at the White House*, 247.
16. "Chandelier Washington," *The Diplomat,* December 1962, 25.
17. Oral history.
18. "Chandelier Washington," the *Diplomat,* December 1962, 25.
19. Christopher Anderson, *These Few Precious Days*, 233, 236.
20. Letitia Baldrige, *A Lady First*, 199.
21. Ruth Montgomery, "Capital Society in Muddle," *Los Angeles Times,* October 24, 1963.

CHAPTER 14

1. Lady Bird Johnson, *A White House Diary*, 16.
2. "Editor's Notebook," the *Diplomat,* January 1964, 18–20.
3. "As the Editor Sees It," the *Diplomat,* February 1964, 17.
4. Letter from Johnson, March 24, 1964.
5. Letters from Miller, November 1, 1967 and from Johnson, November 7, 1967.
6. Memo to Johnson, February 16, 1967.
7. "Editor's Notebook," the *Diplomat,* October 1964, 18–20.
8. "Editor's Notebook," the *Diplomat,* July 1964, 21.
9. "Editor's Inaugural Notebook," the *Diplomat,* February 1964, 33–34.
10. Johnson, *A White House Diary*, 227–28.
11. Ibid., 229.
12. Oral history.
13. Sue Smith, "Hope Recalls Capital Life," *Chicago Tribune,* April 19, 1969.

14. Oral history.

15. Marilyn Berger, "John W. Kluge, Founder of Metromedia, Dies at 95," *New York Times,* September 8, 2010, and Terence McArdle, "John W. Kluge, 95, dies; self-made billionaire created Metromedia conglomerate," WP, September 9, 2010.

16. Richard Severo, "Igor Cassini, Hearst Columnist, Dies at 86," *New York Times,* January 9, 2002.

17. Paul Herron, "Diplomat Sold by Metromedia," WP, November 24, 1966.

18. "Indira Gandhi at the White House," the *Diplomat,* July 1966, 56

19. Eve Tibby, "Murder on Bleecker Street," the *Diplomat,* July 1966, 54.

CHAPTER 15

1. Oral history.

2. *Embassy Row,* 5

3. Ibid., 14.

4. Ibid., 131–32.

5. Ibid., 241.

6. *Embassy Row,* 239, and "Report that Hans Thomsen is new Nazi envoy," WP, February 26, 1943.

7. *Embassy Row,* 128.

8. Ymelda Dixon, "Moving Along the Party Row with Hope," *Evening Star,* February 24, 1969.

9. "All That Glitters," by Paul Douglass, *Orlando Sentinel,* February 16, 1969.

10. Letitia Baldrige, "Protocol finesse and gin on Embassy Row," *Chicago Sunday Sun Times,* February 23, 1969.

11. Typed notes to an undated speech.

12. Betty Beale, "New Book to Reveal Scandals of American Presidents," *Cincinnati Inquirer,* September 16, 1973.

13. *Kirkus Review,* August 15, 1973.

14. Dorothy Marks, "Private Lives of Presidents," *The Robesonian,* Lumberton, NC, November 4, 1973.

15. *Scandals in the Highest Office,* 246.

16. Ibid., 250.

17. Ibid., 260.

18. Charlotte Hays, "Scandals at the Top," WP, October 26, 1973.

19. Ruth Montgomery, *A Search for the Truth,* 74.

20. Oral history.

21. Ruth Montgomery, *The World to Come,* 130.

22. "About Washington," WP, October 14, 1943.

23. "Miss Skariatina's Ambition," WP, August 30, 1944.

24. *Treasure! The Hope Diamond,* Greystone Communications, Inc., A&E Television Network, 1998.

25. "The Many Sided Kennedys," the *Diplomat,* February, 1961, 29.

26. Bob Colacello, *Ronnie & Nancy,* 255.

27. Kitty Kelley, *Nancy Reagan: The Unauthorized Biography,* 213.

28. "Keeper of the Lists," *Dossier Magazine,* June 1982, 21.

29. "Have a Classy Christmas," *Sun Sentinel,* November 8, 1987.

30. Sarah Booth Conroy, "Splendid in the Spring" WP, April 7, 1997.

31. David Brinkley, *Washington Goes to War*, 141, 161, 142.

32. Gore Vidal, *Washington, D.C.*, 88.

CHAPTER 16

1. Matt Schudel, "Washington Society Chronicler Hope Ridings Miller Dies at 99" WP, May 5, 2005.

2. Henry Van Dyke, "America for Me," 1909.

BIBLIOGRAPHY

Allen, J. Taylor. *Early Pioneer Days in Texas*, Dallas: Wilkinson Printing Company, 1918.

Anderson, Christopher. *These Few Precious Days: The Final Year of Jack with Jackie*. New York: Gallery Books, 2013.

Andrews, Maxene, and Bill Gilbert. *Over Here, Over There: The Andrews Sisters and the USO Stars in World War II*. New York: Zebra Books, 1993.

Baldrige, Letitia. *A Lady, First*. New York: Viking, 2001.

———. *Of Diamonds & Diplomats*. Boston: Houghton Mifflin Company, 1968.

Bankhead, Tallulah. *My Autobiography*. New York: Harper & Bros, 1952.

Beale, Betty. *Power at Play*. Washington, DC: Regnery Gateway, 1993.

Beasley, Maurine H. *Eleanor Roosevelt and the Media*. Urbana: University of Illinois Press, 1987.

———. *Women of the Washington Press*. Evanston, IL: Northwestern University Press, 2012.

———. *The Women's National Press Club: Case Study in the Professionalization of Women Journalists*. Paper presented at the Annual Meeting of the Association for Education in Journalism and Mass Communication, August 3–6, 1986.

Beasley, Maurine and Holly C. Shulman and Henry R Beasley. *The Eleanor Roosevelt Encyclopedia*. Westport, CT: Greenwood Press, 2001.

Brinkley, David. *Washington Goes to War*. New York: Alfred A. Knopf, 1988.

Carpenter, Liz. *Ruffles and Flourishes*. Garden City, NY: Doubleday & Co., 1970.

Caro, Robert A. *The Years of Lyndon Johnson: The Passage of Power*. New York: Alfred A. Knopf, 2012.

Cassini, Igor with Jeanne Molli. *I'd Do It All Over Again: The Life and Times of Igor Cassini*. New York: G. P. Putnam's Sons, 1977.

Champagne, Anthony. *Congressman Sam Rayburn*. New Brunswick, NJ: Rutgers University Press, 1984.

———. Interview with Hope Ridings Miller. Rayburn Library, 1986.

Clapper, Oliver Ewing. *Washington Tapestry.* New York: Whittlesey House, McGraw Hill, 1946.

Cohen, Judith R. *The Mayflower Hotel: Grande Dame of Washington, D.C.* New York: Balance House, 1987.

Colacello, Bob. *Ronnie & Nancy: Their Path to the White House 1911 to 1980.* New York: Warner Books, 2004.

Conant, Jennet. *The Irregulars: Roald Dahl and the British Spy Ring in Wartime Washington.* New York: Simon & Schuster, 2008.

Cordery, Stacy A. *Alice: Alice Roosevelt Longworth, from White House Princess to Washington Power Broker.* New York: Penguin, 2007.

Cutlip, Scott. *The Unseen Power: Public Relations, A History.* Hillsdale, NJ: Lawrence Erlbaum Associations, 1994.

Dorough, C. Dwight. *Mr. Sam.* New York: Random House, 1962.

Edwards, India. *Pulling No Punches.* New York: Putnam, 1977.

Felsenthal, Carol. *Power, Privilege and the Post: The Katherine Graham Story.* New York: Seven Stories Press, 1993.

————. *Alice Roosevelt Longworth.* New York: Putnam, 1988.

Frank, Judy and Mary Beth Larrabee, eds. *The Sulgrave Club's First Fifty Years.* Washington, DC: Sulgrave Club, 1983.

Gillette, Michael. *Lady Bird Johnson, An Oral History.* New York: Oxford University Press, 2012.

Goode, James M. *Best Addresses: A Century of Washington's Distinguished Apartment Houses.* Washington, DC: Smithsonian Institution, 1988.

Gottlieb, Agnes Hooper. "Society Reporting" from *Encyclopedia of American Journalism* by Stephen L. Vaughn, ed. New York: Routledge, 2007.

Graham, Katharine. *Katharine Graham's Washington.* New York: Knopf, 2002.

Halsell, Grace. *In Their Shoes.* Fort Worth: Texas Christian University Press, 1996.

Hardeman, D.B. and Donald C. Bacon. *Rayburn: A Biography.* New York: Madison Books, 1987.

Healy, Paul F. *Cissy: The Biography of Eleanor M. "Cissy" Patterson.* Garden City, NY: Doubleday, 1966.

Hurd, Charles. *Washington Cavalcade.* New York: E. P. Dutton & Co. 1948.

————. *When the New Deal Was Young and Gay: FDR and His Circle.* New York: Hawthorn Books, Inc. 1965.

Johnson, Lady Bird. *A White House Diary.* New York: Holt, Rinehart & Winston, 1970.

Jones, Marvin. *Memoirs.* El Paso: Texas Western Press, 1973.

Kelley, Kitty. *Nancy Reagan: The Unauthorized Biography.* New York: Simon & Schuster, 1991.

Li, Laura Tyson. *Madame Chiang Kai-shek: China's Eternal First Lady.* New York: Atlantic Monthly Press, 2006.

Lobenthal, Joel. *Tallulah! The Life and Times of a Leading Lady.* New York: Harper Collins, 2004.

Martin, Joseph W. *My First Fifty Years in Politics.* New York: McGraw-Hill, 1960.

Martin, Ralph G. *Cissy: The Extraordinary Life of Eleanor Medill Patterson.* New York: Simon & Schuster, 1979.

Maxwell, Elsa. *How to Do It: The Lively Art of Entertaining.* Boston: Little, Brown & Co., 1957.

May, Irvin M. *Marvin Jones: The Public Life of an Agrarian Advocate.* College Station: Texas A&M Press, 1980.

McClendon, Sarah. *Mr. President, Mr. President! My 50 Years of Covering the White House.* Los Angeles: General Publishing Group, 1996.

McClinsey, Keither. *Washington, D.C.'s Mayflower Hotel.* Charleston, SC: Arcadia Publishing, 2007.

McKelway, St. Clair. *Gossip: The Life and Times of Walter Winchell.* New York: Viking Press, 1940.

McLean, Evalyn Walsh. *Father Struck It Rich.* Boston: Little, Brown & Co., 1936.

McLendon, Winzola and Scotti Smith. *Don't Quote Me! Washington Newswomen & the Power Society.* New York: E. P. Dutton & Co., 1970.

Mesta, Perle. *Perle, My Story.* New York: McGraw-Hill, 1960.

Meyer, Eugene. Oral history, Columbia University Library.

Miller, Hope Ridings. *Embassy Row: The Life & Times of Diplomatic Washington.* New York: Holt, Rinehart & Winston, 1969.

———. *Great Houses of Washington, D.C.* New York: Clarkson N. Potter, 1969.

———. "A Long Way From Coffee Mill Creek," *Speak, Mr. Speaker*, Rayburn Library Newsletter, September, 1986.

———. Oral history. Austin College Archives.

———. *Scandals in the Highest Office: Facts and Fictions in the Private Lives of Our Presidents.* New York: Random House, 1973.

Montgomery, Ruth. *A Gift of Prophecy: The Phenomenal Jeane Dixon.* New York: William Morrow & Company, 1965.

———. *Hail to the Chiefs: My Life and Times with Six Presidents.* New York: Coward-McCann, Inc., 1970.

———. *A Search for the Truth.* New York: William Morrow & Co., 1970.

———. *Strangers Among Us.* New York: Coward, McCann & Geohegan, 1979.

———. *The World to Come.* New York: Harmony Books, 1999.

Morris, Sylvia Jukes. *Price of Fame: The Honorable Clare Boothe Luce.* New York: Random House, 2014.

———. *Rage for Fame: The Ascent of Clare Boothe Luce.* New York: Random House, 1997.

Owens, William A. *This Stubborn Soil.* New York: Charles Scribner's Sons, 1966.

———. *A Season of Weathering.* New York: Charles Scribner's Sons, 1973.

Pakula, Hannah. *The Last Empress: Madame Chiang Kai-Shek and the Birth of Modern China.* New York: Simon & Schuster, 2009.

Phillips, Edward H. "The Sherman Courthouse Riot of 1930," *East Texas Historical Journal*, Vol. 25, Issue 2, 1987.

Radlovic, I. Monte. *Etiquette & Protocol*. New York: Harcourt, Brace & Co., 1956.

Reagan, Nancy, with William Novak. *My Turn: The Memoirs of Nancy Reagan*. New York: Random House, 1989.

Ridings, Grace Dupree. *By the Light of the Lone Star*. Dallas: Kaleidograph Press, 1936.

———. *Shawl of Song*. Dallas: Kaleidograph Press, 1934.

Roberts, Chalmers M. *The Washington Post, the First 100 Years*. Boston: Houghton Mifflin Co., 1977.

Roosevelt, Eleanor. *The Autobiography of Eleanor Roosevelt*. New York: Harper & Brothers, 1961.

Simpson, Peggy A., "Covering the Women's Movement," *Nieman Reports*. Cambridge: Nieman Reports, 1979.

Smith, Amanda. *Newspaper Titan: The Infamous Life and Monumental Times of Cissy Patterson*. New York: Alfred A. Knopf, 2011.

Steinberg, Alfred. *Sam Rayburn: A Biography*. New York: Hawthorn Books, 1975.

Stuart, Lyle. *The Secret Life of Walter Winchell*. New York: Boar's Head Books, 1953.

Swain, Martha H. *Ellen S. Woodward: New Deal Advocate for Women*. Jackson: University Press of Mississippi, 1995.

Swift, Will. *The Roosevelts and the Royals*. Hoboken, NJ: John Wiley & Sons, 2004.

Thomas, Helen. *Dateline: White House*. New York: Macmillan Publishing Co., 1973.

———. *Front Row at the White House: My Life and Times*. New York: Scribner, 1999.

———. *Thanks for the Memories, Mr. President*. New York: Scribner, 2002.

Vidal, Gore. *Washington, DC*. New York: Random House, 1967.

Weiner, Edward Horace. *Let's Go to Press: A Biography of Walter Winchell*. New York: Putnam, 1955.

Yellin, Emily. *Our Mothers' War, American Women at Home and at the Front During World War II*. New York: Free Press, 2004.

INDEX

Photos are indicated by *p* and their respective number in order of presentation

219

Women's National Press Club (WNPC), vii–viii, xi, 35–37; British royalty and, 53, 83–84; Duchess of Windsor at, 83–84; headquarters for, 134–35; Kennedy, J. P., at, 49; Lady Lindsay at, 60; Luce, C. B., at, 116–17; president of, 52; Roosevelt, E., and, *p*10, *p*12, 35–36, 52–54, 119–20; speakers at, 52–53; stunt parties at, *p*8, *p*15, *p*24, 35–36, 53, 60, 80, 132, 159–60
Woodring, Harry H., 47

Works Progress Administration, 33, 54
world issues, in *Diplomat* magazine, 149
The World to Come (Montgomery), 183
Worthington House, 178
Wright, Frank Lloyd, 143
Wright, Jim, viii, 156
writing, 5; automatic, 182; definition of, 173; diary, 192; hatred of, 195–96; memoirs, 177, 196. *See also* journalism

Young, Elizabeth, 23

ABOUT THE AUTHOR

JOSEPH DALTON has been a general arts reporter and classical music critic for the *Times Union* in Albany, New York since 2002. He earned a first-place award for arts and entertainment writing from the New York Associated Press, and he has twice received the ASCAP Deems Taylor Award for music journalism. A native of Fort Worth, he earned degrees in music (Catholic University of America) and arts administration (Southern Methodist University). Dalton launched his career in the record business working for three years in A&R administration at CBS Masterworks/Sony Classical. For 10 years he was executive director of the indie classical label Composers Recordings, Inc., where he produced 300 CD titles, two of which earned Grammy nominations. As a writer, Dalton has also been a contributor to *The Washington Post, Time Out New York, Opera News* and *The Advocate*, among other publications. Hope Ridings Miller and Joseph Ridings Dalton were first cousins twice removed.